Theodore Dreiser

HIS WORLD AND HIS NOVELS

RICHARD LEHAN

Southern Illinois University Press   *Carbondale & Edwardsville*

Feffer & Simons, Inc.   *London and Amsterdam*

Library of Congress Cataloging in Publication Data

Lehan, Richard Daniel, 1930-
    Theodore Dreiser: his world and novels.
    (Arcturus books, AB121)
    Includes bibliographical references.
    1. Dreiser, Theodore, 1871-1945.
[PS3507.R55Z66 1974]   813'.5'2   73-12637
ISBN 0-8093-0663-8

ARCT
~~URUS~~
BOOKS ®

Copyright © 1969 by Southern Illinois University Press
All rights reserved
First published December 1969
Second printing October 1971
Arcturus Books Edition February 1974
This edition printed by offset lithography
  in the United States of America

To my Mother and the Memory of my Father

TABLE OF CONTENTS

LIST OF ILLUSTRATIONS
Between pages 112–113

A CAVEAT TO THE READER

Theodore Dreiser: His World and His Novels is primarily a critical study of Dreiser's novels. My concern is with the genesis and evolution of the novels, their pattern, and their meaning. In order to focus on the meaning, I have examined some of the influences which most shaped Dreiser's imagination—especially his family, the city, his work as a journalist and free-lance writer, his reading, and his reaction to the politics and the scientific ideas of his times.

Dreiser tried his whole life to explain the world in which he lived. He was in awe of its vastness, was fascinated by the modern Prometheus who tapped its great energy, and was concerned with the ways this power was being put to use and misuse. The titan not only changed the landscape; he also changed the motives of modern man, created the imbalances that shaped the destiny of a Cowperwood at one extreme and a Hurstwood at the other. These imbalances concerned Dreiser, who began to feel that the Christian ideals of love, charity, humility, and poverty had little or no relationship to his times.

Like his contemporaries Henry Adams and Frank Norris, Dreiser was fascinated with political and technological power. He could both admire and scorn a Charles Yerkes and the other titans of the Gilded Age. He believed that Yerkes's success was a form of realized power, but he was not certain whether the new technology should benefit a privileged few or the masses. He could not, in other words, reconcile his own sense of ego with an abiding altruism. He also could not reconcile his own love of beauty with his desire for money, and his esthetics conflicted with his materialistic nature. Dreiser's ideal man was the artist who worked for social justice—not the titan who worked for his own self-fulfillment. Yet both men warred within Dreiser himself. His artist was part titan, and the titan part artist; and when these concerns conflicted in his fiction, Dreiser's characters felt a sense of displacement which was Dreiser's own.

Dreiser was unable to reconcile his own romantic aspirations with his belief in a world of physical limits, and this led in his fiction to the displaced character—the man whose desire for self-fulfillment is in conflict with his environment. These characters yearn in a world of limits; their struggle seems to bring into operation destructive counter-forces. They believe that they are independent creatures of free will, but they are victims of their appetites, of physical needs, of other men, and of the universe. These characters are men of romantic illusions, often duped by a sense of power and strength they do not have, intent on realizing a kind of essential self, a feeling of capacity that drives them to the big city where, without ever looking back, they rush headlong into the future like lemmings to the sea. While the story often begins with an accident, the accident is only a catalyst which brings into operation a fatal quality of mind and temperament. Much like the doomed characters of tragedy, they often blindly cooperate in the process of events which brings them to a fate they are trying to avoid.

Dreiser externalized his own sense of conflict in his fiction. Even in his last days, when his own views were mellowing, he felt that fate was outside him, that the story of Hurstwood and Clyde Griffiths was the story of all men. Dreiser's final image of the universe was that of a greedy self, fulfilling its being at others' expense, and he believed this even as he contradicted himself by working for political causes that promised a better tomorrow.

For the last twenty years or more, many, if not most, of the literary critics have been concerned, even obsessed, with matters of myth, symbol, and stream of consciousness, and it is not surprising that, given this interest, Dreiser's reputation as a novelist has declined. Dreiser's literary technique seems more Victorian than modern—closer to Dickens than to Joyce. Dreiser did not endow his characters with a Joycean consciousness, with double-track minds that work back and forth in time, violating chronology. His characters do not think in terms of the haunted past or symbolic systems. As a result, we tend to lose sight of the immense influence that Dreiser has nevertheless had on a number of more recent writers. In the copy of *U.S.A.* that he sent Dreiser, John Dos Passos, for example, wrote on the flyleaf:

Dear Dreiser:

    I just want you to know that I still feel that if it hadn't been for your pioneer work none of us would have gotten our stuff written or published.

Norman Mailer has been even more specific in describing the legacy of Theodore Dreiser. "There was something going on in American life," Mailer writes, "which was either grand or horrible or both, but it was going on—at a dizzy rate—and the future glory or doom of the world was not divorced from it." The novelist of manners could not depict these matters. "So the job was left to Howells, Stephen Crane, to Dreiser, and in lesser degree to such writers as Norris, Jack London, Upton Sinclair—let us say that it was left to Dreiser." The genteel writers never understood how the new power worked, could not grasp its secrets, and they wrote "about courtship and marriage and love and play and devotion and piety and style, a literature which had to do finally with the *excellence* of belonging to their own genteel tradition." Dreiser came "closer to understanding the social machine than any other American writer who ever lived." Mailer's words are to the point. In fact, Mailer's fiction shares with Dreiser's the man of power who tries to over-leap himself and transvalue all values in the name of his own ideals, and to this extent, Dreiser's fiction is more modern than many of his critics have realized.

More than any other novelist in the twentieth century, Dreiser has been criticized for his view of reality, for his ideas. As inchoate as his ideas may be, they are not inchoate in his fiction, and the primary purpose of this book is to show how Dreiser moved from idea to fiction—a fiction which is its own justification.

In the course of writing this book, I have asked for many favors that I should like to acknowledge. First, Mrs. Neda M. Westlake, curator of the rare book collection at the University of Pennsylvania, allowed me to use the Dreiser papers and to quote from the letters of Dreiser and the holographs and typescripts of the novels and "Notes on Life." I am very grateful to her and her fine staff for their generous help. In great part, because of their cooperation, my wife and I can think back fondly of the almost four months we spent with the Dreiser papers in Philadelphia. Second, I should like to thank the World Publishing Company for permission to quote from Dreiser's works, *The Financier, The Titan, The "Genius," An American Tragedy, A Hoosier Holiday, Dawn, Newspaper Days*, and *Hey Rub-A-Dub-Dub*. I am also grateful to Doubleday & Company and to Mr. Harold J. Dies, trustee of the Drieser Trust, for permission to quote from *The Bulwark* and *The Stoic*.

My thanks go to Benny Hudnall who helped me track down obscure Dreiser articles and get them on xerox, to Virginia Tufte who helped at the early stages of the bibliography, and to Fran Kunkel and Kapaka Senko who helped with proofreading. I am also grateful to P. Albert Duhamel of the Boston *Herald*, Richard Seamon of *Time-Life*, and Miss Grenwald of the Los Angeles Public Library, who helped me locate a number of Dreiser photographs.

I am particularly indebted to John Espey, Donald Pizer, and Charles Shapiro who read the entire manuscript and made many useful suggestions. A simple acknowledgment cannot satisfactorily express my feeling of appreciation for their time and care.

My greatest appreciation, however, is to my wife, Ann, who was with me in this project every step of the way—from the time that we read and reread the Dreiser papers in Philadelphia to the final reading of proof. If a steady sense of encouragement is half the motives behind writing a book, then this is as much her book as it is mine.

Richard Lehan

University of California, Los Angeles
February 14, 1969

Theodore Dreiser: HIS WORLD AND HIS NOVELS

1

The Family

When Theodore Dreiser finished writing the story of Hurst-wood's suicide in the holograph of *Sister Carrie*, he wrote "The End" and then the date and hour: "Thursday, March 29, 1900 —2:53 p.m." He later added a long epilogue to *Sister Carrie*, treating a variety of subjects, most of which he then deleted, ending the novel almost as he had first intended. March 29, 1900 is an important date in American literary history. In writing *Sister Carrie*, Dreiser broke with the tradition of the senti-mental romance, wrote a new and "realistic" novel, and created a work that was in subject matter more original than even Stephen Crane's *Maggie*. Although it shocked Mr. Doubleday and later critics, the subject matter was hardly startling to Dreiser himself, who was merely telling the story of his own family and writing out of his own sense of experience.

The themes of *Sister Carrie*—the rejected family, the jour-ney to the towering city, the struggle against poverty, the de-sire for wealth, the illusion of limitless opportunity, the conflict between personal desire and conventional restraint, the urge to reject such convention, the effect of cosmic and social forces upon ignorant man, and the sweep of the tide of humanity toward a mysterious and hidden shore—these and other key themes dominate Dreiser's fiction from *Sister Carrie* to *The Stoic*. Dreiser's first novel was twenty-nine years in the making because it was twenty-nine years in the living. Time and new experience never radically changed Dreiser's literary concerns and emphases. In fact, by 1912 or soon after, he had roughly in mind the plots of all the novels that he was to write. *An American Tragedy* took a dozen years from inception to completion, and *The Bulwark* and *The Stoic* took over thirty years. Although Dreiser changed and rechanged the details of these novels, he remained remarkably faithful to his original conception of narrative pattern. In fact, while he became more competent in his craft, and while his concerns shifted as the world about him changed, the pattern remained, just as a skeleton remains while the flesh alters. Over and over, Dreiser wrote about a character's ordeal with his family, with the city, with money and poverty, with sex, with conventions and the law; and he set these characters in a complex political and social world where the laws of the universe—the mechanistic universe that so fascinated him—were forever working.

Perhaps the most important influence on Dreiser—one that would always remain—was his family; and a strange family it was. In fact, when Dreiser published *Dawn* in 1931, he deleted many of the intimate details, because he still found them embarrassing.

Dreiser's father, John Paul Dreiser (September 28, 1821—December 25, 1900) was born in Mayen, Germany, a small town surrounded by a large wall, geographically isolated from the big cities, and closer to Middle Ages than to the modern world. In the district of Moselle, Mayen was fifteen miles from Coblenz, part of the Rhineland, a region bordering Belgium, the Duchy of Luxembourg, and Alsace-Lorraine. Dreiser's father came to America in 1844, when he was twenty-three, to escape German conscription. Whereas his children would work their way from the rural Midwest back to the big city, he drifted from New York to Connecticut, and then to Dayton, Ohio, where he met Dreiser's mother.

Sarah Mary Schänäb (May 8, 1833—November 14, 1890) was the daughter of Henry Schänäb and Esther Schaub, of Pennsylvania German (or Dutch) origin and of the Dunkard or Mennonite faith. Against her father's will (he, in fact, disowned her), Sarah married John Paul Dreiser on January 1, 1848, when he was tweny-seven and she not quite sixteen years old. Dreiser's interest in rural Pennsylvania—an interest that culminated in *The Bulwark*—stemmed from a concern with his mother's religious and geographical background.

Dreiser never loved anyone else as much as he did his mother. Her death in November of 1890, when he was nineteen years old, was the shock of his life; and Dreiser was forever in search of women who would mother and love him. In the manuscript of *Dawn*, he says, in my youth "No one ever wanted me *enough*, unless it was my mother." [1] Dreiser's later promiscuity was, perhaps, an attempt to find a woman who could take her place. In the typescript of *Dawn*, he wrote and later deleted that his mother had "little moral and social sophistication" and was "a strange, sweet, dreamy woman." He goes on to say that "In *Jennie Gerhardt* I have indicated the type." [2] Mrs. Dreiser was to appear in many other of Dreiser's works, particularly in *An American Tragedy* (as Mrs. Asa Griffiths) and in the short story "Her Boy." As these works indicate, Dreiser thought of her as the always-loving mother who stood by and could never abandon the wayward son.

Dreiser was zealously attracted to his mother, perhaps because his father was the source of constant disappointment. Theodore was the eleventh child in a family of thirteen, counting the three oldest children who died before he was born on August 27, 1871 in Terre Haute, Indiana. The senior Dreiser, who was an experienced wool manufacturer, rented a factory in Sullivan, Indiana which burned to the ground in 1869, two years before Theodore was born. Uninsured, he insisted on paying the farmers who had lost their season's fleece in the burned sheds because, as a devout Roman Catholic, he believed his salvation depended upon it. When the mill was being rebuilt, a heavy beam fell and struck him, injuring him seriously. When Dreiser came to this event in the manuscript of *Dawn*, he described what happened to his father and then went back and added a relative clause, making it clear that it was a beam "which was being placed under his [his father's] architectural direction." Dreiser felt that his father's incompetence was responsible for the miserable plight of the family. "I looked upon him as mentally a little weak," he said; and he described in his novels the man of meager talents—George Hurstwood, Mr. Gerhardt, Asa Griffiths—who never fully recovers from a reversal of fortune.

The father and mother were a fixed point of reference in his mind. A man subject to fits of deep depression, Dreiser at some moments gave way to black moods based on fear of failure and death by poverty. A man who was also excited by the panorama of life, Dreiser at the next moment would be euphoric and trust completely in himself and a future of boundless possibility. Here he was very much the product of two very different parents. He saw his father as self-pitying and ineffectual, as a man of severe religious temperament whose demand for authority was undercut by his defeat in a world that was too much for mere man. He saw his mother as selfless and expedient, as a woman warmly devoted to her family whose emotional strength and trust in the future stemmed from her joy in the color of life.

The influence of his mother and father played a large part in Dreiser's later social and political ideas. He was obsessed with the psychology—"the mechanism," would be Dreiser's word—of both success and failure. He was fascinated with the way a Frank Algernon Cowperwood—who was everything his father was not—clawed and clamored his way to power and fortune. He was equally concerned with the way Asa Griffiths was destined to be overcome by life. Asa is modeled on a real-estate broker (Asa Conklin) for whom Dreiser worked in Chicago. He is also modeled on his own father, as a discarded version of *An American Tragedy* proves. Dreiser would always be fascinated by how life could turn out men as different as Cowperwood and Asa Griffiths, how men could so differ in individual temperament and physical drive. While he could never warm to the inept and fumbling father, he always sympathized with him, primarily because the helpless mother was also the victim of poverty. Poverty was too much a part of Dreiser's life—both when he was a child and when he was a struggling hack-writer in New York City—for him to turn his back on the poor. "As a child I was more than once hungry," he says in the manuscript of *Dawn*. "But through no want or effort on the part of the woman whose memory I adore," he hastened to add.[3] While Dreiser believed that some men were born to fail, and while he maintained that forces and counter-forces within nature kept the Cowperwoods from becoming too strong and powerful, he was moved by poverty and suffering and wanted desperately to change the economic structure of America. As he says in *Dawn*:

> I . . . recall long, dreary, grey cold days, meagre meals (only fried potatoes or fried mush at times), and my mother and father going about in shabby clothes. Life has long since schooled me in its bitter aspects . . . I can never look on crowded tenements or small, shabby cottages in cheap, mean streets, without reverting in thought to this particular period in our lives and wishing . . . life might be [different].[4]

Many critics maintain that Dreiser was an inconsistent mechanist, that he contradicted his belief in a world over which man had no control when he fought for social reform and when he joined the Communist Party in 1945. From one point of view, the critics are right: Dreiser suggests that man has both the will and the means to change his world. Yet Dreiser never really believed this. He did not accept communism with any hope for a new Utopia, nor did he believe it would change the nature of man. Life preyed on life, the struggle was fierce, and the strongest survived. But his heart conflicted with his head. In late nineteenth- and early twentieth-century America, Dreiser felt that the wealthy and the strong had luxury and power out of reasonable proportion to the masses. Far from everyone having an equal chance in America, he came more and more to believe that democracy protected invested interests. A privileged sixty families, as Ferdinand Lunberg maintained in *America's 60 Families*, controlled the country, exploited the land and the people, and they were intent on keeping America the way it was.

Dreiser believed that change had to come, that rebellion had come about in every such society from the old Roman to the new Russian, and that the balance would be restored, at least for a moment. "The dawn was in the East," he said, giving this title to a long argument in which he maintained that the modern civilization would not die but that communism—a mechanistic counter-force engendered by capitalism—would bring needed change. The important idea here is "change." Communism would change, not save, the world; and Dreiser had reservations about the Communist Party, even at the time he joined it in 1945. His attitude toward politics was more emotional than intellectual. He drifted into the Party with no philosophical or intellectual theory of life (although he had one, if called upon to give it) but because he remembered his own early years, especially his mother in her "shabby clothes," and particularly the day he cried when he saw her with holes in her shoes.

The poverty of Dreiser's parents also influenced his life-long interest in mechanistic philosophy, and perhaps even accounts for the fundamental inconsistencies in his thinking. On the one hand, Dreiser insisted that life was nothing but energized matter, completely indifferent to man. On the other hand, he maintained that all matter was moved by a creative intelligence. Because he had a mere factotum for a father, he all too easily consented to the insignificance and the helplessness of ignorant men who were the mere victims of a mysterious cosmic cause and effect process. He believed that matter was energy continually being discharged and renewed, that man was an insignificant part of the universe—a mere tool of a mysterious cosmic process, that man was devoid of will power and completely subject to physical laws and environment, and that the world in flux led to a continued process of change and contrast which gave life texture and pattern. When Dreiser, in fact, came to describe the nature of the atoms in flux, he compared them to a multitude of men—the George Hurstwoods who were so like his father—out of work. And yet

Dreiser had the continued attention of an affectionate mother, and he could also believe that a creative intelligence—some "thing" that cared—might be behind the "electro-chemical phenomena of life," as he called it in his unpublished manuscript, "Notes on Life." Here he suggested that a mind revealed itself in the workings of the universe, a mind which was immanent in nature and which unfolded before us as the petals of a rose unfold. Suddenly Dreiser's universe became more than mere energized matter: it was also alive with human emotion and sympathy, as compassionate as a loving mother. "Joy must be innate in energy itself," Dreiser said in "Notes on Life." "It cannot be elsewhere. The response of man, animal, bird . . . to sunlight, dawn, the new day . . . demonstrates that." [5] Dreiser's theory of both the universe and society has a strong corollary to his own sense of experience—and in particular to his experience within his family.

Along with his parents, Dreiser's brothers and sisters play an equally important part in his later life and in the subject matter of his novels. Mrs. Dreiser gave birth to her children with devastating regularity, almost all coming eighteen months apart from January to April of one year (Paul, Rome, Emma, Sylvia) followed by another from June to August of the next year (Mame, Theresa, Al, Theodore, Ed). Only Paul and Rome (who were born two years apart) and Claire (who was born in November) break the pattern.

The most famous of the brothers was Paul. A large, jovial, carefree man, Paul had been sent by his father to St. Meinerts novitiate in Kent, Indiana to study for the priesthood. From there he ran away, hiking sixty miles to Indianapolis, where he joined a vaudeville group and traveled over Ohio, Illinois, and Indiana before unexpectedly returning to Sullivan. Paul supported the family in Evansville, Indiana, when Dreiser was eleven years old, and there Paul kept his mistress—Annie Brace, a local madame, who went by the name of Sallie Walker and who was the subject of the song "My Gal Sal," which was later adapted into a successful movie. Paul eventually moved to New York, where he went into business with Howley, Haviland and Co., successful song producers, for whom he wrote such pieces as "The Letter that Never Came," "I Believe It for My Mother Told Me So," "The Convict and the Bird," "The Pardon Came Too Late," "Just Tell Them that You Saw Me," "The Blue and the Gray," and "On the Banks of the Wabash," for which Dreiser wrote the lyrics and which became the official state song of Indiana.

Paul coaxed Dreiser to leave his job on the Pittsburgh *Dispatch*, met him in New Jersey in the summer of 1894, and introduced him to New York, especially to Broadway, a moment that Dreiser never forgot. In fact, Dreiser wrote a long and excited essay about Broadway, "Whence the Song," based upon his experiences.[6] When Sister Carrie moves to a more heightened world, it is that of the Broadway stage. Dreiser was here looking through Paul's eyes, just as he had seen so much of Carrie's other experience through the eyes of his sister, Emma. Paul made a lot of money on Broadway, but when he died in 1906, he was bankrupt, and there was a family feud over the expense of burying him in Chicago's St. Boniface cemetery, in a plot near his parents (his remains were later removed to Terre Haute, Indiana, when a monument was built in his memory).

A second brother, Marcus Romanus (Rome), was the black sheep of the boys. A wastrel and a drunkard, he would disappear for years and then suddenly reappear in places like Evansville or Warsaw, thoroughly embarrassing the family. Dreiser never liked Rome. In the holograph of *Dawn*, he deleted a five-page attack in which he described Rome's self-centered and vicious ways; and in the final version of *Dawn*, he described Rome trying to borrow money from his sister's admirer in order to play the lottery. Dreiser used this incident in the first version of *Jennie Gerhardt*—Jennie going to Senator Brander for help when her brother, a bill collector, loses a large sum of his payments in a card game—but he also deleted this from the final text of the novel. When Dreiser was writing *Dawn* (and he had begun the writing as early as 1912), he said that Rome had met a drunkard's death. When the autobiography was published in 1931, he was embarrassed not to have deleted this passage from the book—for Rome had long since been discovered as much alive as could be hoped. In fact, when *Dawn* was finally published, Dreiser was supporting him in a Chicago rest home.

Dreiser used the pattern of both brothers' lives in his fiction: he admired Paul, and his characters want very much to be like the brother who left the small town and achieved relative success in the big city. He feared Rome, and his characters stand in dread of the brother who could die alone and unknown at any drunken moment in a cold river or a dark alley of a strange city. Dreiser wrote in horror about such a fate in "The River of the Nameless Dead," [7] the study of a man, much like George Hurstwood, whose unidentified body is found floating in the East River at Twenty-fifth Street.

If Rome was a source of embarrassment to the young Dreiser, his sisters were even greater ones. The oldest—ten years older than Dreiser—was Mary Frances, called Mame, born on July 7, 1861. A buxom, voluptuous girl, her story becomes, in part, the story of Jennie Gerhardt. Dreiser tells us in *Dawn*, where he refers to Mame as "Eleanor," that she took money from a prominent Terre Haute lawyer and politician, that she convinced Mrs. Dreiser that the family needed and should keep the money, and that she became the lover of this influential citizen after he helped get Paul (who had been arrested for forging a check) out of jail. Dreiser later used these incidents in *Jennie Gerhardt*.

When Mrs. Dreiser took the youngest children to Sullivan, Mame, who remained in Terre Haute with the father and the older sisters, worked in a local dry goods store, her salary generously supplemented by her lover who, like Senator Brander in *Jennie Gerhardt*, wanted to send her to a private school. Like Jennie Gerhardt, Mame becomes pregnant. Unlike Jennie, whose lover dies before he can marry her, Mame is deserted by her lover, who merely gives her one hundred dollars and the name of an abortionist. In the holograph of *Dawn*, Dreiser discussed Mame's pregnancy at length, although in a later version of the autobiography—perhaps to save Mame from further embarrassment—he attributed the events to one Kitty Costigan, supposedly Mame's closest friend. In both versions of the story, when the girl discovers that the abortionist has died, she goes to Dreiser's mother, who consoles her, moralizes over the situation ("Perhaps you will be a better girl for it," the same words Mrs. Gerhardt speaks to Jennie), and delivers her of a stillborn child.[8]

These events took place in 1879–80. Although Dreiser was not yet ten years old at this time, his sister's experience left an indelible mark. In a passage that he later deleted from *Dawn*, Dreiser said, "I give these incidents in their detailed form . . . [because] they colored the atmosphere in which I moved and made life seem the strange, unmoral [*sic*], rhymeless spectacle that it is." He then maintained that there was no relationship between the passions that moved the young—especially those who were from destitute and "under-dog families"—and the moral laws by which they were supposed to live. The real and the ideal, he maintained, are mutually exclusive, and man in America is haunted by a moral image of himself which cannot and does not exist in reality.

The religious dictates of the father were, needless to say, not very convincing to the children. Mame continued her wayward life until, in 1884, when she was in Chicago, she met Austin Brennan (called Walter Tisdale in *Dawn*) who introduced her to an elderly widower named Joseph H. Bull, a wealthy coffin manufacturer. Mame, however, showed little interest in Mr. Bull and eventually returned to Brennan, married him, and together they moved to St. Louis and later to New York. When Mame rejected Bull's proposal of marriage, he turned his attention to Theresa, the third oldest of the Dreiser girls, and he eventually seduced her. Theresa, whom Dreiser refers to as "Ruth" in *Dawn*, was born on August 3, 1864 (Dreiser himself was confused about the year). Although she was as promiscuous as her other sisters, she never became pregnant. After this affair, she lived for a long time with a painter (for whom Dreiser worked briefly) and was hit and killed by a train on October 22, 1897, at the age of thirty-three.

The second daughter, baptized Emma Wilhelmina Dreiser, led a life as hectic as Mame's. Dreiser wrote about her early years in *Dawn*, where he called her "Janet," but treated in *A Book About Myself* (Dreiser had really intended to entitle this *Newspaper Days*) the events in her life which became the basis for *Sister Carrie*, events that he had deleted from the pub-

lished work. In 1885, when she along with Mame and Theresa
was in Chicago, Emma met L. A. Hopkins, whom Dreiser describes as "a man somewhere near fifteen years older than herself and moderately well versed in the affairs of the world."
According to Dreiser's further account, Hopkins was "reasonably placed socially, married, and the father of two or three
children . . . all but grown to maturity," exactly the details
Dreiser used to describe Hurstwood. While Dreiser made him
the manager of a wholesale drug company in *Newspaper Days*,
Hopkins in reality was a mere clerk in a Chicago tavern, Chapin
& Gore (the Fitzgerald and Moy's of the novel) from which he
stole thirty-five hundred dollars (Hurstwood stole ten thousand
dollars),[9] taking Emma by way of Montreal to New York. Like
Hurstwood, Hopkins also returned part of the stolen money.

At this time Emma cut herself off from the family. Unlike
Carrie, however, she did return home twice: once in 1886 when
Mrs. Dreiser was ill in Warsaw, Indiana and again in 1890
when Mrs. Dreiser died in Chicago. Emma, however, was
hardly as resourceful as Carrie, and she did not rise above her
husband who, in fact, often beat her and whom she ended up
supporting. When they first arrived in New York, Hopkins
forced Emma to take in girls off the streets and soon they were
running a profitable house of prostitution, renting rooms in
shifts at between two to twelve dollars, grossing between one
hundred and fifty and three hundred dollars a month.[10] Later,
living on 15th Street in New York, Hopkins became a small-
time politician, a second deputy in the New York Street Clean-
ing Department, losing his job when the Tammany adminis-
tration was exposed by the Lexow Committee.

The later years of "Sister Carrie" are hardly illustrious. On
November 18, 1897, she was running (with less profit it seems)
another boarding house in Bayonne, New Jersey, where she
invited Dreiser (with no success) to take a room. On February
9, 1901, she had read *Sister Carrie*, but the best she could say
about her own story was "I liked the book very much." Like
the rest of the Dreisers, she was intensely superstitious, and
on April 20, 1908 she advised Dreiser to visit an astrologer, urg-
ing him to "go by what he tells you, . . . keep a close[d]
mouth, and believe in yourself." Her last letters reflect her

dismal conditions. On January 14, 1909, she pleaded with Dreiser to help her son George, who seemed to be as much a vagabond as Rome, to get a job "and . . . an old coat if you have one—and underwear." Over a year later, on October 25, 1910, Gertrude Hopkins, Emma's daughter, wrote Dreiser to complain about the lack of money, about "a quarrel every other day" with Hopkins, and about her mother who told her "that God will direct us." Two years later, on January 22, 1911, Emma herself told Dreiser that she was "most unhappy," and threatened in the letter to leave Hopkins and try to "meet some middle aged *sane* man who would appreciate a good home." [11]

Dreiser had lived with the Hopkinses when he first came to New York in 1894; and six years before the publication of *Sister Carrie*, he had anticipated these events. The ending of the novel reflects less his concern with the fate of Emma and more his belief in the compelling urges of the yearning heart, urges which move all the Emmas and all the Carries alike, whatever their end.

The fourth daughter, baptized Cecilia but called Sylvia, was the prettiest of the Dreiser girls. Dreiser, who referred to her as "Amy" in *Dawn*, said that in temperament Sylvia was most like Emma, and these sisters were in fact very close. When they both promiscuously encouraged the local streetcorner boys in Warsaw, Mr. Dreiser raged and fumed, as usual, finally forcing Emma to leave for Chicago, because he believed that she was a bad influence on Sylvia. A lot of boys wanted to marry Sylvia, including her cousin, Oliver Snepp (a corruption of Schänäb), the son of Mrs. Dreiser's brother, a bishop in the United Brethren Church. Mrs. Dreiser disapproved, but Sylvia still had an affair with Oliver, who (Mrs. Dreiser thought it divine intervention) died three years later of tuberculosis.

During this time, Sylvia also had an affair with Don Ashley, from one of the more prominent Warsaw families, who left town when she became pregnant and whose family haughtily dismissed Sylvia's pleas for help. This event, in a rough way, supplied the Lester Kane-Jennie Gerhardt plot in Dreiser's second novel. With a pregnant, unmarried daughter once again on her hands, Mrs. Dreiser appealed for help to Mame and Theresa, living in Chicago. Mame, in turn, appealed to Emma, whom she knew was well situated in New York, but whom she did not know was running a house of prostitution. Emma was willing to help, and Sylvia had her baby in New York where she stayed, sending the child back to Warsaw. Mr. Dreiser once more raged and stormed, eventually accepting the situation and growing to love the child.[12] Dreiser used these events in his novels: in *Jennie Gerhardt*, Mr. Gerhardt raged in exactly the same way; and in *An American Tragedy*, Russell, the illegitimate son of Clyde's sister, comes to live with the family.

Dreiser had been less than ten when Mame had her illegitimate child. He was over fifteen during Sylvia's ordeal, understood more of what was happening, and resented being in a family that was a town scandal. He brooded over these events for the next thirteen years, struggled to make sense out of them in *Sister Carrie* and *Jennie Gerhardt*, depicted the agony of his mother in *An American Tragedy* (a novel in which all events lead up to and away from the moment of seduction and inevitable pregnancy), and described once again morally rebellious children from the bewildered point of view of the religious father in *The Bulwark*.

As a realist, Dreiser felt almost compelled to stick to the actual facts of these catastrophes, especially in *Sister Carrie* and *Jennie Gerhardt*. Yet in *Jennie Gerhardt*, he made Jennie into a loving mother who dotes on her child. In real life, Sylvia reacted exactly the opposite. Dreiser was more shocked when Sylvia callously rejected her own child than when the child was born. Sylvia literally had nothing to do with her son after his birth, turning him over to her mother, who eventually gave him to Mame, still living in Chicago, where he died at the age of sixteen.[13]

These events were driving a wedge between the young Dreiser and his family. Although Dreiser helped support Rome, Mame, and Emma through their last years, he reached a point in his career when he could never go home again, when he had to move away from the turbulent lives of his brothers and sisters. Yet, in another sense, Dreiser never left home, never escaped the effects of the twenty years he spent with the family. When he left the Chicago *Daily Globe* in 1892 for the St. Louis *Globe-Democrat*, he was a man of many contradictions: he was superstitious and yet distrusted religion and moral conventions; he was filled with parochial prejudice and yet developing a political consciousness based on his sympathy for the poor; he was enraged by his father and yet so guilt-ridden that he would need to describe in a confessional way these early experiences as if the telling could somehow wash him clean; and he was suspicious of everyone and yet in dire need of the mother's love he had lost. In 1892, he was both apart from and a part of the family.

In a discarded version of *An American Tragedy*, Dreiser used a number of his childhood experiences in a less disguised way than they now appear in the final draft of that novel. At one point in this early draft, just after he had described how Clyde's family reacted when they discovered his unmarried sister's pregnancy, Dreiser says that Clyde began "to develop a peculiar and yet rather well concealed sombreness or morbidity which grew directly out of the wounds inflicted upon a sensitive and decidedly responsive psyche." [14]

Despite the jargon, this is an effective description of Dreiser himself. He would never come out from under the cloud of these early years: life would always be a dour matter, punctuated by occasional moments of drama and color, and structured upon the hope—the eternal yearning—for the riches and pleasures that money can buy. Dreiser would always suffer from a poverty complex: even when he had money in later years he would walk miles to avoid paying for a taxi or to find a place where he could get a cheaper haircut. His fear of poverty made him continually suspicious of even his best friends, who he thought were trying to use and cheat him. This led to breaks or at least unpleasantness with Arthur Henry (who encouraged him to write *Sister Carrie*), Grant Richards (who maneuvered Dreiser's 1912 trip to Europe), H. L. Mencken, Horace Liveright, Harold Hersey (who helped him fight *The "Genius"* battle), Hy Kraft (who tried to rewrite *Sister Carrie* for the stage and to help rewrite *An American Tragedy* and *Tobacco* for the movies), and William Lengel.

In the same early version of *An American Tragedy*, Clyde becomes more and more the dreamer, more the introvert as his family situation becomes more intolerable. Dreiser did the same, retreating into himself, cutting himself off from all but a very few friends, and distrusting even these. In 1894, working for the Pittsburgh *Dispatch*, Dreiser read Huxley, Spencer, Darwin, and Balzac, and he retreated after this reading into an abstract realm from which he would never emerge. The ideas of Huxley, in fact, were as real as the bleak, soot-stained Pittsburgh factories and workers' homes. Dreiser's life-long interest in science—an interest in later years that became an obsession —marked his way of trying to cope with, of trying to explain, the world that so baffled him even as a boy. His interest in science, his attempt to fathom man's insignificant place in a whirling universe, also marked his attempt to explain the ineptitude of his father and to dismiss once and for all the God of thunder to which his father had given total assent.

Unlike Clyde Griffiths, who only rejected his father emotionally, Dreiser was to reject him both emotionally and intellectually. The fact that he had to reject him reveals, of course, how persistent the father's influence was throughout Dreiser's life. Like so many other American novelists, Dreiser would continue to live in a house haunted by his father. As a young man, he could not wait to escape from that house, and his restlessness stemmed from his dissatisfaction with the home after his mother's death and with his belief that his destiny lay elsewhere. Like so many of Dreiser's characters, he believed that he had an essential self—a genius that made him superior to his family and to his boyhood friends. Like so many of Dreiser's characters, he also believed that he could realize this essential self only in the city. As he once said, "Those mystic cities! Already they were calling me." [15]

2

The New Man & the New City

Like Dreiser's novels, *Dawn*, the autobiography of his youth, is a story of becoming—of growth, of hope, of expectation, and of trust in oneself. Here Dreiser showed what it was to want and not to have, and no other literary work has ever described so well the psychology of desire. We see Dreiser as a boy more clearly than we will ever see him again—a youth of not remarkable intelligence, hopelessly shy, freighted with religious and racial prejudice, interested in the meaning of life and yet totally superstitious. We see him excited by the rush and flux of life, gifted with an eye for beauty in both nature and the city, tortured by the quickening of his own sexual blood, and trying in a stumbling way to find the means to satisfy all his longings.

Dawn reflects both the growth of an artist and of a young man who could have become a George Babbitt. Dreiser moved away from middle-class values as they victimized him. Throughout his autobiographies, he compared himself to a flower grow-

ing in a dark cellar. He saw himself suppressed by the family's
poverty and his father's fanatical beliefs. His father's dark authority hung over the family—even when the father was not
there—and blighted Dreiser's early days in Terre Haute, Vin-
cennes, Sullivan, Evansville, Chicago, Warsaw, and finally
back in Chicago. When Dreiser rejected his father, he rejected
the Roman Catholic Church, believing that it was responsible
for his father's blind faith, for his father's ineptness, and for
his own intellectual blindness. His years in Warsaw were somewhat more pleasant, primarily because his mother put him, his
brother Ed, and his sister Claire into a public school, the first
one he had ever attended. To his delight, he met a young and
pretty teacher who contrasted with the black-garbed nuns that
"terrorized me . . . with their ultra-solemn countenances and
their dull, dogma-repressed minds." [1] Dreiser's enthusiasm with
the public schools marks a break with the values of the family
—particularly his father's religion. His teacher, May Calvert,
became a life-long friend; and his second teacher, Mildred
Fielding, sent him for a year to the University of Indiana at
her own expense.

Dreiser found little to admire at the university. He looked
with philistine eyes upon men who pursued knowledge for its
own sake, was not moved by intellectual curiosity, and was
both impressed and depressed—as a Babbitt might be—by pro-
fessors like Arthur Peddoe Gats and Walter Deming Willikus
whose knowledge of the past, he felt, was dry and of little use
—"narrow, dull, even futile." [2] He was perhaps too much interested in the drama of life to be impressed with an academic interest in knowledge, although he would spend his last fifteen
years speculating about the nature of life and the universe. His
later scientific research stemmed from a compulsive desire to
find the answers that would finally justify the way he rejected
his father's Catholicism; but in 1889 he was more interested in
a vocation than in a theory of life.

Dawn is, in fact, a description of how Dreiser tried to find
his vocation. As a boy, he read *Diamond Dick, Brave and Bold,
Pluck and Luck, Work and Win*—that is, all the Horatio Alger
stories—and he believed in a world where wealth and romance
were only a dream away from poverty and hardship. At one

point in his autobiography, he wished that he were from an established family with business connections so that his future
would be fixed, so his vocation would have been dictated by
his birth. Dreiser would always distrust democracy, believing
that the wealthy still had the privileges of the old aristocracy
and that the poor had never found their sense of place. *Dawn*
is the study of a young boy who is trying to establish a sense of
place, trying to find himself in the modern world.

As Dreiser's father was a source of embarrassment, so was
the small town—and the next step in his growth was to reject
it. Even as a child in Sullivan, Indiana, he was discontent with
the small town. He was fascinated at this time by the trains
that passed in the night not far from his house, the eight-thirty
going to Nashville and Memphis, the eleven to Indianapolis
and Chicago. He yearned to be on them—to be away—and he
asked himself "when, ah, when, would come the day when I
should be setting forth on such a train to see the world?" [3]

Paul, Dreiser's oldest brother, had traveled all over America, and so had Rome, whose stories of St. Louis, New Orleans,
Galveston, Santa Fe, St. Paul, and Chicago thrilled Dreiser,
despite the fact that he was never fond of his alcoholic brother.
After Rome's visit, Dreiser's imagination took flight, and the
trains—even the birds—that streamed by became symbolic of
a life elsewhere, a world apart. Chicago, particularly, interested him. In 1880, it was a city with a population of less than
four hundred thousand, "but obviously already the up-and-
coming centre of the middle west, New York's only important
rival." [4]

As Dreiser rejected Catholicism emotionally before he rejected it intellectually, he also rejected the small town emotionally and longed for the big city as a source of escape. While
he liked the public schools of Warsaw, he was embarrassed
there by his sisters' promiscuous reputations. Moreover, he
could not find work in Warsaw, his one attempt at a farm job
ending in failure. The city called, and he told his mother that
he was going to Chicago: "I don't want to sit around this place
any longer. We can't get anywhere here. People only talk about
us." [5]

Dreiser had lived in Chicago before, his mother taking the

family there from Evansville in 1882, only to move on to Warsaw in 1883 when Chicago proved too expensive. Even though
Mame and Theresa still lived in Chicago, Dreiser was going
back alone, to make his separate way, and he was going back
as a modern-day Romantic, full of hope. The Chicago of 1887,
as Dreiser wrote about it in 1914, was an unreal city, and he
came to it "like a scene in a play: an Aladdin view in the Arabian nights . . . [a] mirage of the heart." [6] The city had become larger than life, had gone beyond reality: "The city of
which I sing," he wrote retrospectively, "was not of land or sea
or any time or place. Look for it in vain! I can scarcely find it
in my own soul now. Hail, Chicago! First of the daughters of
the new world!" [7]

The city not only became the source of Dreiser's motives,
it also became, logically enough, the subject matter of his writing. Interested in Chicago even as a boy, Dreiser read Eugene
Field's column about that city in the *Daily News* and realized
that he "wanted to write, possibly something like that." [8]

Dreiser eventually worked for the Chicago *Daily Globe*,
the St. Louis *Globe-Democrat*, the St. Louis *Republic*, and the
Pittsburgh *Dispatch*. His early journalism reveals a speculative
mind as well as a sharp eye for detail and the rhythms of life.
He wrote, for example, a series of articles for the *Republic*, entitled "Overheard in the Corridors," which were mostly imag-
inary interviews that allowed his imagination to take flight.
Basing his column on fictitious travelers who were supposedly
staying at the various St. Louis hotels, Dreiser was really inter-
viewing and even debating himself. The column always followed the same format. Dreiser would begin with a quote:

"I was the first to discover gold in the Ember district of New
South Wales," said Harold Meyer, a wealthy citizen of Australia,
who is stopping at the Lindell.

And

"It is a subject of wonder to many, including myself," said
Spencer Harding, who is at the Lindell, "that rays of light and
heat should pass through intense darkness and cold and still
retain their primal condition of light and heat."

The guest would then develop his ideas, and conclude aphoristically:

> "I do believe that there is a great deal more of the ridiculous in this world than there is of the sublime," said Philip Durham.[9]

Dreiser usually limited these discussions to three subjects—money (he had columns on credit buying, foreign merchants, and strikes and the economy), science (he had columns on instincts in animals, wind storms in Chicago, and the nature of earthquakes), and the meaning of life in general (he had columns of pessimism and optimism, music and the emotions, and why people give impractical gifts). Some of these topics were to have a life-time interest for him.

Unquestionably, Dreiser's best journalism at this time were the mood pieces in which he related his own feelings to city scenes and situations that he often brilliantly described. He would try to catch "the idle summer mood of the city";[10] and he wrote for the *Republic* a series of articles which were entitled "Pictures from Real Life," many of which are among his papers at the University of Pennsylvania.[11] Dreiser's writing at this time revealed a kind of inverted romantic esthetic: where the romantics believed that beauty was inherent in nature, Dreiser believed that beauty was inherent even in the city's ugliness, and that heroic drama went on in the slums. All experience, he felt, could be reduced to feelings, and each emotion had its relevant beauty. When Dreiser was sent, for example, to cover the story of a Negro stevedore who attacked his unfaithful girl friend with a razor, he tried to capture the mood of the scene: "the hot river waterfronts . . . the crowded Negro quarters . . . the sing-song sleepiness of the levee boat-landing, the stevedores at their lazy labors, the idle dreamy character of the slow-moving boats . . . the barbaric character of the alley in which it [the slashing] occurred." The scene "moved me," Dreiser tells us, "to a poetic frenzy." [12]

This early journalism leaves no doubt that Dreiser had a keen eye for detail and that he was trying to catch the sights and sounds of the city—the very flow of life itself. In a series of vignettes for the Pittsburgh *Dispatch*, for example, he described the different kinds of music one heard through open windows and in the parks on hot Pittsburgh nights;[13] how the Pennsylvania countryside looked on a day in which many people were out riding;[14] how General Booth of the Salvation Army looked when he last appeared in Pittsburgh;[15] how the spirit of the Fourth of July dominated a parade at a reform school.[16]

When he talked about abstractions, it was always from the point of view of people living and working in the city. He wrote, for example, fictitious conversations about books, including one with a literary janitor. He was fascinated by the flux and movement of the city—especially by the process of change; and he decried the loss of two, three, and five-cent silver money, one-cent and nickel pieces, and one, three, and fifty-dollar gold coins.[17] Many of these articles are quite serious, revealing a concern with the cruelties and enigmas of life. He described, for example, the city coming to life on Monday— the clerks trying to escape the plight through "Arabian Night" dreams, the factory workers trudging once again to work, the women at their wash, and poor O'Rourke sentenced to thirty days in jail because the magistrate suffered from the perversity of "blue Monday." [18] He also described a man named Fintz dying in a hospital while life went on around him, strangers laughing and jesting in the courtyard below. In all these pieces, Dreiser had an eye for contrast, but particularly here, as he contrasted the world of the living with the ordeal of dying. As in Dreiser's writing in general, the descriptive details here generate their own peculiar emotion and arrest the moment:

> Even while [Fintz's eyes] were yet strained the glassiness crept into them, and the watching attendant closed the lids. Then the loosened jaw was bound shut, the arms folded and the body wrapt in rough linen.[19]

Dreiser's journalism was prelude to a long career as a free-lance writer. When he left St. Louis, he had gone to Grand Rapids, Ohio, where he hoped to become a partner in a small-town newspaper. Reluctant to become trapped in the small town, he had drifted to Toledo, Ohio (where he met Arthur Henry, who would soon become his closest friend), then had moved on to Cleveland (where he was in awe of the beautiful homes on Euclid Avenue), then to Buffalo (where he once again failed to find a job), and then to Pittsburgh and his job with the *Dispatch*.

In the late summer of 1894, Paul invited Dreiser to New York, met him in Jersey City, and took him across the river on the ferry. Suddenly Dreiser was in New York. The city at first seemed dirty and crowded and did not impress him; but when Paul took him to Broadway, Dreiser changed his mind. It had taken him twenty-three years to get to New York; the journey had been circuitous; but once there he knew that he wanted to live no place else. When he left Paul, Dreiser returned to the *Dispatch*, but he now found Pittsburgh intolerable; and in November of 1894, when he was twenty-three, he quit his job and came to New York to seek his destiny once again in the big city.

His early efforts met with disappointment. When he finally got a job with the *World*, it was on "space," which meant that he received $7.50 a column. Because he was seldom given a significant assignment, he seldom wrote a column; and when he stumbled upon big news, the story was taken from him and given to one of the regular reporters. On his first day, he made $1.86, and some days he would make even less.[20]

From the *World* he went to *Ev'ry Month* (a magazine financed by Howley & Haviland Co., Paul's firm, to promote their songs), where he wrote a philosophical column called "Reflections" which he signed "The Prophet." At this time, Arthur Henry had given up his editorial job on the Toledo *Blade* and come to New York. In *Lodgings in Town*, Henry recorded his first impressions of New York, his excitement in being in the city, his concern with the effects of poverty, his anxiety about becoming a successful writer—and his book superbly portrayed the spirit of New York at the turn of the century. Henry also portrayed Dreiser at work at *Ev'ry Month*. As he entered the offices of Howley & Haviland, Henry first saw in one corner "a lady with a very droll countenance, very blonde hair and a gorgeous hat and gown" singing beside a piano. In another corner he saw "a very fat man," surely Paul Dresser, "hanging . . . over the keys" of another piano, "thrumming and humming a song he was composing." The song was sad, and "I . . . saw a tear roll down his big fat face as, verse completed, he sang it softly through." Climbing some stairs that led to "a dingy little room, just large enough for two chairs and a table," Henry found Dreiser at work on the next issue of *Ev'ry Month*. Henry showed Dreiser an article that he had just written, and Dreiser bought it for fifteen dollars, the two cashing the teller's check before going to lunch, during which Dreiser told Henry to write an essay on the New York Foundling Asylum, how it cared for young orphans and even unmarried mothers—a concern that obviously stemmed from Dreiser's own experience with his three sisters and their illegitimate children. Dreiser was not at all happy at this time. "I am drawing a good salary," he told Henry, but "the things I am able to get the boss to publish that I believe in are few. The rest must tickle the vanity or cater to the foibles and prejudices of readers. From my standpoint, I am not succeeding." [21]

The desire to succeed was becoming an obsession; and when Dreiser fell out with Paul, he abandoned *Ev'ry Month* and began to free-lance. One of his most profitable sources at this time was Dr. Orison Swett Marden's *Success*, for which Dreiser interviewed John Burroughs, Andrew Carnegie, Thomas Edison, Marshall Field, Frank Gunsaulus, William Dean Howells, Philip D. Armour, Joseph H. Choate, Chauncey M. Depew, Lillian Nordica, and many others. Soon Dreiser was making more money free-lancing than he had as a reporter.

Seemingly secure, he thought of getting married. When he had been in St. Louis, he had met Sara White, an attractive school teacher from Montgomery City, Missouri, whom he had accompanied to the Chicago World's Fair when she, along with a dozen other Missouri school teachers, won a popularity contest held by the *Republic*. Shy and parochial, two years older than Dreiser, Jug (as Dreiser called her) embodied the deeply religious and highly conservative mentality that he would spend the rest of his life trying to overcome. Yet, to his eventual regret, on December 28, 1898, Dreiser and Sara were married by a Methodist minister on Massachusetts Avenue in Washington, D.C.

The Dreisers spent the summer of 1899 with the Henrys in Maumee, Ohio, where Dreiser wrote his first short story, "Mc-

Ewen of the Shining Slave Makers," and began *Sister Carrie.* The story (one that Dreiser had great trouble getting published) is an allegory wherein men are reduced to ants, which is exactly the way Dreiser was beginning to think of men in general. Significantly, two ants help each other in the battle of life, which is symbolically the way he thought of himself and Arthur Henry at the time he wrote the story. "Nigger Jeff," the next story that he was to write, reveals Dreiser as a newspaper reporter, turning from a cold observer to a humanitarian, moved by calamity and infused with the desire to do something about the suffering he sees. The reporter in the story becomes aware of the double standard of justice when he sees a Negro lynched by a mob. He is further moved by the agony of the Negro's suffering mother—a subject that always affected Dreiser. In some ways, "Nigger Jeff" was Dreiser's own nightmare vision of what might happen to him, or to any man of passion, who was suddenly carried away by impulse and committed a crime, his fate a source of horrible pain to the mother. Dreiser would use this same story over and over, making best use of it, of course, in *An American Tragedy.*

After that summer in Maumee, Dreiser and Henry returned to New York, where they collaborated on articles and where Dreiser finished *Sister Carrie* in March of 1900. The approaching summer was a disastrous one for Dreiser. Visiting with Jug's family in Montgomery City, he received word, first from Henry, then directly from the publisher, that Doubleday, Page was trying to break their contract to publish *Sister Carrie.* Following Henry's advice, Dreiser forced Doubleday, Page to publish his novel. Although he later said that the publisher refused to sell a copy, this was not true. From the correspondence in Dreiser's own file, we know that on February 1, 1901, Doubleday, Page had received 558 copies from the bindery, of which they sold (at $1.50 apiece) 334 copies and distributed 127 "editor's copies" for review, leaving 97 copies on hand, and netting Dreiser $50.10 in royalties. On August 1, 1901, Doubleday, Page bound another 100 and sold (including some of the 97 on hand) 117 more copies, leaving (after two editor's copies) 78 on hand, netting Dreiser $17.55 in royalties. On

February 1, 1902, Doubleday, Page bound another 350 copies and sold 423 to J. F. Taylor. At this time, Dreiser received a check for $84.78 from the English sales of *Sister Carrie*. While Mr. Doubleday did nothing to promote *Sister Carrie*, he also did nothing to suppress it, even though years afterwards Dreiser would insist differently.[22]

The end of the first year of the new century was a nightmare for Dreiser—one that literally taxed his sanity. Along with his disappointment over *Sister Carrie*, his friendship with Arthur Henry hit a snag. Moreover, his father had died on Christmas day of 1900, and Mame and Brennan were squabbling with him over the cost of the funeral. When Dreiser sent *Cosmopolitan Magazine* his article, "The Problem of the Soil," there were still twenty-five cents due on the postage. *Cosmopolitan* rejected the article but would not return the manuscript until Dreiser paid the charges. Furious, he wrote a blistering letter to Mr. Vassault, one of the editors. H. H. Boyesen replied that he was sorry for Dreiser's "long record of trouble with *Cosmopolitan*," and, in what must be gigantic understatement, concluded that "your letter to Mr. Vassault displayed very little warmth indeed."

While Dreiser wrote easily, he was careless about details; and during his free-lance days he often found himself in trouble. When he wrote an article on fire arms and cartridges for *Cosmopolitan Magazine*, H. J. Miller wrote the editors that much of it had been plagiarized from a catalogue of the Winchester Arms Company. Dr. Marden of *Success* wrote him (July 11, 1900) that "I have a letter from Mr. Reed who is very angry about your interview published in *Success*, which he says he never gave." When Dreiser wrote an article, "Advance of the Trolley Car," for *Pearson's Magazine*, the editor's paid him ninety-five dollars and then wrote (June 28, 1901) that his maps were all wrong and "It is not possible at present to go from New York to Sing Sing by trolley; there is no trolley as a matter of fact along the Eastern bank of the Hudson River after Hastings, which is this side of Tarryton."

Life was indeed gray. One can only imagine how Dreiser responded to a letter from *Harper's* (June 24, 1902), just before his nervous breakdown, asking him to write an article on "Christmas in the Tenements," adding: "We don't want much misery," but something "bright and cheerful."

These were years of doubt and depression, of flight from poverty and a search for stability. He was drifting—as his list of addresses reveals. He lived for a while with Emma at 232 West 15th Street, then moved to the Salmagundi Club at 14 West 12th. After the summer with the Henrys, Sara and he lived at 6 West 102nd Street, from which they moved to 1599 East End Avenue (at 82nd Street). Although he was working on a draft of *Jennie Gerhardt* at this time, he brought it with him to Bedford City (outside of Roanoke) Virginia. From there he went with Jug to Missouri, to spend the end of December with the Whites, and from there to the Gulf coast which they left in early February, 1902 for Hinton, West Virginia, stopping after that at Lynchburg, Virginia before they spent April and May at Charlottesville, Virginia, where Dreiser finished Chapter 10 of *Jennie Gerhardt*. When the novel bogged down, Dreiser started out alone on a walking trip that took him three hundred miles, ending in Rehobeth, Delaware. From there he walked on to Philadelphia, where he lived at 3225 Ridge Avenue before Jug rejoined him and they moved to 210 Summac Avenue, where they lived until February, 1903. At this point, Jug left for Montgomery City and Dreiser for New York, where he hoped to write himself out of poverty.

When he moved into a $2.50-a-week bedroom at 113 Ross Street in Brooklyn, he feared he was going insane. On the verge of suicide, he visited Mame, who was so upset with his ragged appearance that she called Paul. When Paul finally found him, he sent Dreiser to a health camp, Muldoon's, just outside of White Plains. From there Dreiser went to work as a laborer for the New York Central at the Spuyten Duyvill shop on the Hudson. In the autobiographical *The "Genius,"* he discussed a love affair he had at this time with his landlady's daughter, probably that of a Mrs. Hughes of Kingsbridge Avenue, Kingsbridge, New York, with whom we know (from a letter dated July 31, 1903) that Dreiser was living at this time. In September of 1903, he had moved in with a

Schill family on Nathalie Avenue, Kingsbridge, New York, where Jug seems to have rejoined him.

Dreiser had considerable editorial experience. He had edited *Ev'ry Month* from October 1895 to September 1897 and was later a consulting editor for both *Ainslee's* and *Success*. When he finally regained his health, he resigned from the railroad on Christmas eve 1903 and became an editor of Munsey's New York *Daily News*. On a tip from Richard Duffy, he left Munsey's and went to work for *Smith's Magazine*. The Smith publishing house, located at 156 Fifth Avenue, consisted of *Ainslee's, Popular Magazine,* and *Smith's Magazine* which had a circulation of two hundred thousand and which Dreiser edited from the fall of 1904 to April of 1906. He then left *Smith's* for the *Broadway Magazine*, located at 3–7 West 22nd Street, owned by Thomas H. McKee, who ironically was the Doubleday, Page lawyer during Dreiser's difficulties with *Sister Carrie*. While Dreiser had a good sense of what would interest his readers (he sent, for example, Charles Fort to Ellis Island to describe the influx of immigrants, and he later commissioned him to write the play "When a Man's Not Working"), he was careless about schedules and unable to manage his staff. In a memo (February 4, 1907) McKee criticized him for his "lack of attention to details," and later wrote (March 29, 1907) that "The managing editor must *manage*. . . . His job is to find the tools that I designate." He concluded, "At no time have I been satisfied with you as managing editor." Dreiser, seeing the handwriting on the wall, left the *Broadway* in June of 1907 for a much better-paying job with Butterick's *Delineator,* where he remained as editor until October 15, 1910.

Dreiser had broken with Arthur Henry in 1904, after Henry published *An Island Cabin,* an account of the few weeks in the summer of 1901 that Dreiser had spent on Dumpling Island off Noank, Connecticut with Henry and Anna Mallon. When Dreiser introduced Anna, who ran a typing service, to Henry, he started a chain of events that led eventually to Henry's divorcing his wife and marrying Anna. Dreiser brought the same emotional intensity to a friendship that he did to a love affair; and when Anna threatened his friendship with

Henry, he turned on her—just as he would turn on George Nathan when Nathan threatened his friendship with H. L. Mencken. Henry recounted Dreiser's attitude that summer— his severity with Anna, his fastidious concern over the cabin's unwashed floor and dishes—in *An Island Cabin,* in which Dreiser is disguised as "Tom." Although Henry also described Dreiser's interest in sea biology, and lauded his power of observation and analysis, the general portrait hurt Dreiser, and he angrily broke with Henry in February of 1904. (Dreiser would get revenge years later when he portrayed Anna and Henry as Rona Murtha and Winnie Vlasto in *A Gallery of Women,* a portrait in which Henry becomes a cruel bully who is merely using Anna for her money and who deserts her when he meets a wealthier woman.)

Three years after Arthur Henry dropped out of Dreiser's life, H. L. Mencken wandered in. Although Mencken lived in Baltimore, Dreiser had become aware of his journalism and his free-lance writing, and before Dreiser actually assumed his official duties at the *Delineator,* he wrote Mencken (April 26, 1907), offering him an editorial position at fifty dollars a week. While Mencken did not accept the job, he did contribute regularly to the magazine, Dreiser writing him (March 4, 1909) to request an article entitled "What Science Has Done for the Sick." Dreiser asked him again (April 10, 1909) to write a series of articles on women: "A Woman as Seen by Others"—her physician, lawyer, pastor, merchant, broker. A bachelor, the cigar-chewing Mencken also collaborated with Dr. Leonard Hirshberg on a baby-column. Dreiser and Mencken became close friends at this time, although they were often at odds. Mencken, for example, had just edited *The Philosophy of Frederick Nietzsche* and tried unsuccessfully to convince Dreiser that Nietzsche was an important thinker. "I can't say that I greatly admire him," Dreiser wrote (April 16, 1909). "He seems to [be] Schopenhauer confused and warmed over."

Dreiser might very well have continued as editor of the *Delineator,* if he could have restrained his passion for Thelma Cudlipp, the seventeen-year-old daughter of an assistant editor. When the affair frightened Thelma's mother, she literally kidnapped her own daughter to keep her from running away with Dreiser. Thelma spent the next year in England and later married Charles Seymour Whitman, who became Governor of New York. In the meantime, Dreiser had lost his job at the *Delineator*—and also his wife. Just before he was fired on the 15th of October, 1910, Dreiser left Jug and moved into the Park Avenue Hotel and then later rented a large room in the Riverside apartment of his friend Elias Rosenthal. Just six months before (April 6, 1910), he had written Charles Battell Loomis, commissioning him to do a *Delineator* article entitled "How to Keep A Wife's Love."

The city was forming Dreiser, acting as a catalyst and bringing out elements dormant in his personality—just as it did with so many of Dreiser's characters. He came to the city in pursuit of his destiny—a self that was waiting to be born. Dreiser was a modern-day romantic, a wanderer in search of the experience or situation by which he could best realize his nature, his very essence. In *The Social History of Art*, Arnold Hauser described "the inner strife of the romantic soul [which] is reflected nowhere so directly and expressively as in the figure of the 'second self.'" The "second self" stems from the romantic tendency toward "self-observation and the compulsion to consider oneself over and over again as unknown, as an uncannily remote stranger." [23] In the romantic's desire to escape from his social situation, he pursued his "double"—that is, he rushed after an ideal image of self. For this reason, the romantic is always in flight, chasing himself down the corridors of time, believing that in the flux of experience some kind of chance occurrence will ultimately bring him complete self-realization. No matter how depressed he became, no matter how bleak the future seemed, Dreiser continued to believe that he would inevitably catch his second and essential self. A curious optimism runs through his autobiographies: he felt that "wonderful things" were "going to befall me";[24] "that I was destined for a great end";[25] that we are all the products of "chance" so that whatever happens "was all a part of my essential destiny";[26] and that his constant desire for new experience, "the unconscionable urge to move and be away," proved "that certain lives are predestined." [27]

The city was the vortex within which he could best realize his essential self. The city also embodied a state of mind. As Dreiser himself tells us, it did not exist in reality but as a "shadow to the glory that was in my own mind . . . [a] strange illusion of hope," [28] "a land of promise." [29] Only Chicago and later New York were equal to his sense of expectation; only the big city was equal to his own inflated sense of self and destiny. Dreiser had gone to find himself, the city supplying the key that would unlock the door of his future, the city grounding the dream:

> in Chicago . . . I took up my seeking—for work as well as the key to my own disposition and life. For in me were bubbling the most ethereal and yet colorful dreams and possibilities. As for Chicago, it seemed stronger, brisker, more colorful even than before. . . . I liked it much, for here one sensed vigorous, definite projects under way, great dreams and great achievements, and behind them strong, definite-minded, if not so terrifically visionful, men at work. It was more money, money, money, and the fame of the same, the great fortune idea.[30]

This is romanticism in the age of big business. Dreiser, in fact, even used Shelley's images, comparing himself at one point to "a harp on which nature strummed her melodies" [31]— only it turned out that the winds that ultimately play over him are those of "money, money, money . . . the great fortune idea." Dreiser inverted the romantics' belief that the spirit of God, the spirit of Beauty itself, was immanent in the universe, and he suggested instead that the spirit of money permeated a city like Chicago. The music to which Dreiser danced was the music of Mammon; and money—or the hope of it—became the motive that directly moved most of his characters.

If Dreiser came to associate the city with money and the promise of success, he also associated it with sex. He was twelve years old when his mother first took him to Chicago, and there, as he tells us, "I felt the tang and pang of love." [32] He goes on to say that from the time he was fifteen until he was thirty-five (and here he is being conservative) he was helpless before beautiful women: "there appeared to be a toxic something in [the female] form itself." [33] Just as Dreiser desired money, so he desired sex. "Persistence in the form of dream and desires eventually produces our typical experience," Dreiser once wrote.[34] This is an extraordinary remark for a novelist who repeatedly showed his characters—Carrie, Jennie, Hurstwood, Clyde, even Cowperwood—as victims of their desires; and yet Dreiser believed personally that as long as one desired something hard and long enough he would eventually get it.

If his early sexual desires were not realized, Dreiser at least said that they were. The women that he longed for came to him, seemingly pulled by the power of his desire. This happens first at Warsaw, when a baker's daughter literally seduces him. It happens again in Chicago—in fact, three times. When he is working in Asa Conklin's real-estate office, a young widow tries to seduce him: "such," says Dreiser, "is the communicative as well as effective power of desire." [35] While still with Conklin, a sixteen-year-old Italian girl "with dark, liquid eyes" offers herself as still another sexual sacrifice, in a scene that has more of the quality of erotic daydreaming than reality.

What we see in this section of *Dawn* is that women exist—either in fact or fancy—as an object of desire: Dreiser longs for, acquires, and then uses them—just as money is longed for, to be acquired, and spent. Dreiser's attitude toward women is identical, in fact, with his attitude toward money. We see this clearly in young Dreiser's feelings toward Nellie Mac-Pherson, one of the clerks in the laundry firm for which he works. Nellie is pretty, pleasant, and affectionate; but she is from an undistinguished family, and he feels that Chicago should and could offer him more. Dreiser discussed in this context the "social supremacy" of Chicago, linked his desire for money with his desire for women, and confessed that he would like "to succeed financially by marriage with some beautiful and wealthy girl." [36] Beauty and wealth, money and marriage —what we have here, of course, is the pattern of a Horatio Alger tale of success. What we have also is the mentality of a Clyde Griffiths. In fact, the metamorphosis from Dreiser to Clyde is complete when Dreiser tells us, "and when I thought of Nellie MacPherson—I am sorry to confess this—she seemed a mere trifle. How quickly I would leave her for something better!" [37]

3

The Opposing Selves

Charles W. Morris in *Six Ways of Life* described six kinds of personalities: the Dionysian who surrenders self to instinct, the Buddhist who annihilates self, the Christian who purifies the self, the Mohammedan who merges the self in a holy war, the Appolonian who conserves traditional values, and the Promethean who conquers his environment through science and technology. Dreiser embodied the Promethean way of life —first through his grudging admiration of the titan and later through his belief in the social and political power of technocracy. Dreiser, in fact, once said that he would rather be a "seeking Prometheus" than a "whimpering slave praying for some Nirvana." [1]

One does not have to look far to see the Promethean quality in Dreiser's thinking. The city compelled him because it was creating, through industry and finance capitalism, a new world. The factories were to him a thing of beauty, and Dreiser identified himself with the new industry and the new city in a lyrical way. Thinking back to the time when he was a boy in Chicago, Dreiser wrote:

> Joy was ever before me, the sense of some great adventure lurking just around the corner.
>
> How I loved the tonic note of even the grinding wheels of the trucks and cars, the clang and clatter of cable and electric lines, the surge of vehicles in every street! The palls of heavy manufacturing smoke that hung over the city like impending hurricanes; the storms of wintry snow or sleety rain; the glow of yellow lights in little shops at evening, mill after mill, where people were stirring and bustling over potatoes, flour, cabbages —all these things were the substance of songs, paintings, poems.[2]

The industrial revolution and the mechanical revolution are, of course, not the same. Factories preceded the machine —in fact, factories existed in the Roman Republic. The old factories, however, depended upon human labor, the new factories on the machine. In 1831, Michael Faraday perfected the principle of the electric dynamo. In 1876, Werner von Siemens built a working dynamo, powered by coal. Between 1840 and 1870 the production of coal and iron had increased eightyfold in north-central England, northeastern France, and in the Ruhr Valley and Silesia in Germany. In 1816, for example, England mined 16 million tons of coal; in 1870 it mined 118 million tons.

The production of coal and steel brought the rise of the modern factory system, and the factories gave rise in turn to the cities. In 1851, more than one half of the British population lived in the cities where factories mass-produced goods, which increased human wants, and which in turn led to both great wealth and dire poverty. As the mills and factories switched to the machine, the new industry demanded more fixed capital to operate. This encouraged the investor and speculator, and the source of wealth shifted from land to corporate securities. When the manufacturers consolidated their efforts, the trusts were born. The trusts (particularly in America) eventually controlled resources (iron and steel), manufacturing, marketing, and transportation (especially the railroads).

1776 was a significant year. Not only did it mark the birth

of America, but it was also the year in which James Watt invented the steam engine and Adam Smith published his *Wealth of Nations.* If the simultaneity of the three events is accidental, the connection between the machine, laissez-faire capitalism, and the new democracy is not. If the American Revolution was anti-feudalistic, it was not anti-property. In fact, in many of the new states the right to hold political office and even to vote was contingent upon owning property. Some historians believe that class power has remained more or less unchanged from, as one commentator facetiously put it, Cotton Mather to the Cotton Exchange, from General Washington to General Motors.[3]

The American Civil War was, among other matters, a fight between two kinds of property owners: the landed gentry and the industrial capitalists—a fight between those who embodied the spirit of the land (the old frontier) and those who embodied the spirit of the machine (the new titan and later the tycoon). The essential difference between the old aristocracy and the new corporation was that one cared for hierarchy and the other for money and power.

Dreiser was always quick to recognize the accomplishments of the new American titan. Astor, he pointed out, laid the way across the country for roads and railroads, which Vanderbilt finally pushed through; Rockefeller and Carnegie developed our natural resources; Armour took us one step from the jungle by mass slaughtering our animals and packaging our meats; Ford and Pullman made it possible for us to cover vast distances of land with some degree of ease.[4] Dreiser once said that he "was tremendously interested by the rise of various captains of industry." He was amazed by their trusts and combinations and by the way they manipulated the railroads, oil and coal fields, telephone and telegraph companies. At the same time, he said that he "could never think of the work being done in any factory or institution without passing from that work to the lives behind it." Dreiser sympathized with the drab lives of the workers, their bare homes and bone-tiring routines, and concluded that "it was the underdog that always interested me more than the upper one."[5]

While Dreiser knew poverty at first hand, and while he

was moved by the plight of the poor, he could not decide whether poverty was a given and determined fact of life or whether it could be eliminated by human effort. In an early *Ev'ry Month* "Prophet" essay he said that "it may be best for the progress of the world that there should be such a gap between the very rich and the very poor." He then went on to say in the very same essay that the highest social ideal in life is to work "for the general good of others." [6] One statement suggests that poverty is inevitable, while the other allows the poor (supposedly with some hope of fulfillment) the possibility of overcoming their condition. Dreiser would always have difficulty reconciling these two positions because they stemmed from two conflicting attitudes toward man, society, and the universe.

On the one hand, he firmly believed in a mechanistic philosophy, believed that all life was determined by forces and counter-forces. These forces worked *through* man, shaping him, supplying his motives, driving him on; and they created the flux, motion, and the change in life. As a result, man had no more individual motives—had no more free will—than the individual bee in the hive. In fact, Dreiser's concept of society was very similar to the biologist's concept of life in the bee or ant kingdoms, where all activity is at best instinctual; man can no more change himself or his society than could the worker, the drone, or the queen bee change the order of life in the hive.

On the other hand, Dreiser knew that to reduce life to this mechanistic level was to destroy man's ideal, to negate aspiration, and to give up in the face of affliction. He did not want to accept the status quo as he knew it, to concede that the masses were helpless against the classes, that the worker had limited rights, and that the puritan and genteel moral and social traditions in America were destined to prevail. In fact, in his early *Ev'ry Month* essays, Dreiser was quick to point out social institutions which, if changed, would lessen the plight of the poor. He attacked in particular the courts where laws "multiply" and "precedents in both corrupt and honorable cases accumulate, and become more complicated," and where justice seems to depend on the "money wherewith to defend it." [7] Dreiser praised the good work of Governor John P.

Altgeld of Illinois (whom he favorably depicted as Governor Swanson in *The Titan*) who was fighting for legal reform—also Clarence Lexow of New York who cleaned up Tammany Hall in 1894 and then turned to investigate the trusts. In both cases, a courageous crusader, with the support of the people, brought about social change and reform—a fact that Dreiser could not completely reconcile with his rudimentary mechanistic definition of man.

Dreiser was particularly sympathetic to Lexow's attack on the trusts because he saw the trusts as the real enemy of the people, as the source of class privilege and mass misery. The trusts "have no heart," he said. They combine to cut down competition, eliminate jobs, fix prices, and increase profits. "The trust, and those who sponsor it," Dreiser concluded, "must be crushed in the struggle. Such a culmination will prove how wrong is the trust, and how right are the many in advocating kindness, love and mercy." [8]

For all its truth about the trusts, this statement is certainly naive in its idealizing of the masses. Here we see the dichotomies around which Dreiser built his politics, even his very early politics. He saw the struggle as a class war, the rich and the poor locked in deadly combat, the rugged individualist and the masses on two sides of an unbalanced scale. When he came to the Pittsburgh *Dispatch*, he was impressed with the homes of the very rich ("Never did the mere possession of wealth impress me so keenly") and depressed with the plight of the poor ("It seemed astonishing to me that some men could thus rise and soar about the heavens like eagles, while others, drab sparrows all, could only pick among the offal of the hot ways below"). [9] These dichotomies, of course, are the old romantic dichotomies. While Dreiser is far from believing that man is innately good, he is nevertheless only a step away from Rousseau's belief that social institutions are corrupt—a step which often led him (as in the *Ev'ry Month* passage above) to sentimentalize the poor.

While Dreiser greatly admired Clarence Lexow and Governor Altgeld who, in relatively minor ways, worked for the people, he never wrote, or even planned to write, a novel about such a culture hero—perhaps because the times had failed to supply him with a convincing model, a model who could be to the people what Charles Yerkes was to big business. In the play *The Girl in the Coffin,* Dreiser came closest to a proletarian hero with John Ferguson, the strike leader modeled on Big Bill Haywood.

In Dreiser's early essays, we find the core of his political philosophy. He did not want to see capitalism destroyed—not even when he was working for communist causes during the thirties. Instead, he wanted reform—a more just "balance" between the very rich and the very poor. As Dreiser said, he would always support the underdog; and it is indeed significant that when he went to Russia in 1927, he attacked the privileges of the Russian laboring class with the same intensity that he attacked the privileges of the American upper class. As a mechanist, he should have accepted the imbalance that he saw before him—but his emotions conflicted with his ideas. He insisted that there were "balances" in nature and that men could bring about an economic balance, an "equity," an idea that contradicted his belief that man was determined by mechanistic forces beyond his control and that man was without free will. Only in the last years of his life, by qualifying his sense of "individualism," was Dreiser able to tell us what constituted the ideal commitment.

He was unable to decide before this because two voices—a Shelley's and a Babbitt's—spoke at the same time; and he was equally torn between a life that pursued money as an end in itself and one that renounced money for "the general good of others" and the pleasures of beauty freed from money. Between the summer of 1898 and the spring of 1899, Dreiser interviewed a series of eminently successful men for a journal called *Success,* published by Orison Swett Marden, who later (without Dreiser's knowledge or permission) republished most of these articles in a series of books.[10] Dreiser, of course, did not have a free hand as long as he was working for Marden: the interviews follow a format and all, by necessity, hold up the rags-to-riches ideal. Yet Dreiser seemed fascinated with his chance to question distinguished men about the role that ability, chance, accident, temperament, and heredity play in the pursuit of fame and success. Dreiser, in fact, asked the same questions over and over: "Were you a bookworm and dreamer?" (Most were not.) "Do you believe that want urges a man to greater effort and so to greater success?" (Most thought it did.) "Do you believe that invention is a gift, or an acquired ability?" (Opinion divides here.) Did your success come through hard work or were "your discoveries often brilliant intuitions" and the result of chance? (To the man, they attributed their success to hard work.)

All of these men either thought and talked alike, or Dreiser made them appear to be alike. They all believed in the virtue of hard work (but few really worked hard), and they all tell us that money does not matter in life (but they all scrambled for it and were immensely wealthy). They all believed one must have a purpose in life, spoke highly of single-mindedness and concentration, maintained America was ripe with continued opportunities, and extolled the importance of honesty, integrity, and public service.

While the answers are predictable, and while Dreiser obviously had to present these men in a favorable light, the questions were his own and reflect his preoccupations at this time. Dreiser, for example, repeatedly came back to the question—a very personal one—of whether or not poverty hinders the pursuit of success:

> "Isn't it possible, Mr. [Joseph H.] Choate," I ventured, "that your having had little or no worry over poverty in your youth might cause you to underestimate the effect of it on another, and overestimate the importance of sticking with determination to an ideal through wealth or deprivation?"
>
> "No," he replied. . . . "I am sure that it is quite often more difficult to rise with money than without." [11]

And

> "If equally valuable opportunities do not come to all," I went on, "hasn't an individual a right to complain and justify his failure?" [Dreiser asked.]
>
> "We have passed the period when we believe that all men are equal," said Mr. Choate [who did not really answer the question that Dreiser asked]. [12]

Dreiser then asked Choate about the aspiring boy—the romantic idealist—who overreaches himself:

> "You believe, of course, that an individual man can overestimate his abilities?"
> "Believe it," he answered, with a deprecatory wave of the hand, "trust the law to teach that." [13]

Dreiser has here brought up an idea that will be an important theme in his fiction: the inevitability of limits. While his immediate interest was with someone like Clyde Griffiths who is limited by his ability, the problem here cannot be separated from that of a character like Cowperwood, Eugene Witla, and Jennie Gerhardt who underestimates his moral environment: one is limited by his individual capacities, the other by his social situation.

The most interesting of all these interviews—primarily because it breaks the pattern—is the one with John Burroughs. In fact, this interview anticipates Dreiser's later interest in Thoreau, which culminated in the long introduction to his edition of Thoreau's works. Even though he was a boyhood friend of Jay Gould, Burroughs had little interest in becoming wealthy, retreated from society, lived close to nature, wrote books about what he observed, and was independent of the work-a-day routine and the social obligations that controlled life in industrialized America. Dreiser saw that the same forces had pulled a Jay Gould and a John Burroughs in two different directions—that money was the motive that repelled one and compelled the other.

Dreiser himself was the victim of these opposing selves: he was impressed, on the one hand, by the heightened life of a man like Charles Yerkes; he was attracted, on the other hand, to the life and ideas of Henry David Thoreau. Burroughs discussed these conflicts in values with Dreiser:

> "I consider the desire which most individuals have for the luxuries which money can buy, an error of mind. . . . Those things don't mean anything except a lack of higher tastes. Such wants are not necessary wants. If you cannot get wealth with a noble purpose, it is better to abandon it and get some-

thing else. Peace of mind is one . . . and finer taste and feelings." [14]

The two desires that Burroughs so nicely described—one "for the luxuries which money can buy," the other for finer [that is artistic] tastes and feelings—would war within Dreiser his whole life, be a source of conflict for many of his characters (we see this very clearly in the first draft of *Sister Carrie*), and supply the context in which the romantic idealist often canceled himself out.

We need not rely upon Dreiser's articles for *Success* to prove that a war of conflicting values was going on within him. In the essay "A Vanished Seaside Resort," Dreiser told how he was over-awed by his first sight of Manhattan Beach, how he envied the prosperous vacationers in their (as he looked back) flamboyant clothes, and how he wanted to change places with the wealthy businessmen and politicians who could spend a whole summer in the expensive hotels. A young Shelley in him began to speak like an eager Babbitt, and Dreiser equated the material world of Manhattan Beach with the highest kind of beauty: "Beauty, beauty, beauty . . . the eternal search for beauty. By the hard processes of trade, profit and loss, and the driving force of ambition and necessity and the love of and search for pleasure, this [that is, Manhattan Beach] very wonderful thing had been accomplished." [15] This essay, which obviously gave consent to the idea of money and success, contradicted Dreiser's own words, written soon after his arrival in New York. In the May 1, 1897 issue of *Ev'ry Month*, a year before his interview with John Burroughs was published in the September, 1898 issue of *Success*, Dreiser attacked the ruthless materialist in Burroughs' terms:

> Those who rise fix their glance upon a star, and then trample onward towards it over the hopes and ambitions of others. . . . There is something wrong in men whom ambition carries thus ruthlessly forward, or there is something radically wrong in ambition. . . . The answer to this is in the heart of every man. If he would justify ambition, he must rid it of the quality that causes it to turn its hand against every other. [16]

While John Burroughs would be a point of reference toward which Dreiser would move, the path that took him there was long and tortuous. His reading of the early muckrakers had much to do with his belief that the classes and the masses were locked in a deadly struggle. The privileges of the new financiers bothered, in particular, Lincoln Steffens, who described the way they controlled franchises, protective tariffs, legislatures, judges, and the police. Steffens insisted that the people had to want bad government to allow such abuses. Whether or not this was true, Steffens did document at length the ways industry and high finance corrupted politics; and he maintained that the system could not be changed until one changed the whole American concept of success.

Steffens's voice was not alone. Two other muckrakers—Charles Edward Russell and David Graham Phillips—had both attacked the senate as "a chamber of butlers for industrialists and financiers." [17] Thorstein Veblen in his *The Theory of the Leisure Class* (1899) argued that the upper classes were parasitical, wasted money conspicuously, and led superfluous lives. The abuses that these men complained about brought into being the more radical political parties in America: first the Populist Party (1891), then the Socialist Party (1901), and finally the American Communist Party (1919) with its various splinter groups.

One of the most important books that Dreiser read early in his career was Charles Edward Russell's *Lawless Wealth* (1908). The book was published by Dreiser's good friend, B. W. Dodge, and much of it had appeared in articles in *Everybody's Magazine,* owned by Erman J. Ridgway (who later became managing editor of Butterick Company, supervising Dreiser who edited *The Delineator* from June, 1907 to October, 1910). Russell devoted much of his book to Charles T. Yerkes, treating Yerkes's rise with Drexel and Company, a banking house, and his dealings with Joseph F. Marcer, who was City Treasurer of Philadelphia at the time Yerkes persuaded him to invest illegally city money in a Chicago traction scheme. When the crash wiped Yerkes out, he was sentenced to two years and four months in jail, Marcer to four years. When Yerkes was pardoned after seven months, he picked up where he left off, this time with P. A. B. Widener, who had taken over Marcer's job. Widener and Yerkes went into the Philadelphia streetcar business along with William L. Elkins and William K. Kemble. They made a fortune by issuing watered stock on the Seventeenth and Nineteenth Tractor Company, it alone amassing a capital investment of over thirty million dollars, while the backers had contributed "next to nothing" out of their own pockets.[18]

In Chicago, Yerkes duplicated this coup by buying a modest streetcar company, The North Side line, for twenty thousand dollars, hypothecating the stock, borrowing on the watered stock, and emerging with the Union Traction Company of Chicago, which controlled all the city lines, except the South Side. While this company was capitalized at one hundred twenty million dollars, it was worth at best sixteen million dollars and, "except for legislation, alderman, and newspapers, it [had] cost Mr. Yerkes nothing," because he had regained his original twenty thousand dollars investment out of watered stock.[19]

Dreiser found in *Lawless Wealth* much of the information he used in *The Trilogy of Desire*. He also found here the basis for another novel, dealing with the American Tobacco Trust, which he never completed. Five leading cigarette makers (Duke, Allen and Ginter, Kinney, Goodwin, and W. S. Kimball) met in New York in January of 1890 and formed the American Tobacco Company, sold twenty-five million dollars in stock (that went for $117 a piece), and destroyed their existing competition. When, in December of 1895, this trust, in a calculated plan, refused to pay a semi-annual dividend, the stock crashed from 117 to 63. The directors then bought the deflated stock, declared a cash dividend of twenty per cent and a scrip dividend of another twenty per cent, pushed the stock to 180 and sold it for an immense profit. At this point, the Union Tobacco Company of New Jersey forced Duke and his party to buy them out for ten million dollars. This rival syndicate had bought into the Liggett and Myers Company, secured an option to buy out that company for eleven million dollars, and sold out to Duke for eighteen million dollars, making a profit of $6,800,000 on that deal alone. So powerful was their hate of the trust that, on the night of December 1, 1906, three hundred tobacco farmers banded together as night raiders and burned 300,000 pounds of tobacco stored in the Tobacco Trust warehouse in Princeton, Kentucky. The story of tobacco in America, the battle between the financiers and the farmers, moved Dreiser as much as the story of wheat moved Frank Norris.

The real villain in Russell's book, however, was not Yerkes or Duke, but Thomas Fortune Ryan and his syndicate composed of Whitney-Widener-Elkins, with Daniel S. Lamont sometimes acting for them. This syndicate secured control of the old New York City Fifteenth Street to Bowling Green railway line, made a fortune on the watered stock, and then bankrupted the New York City Railroad Company. Behind this railway company was their State Trust Company, which secured money from an unsuspecting public and then loaned it to the syndicate (including a two million dollar loan to one Daniel H. Shea, Thomas F. Ryan's fifteen-dollar-a-week office boy) or used it for traction speculation. Of the almost fifteen million dollars of the people's money deposited with this trust company, it had illegally "loaned" to themselves as directors over five million dollars. While the courts worked effectively to send petty thieves to jail, no action at all was taken in these high-handed and flagrantly criminal dealings.

These stories outraged Dreiser, who both admired and hated these tycoons. Although he was impressed with the financial cunning of a Yerkes, Dreiser felt that justice had been served when the people, angered by high fares and impatient with too few and hopelessly overcrowded cars, stormed the Chicago city council and prevented Yerkes' "hired" politicians from extending his franchise for fifty years. Yerkes made forty million dollars on the watered stock of the Chicago street railroad, money which the people eventually had to make up through high fares and poor service. The situation in Philadelphia and New York was exactly the same. The citizens most affected, of course, were the Sister Carries, the shop-girls who had to ride the overcrowded streetcars and to pay the inflated fares that built the palaces on upper Fifth Avenue, on Girard Street, and Michigan Avenue. The people's satisfaction was also Dreiser's when, at the end of *The Titan,* the masses worked in concert to pull down a financial giant. Here was nature working most magnificently—the people and the titan locked in a battle that revealed an ultimate, perhaps even cosmic balance.

4

The Romantic Dilemma

Dreiser was caught between a world of dreams and a world of reality. He worked hard for social change and yet for most of his life he believed that man was the victim of an environment over which he had no control. As a romantic, he believed that it was possible for him to pursue an idealized self. As a Spencerian naturalist and later as a mechanist, he also believed that he functioned within fixed and prescribed limits. The contradictions in Dreiser's thinking would even be greater if Herbert Spencer's philosophy were not so highly romantic, if Spencer himself had not tried before him to reconcile the romantic and naturalistic mind.

Dreiser began reading Spencer in the summer of 1894 when he was a reporter on the Pittsburg *Dispatch*. Spencer's *First Principles* (the introductory volume to *Synthetic Philosophy*) "quite blew me, intellectually, to bits," says Dreiser.[1] One can imagine the young Dreiser, totally unfamiliar with the complex problems of metaphysics and science, having trouble with

Spencer's writing. *First Principles* is not an easy book to read, and the fact that Dreiser read it—and supposedly profited from the reading—proves how eagerly he must have been looking for answers to his religious questions. Certainly, Spencer would have been talking to him on an emotional as well as an intellectual level because Dreiser would find in Spencer's writings just what he wanted to find.

Spencer begins *First Principles* by questioning the logic of religious absolutists, those who cannot conceive of a self-existent universe and yet insist that a self-existent creator is at the source of the universe.[2] Spencer was not, however, directly attacking religion but was trying, in part, to reconcile religion with science. He insisted that an "Inscrutable Power" existed and that its presence was "manifested to us through all phenomena."[3] Like the romantics, he believed in a "Reality which is behind the veil of appearance,"[4] was concerned with how this "Reality" could be perceived and interpreted, and insisted that "our knowledge of the external world can be but phenomenal . . . the things of which we are conscious are appearances."[5]

Physical matter thus holds the secrets of life—a romantic idea; but at this point Spencer begins to deviate from romantic thought. He maintains first that matter "is expressed in terms of the quality of chemical force it exerts."[6] Motion thus becomes force, and Spencer's real concern is describing the various forces which are in conflict for "any force manifested implies an equal antecedent force from which it is derived, and against which it is a reaction."[7]

Since an action engenders a reaction, force is constant, and matter is in constant motion. The sun's heat will raise vapor to a height at which it condenses and falls as rain, the rain being in direct relation to the gravitational force the sun's heat overcame in raising the atoms of water to a condensation point. Spencer uses this example to illustrate how two opposite forces (the heat of the sun and the temperature of the atmosphere) are here at work, interacting upon the other, and the effect of the two producing the chemical reaction we call rain.

If matter in motion is really chemical force at work, and if man is composed of matter, then man too must be controlled by chemical force. By this logic, Spencer destroys the religious definition of man and reduces him to a chemical organism. In fact, Spencer believes that intelligence in man is directly related to "the proportion of phosphorous present in the brain" which is at a minimum "in infancy, old age and idiocy, and the greatest during the prime of life." [8]

Dreiser's use of Spencer's ideas led him directly into the romantic dilemma. Dreiser maintained, on the one hand, that man is "incurably romantic" and that "it is only by acting in the name of . . . an ideal that . . . [the ideal] is brought to pass." [9] On the other hand, he also maintained, unaware that he was contradicting himself, that man could not realize his ideals because "at his best he is a product of heat and gases generated in amazing variety by so infinitesimal a thing as the sun" and that man is born "to desire that which he has not" and to press "pathetically against his wretched limitations, wishing always to know more and more, and as constantly being denied." [10]

Dreiser's inability to reconcile his romantic aspirations with his belief in a world of physical limits led in his fiction to the displaced hero—the man whose desire for essential self-fulfillment is in conflict with his environment. A destructive principle inheres in Dreiser's thinking: man is born to yearn and desire, and yet he lives in a world of limits. He is born to be one step behind himself, urged on by desire; and yet such struggle brings into operation a destructive counter-force. He believes he is independent, a creature of free will; and yet he is a mere tool of his appetites, of physical needs, of other men, and of the universe. Dreiser, in short, believed that man was a creature of illusion, who longed for an ideal commitment in a world where force and circumstance canceled out ideals.

Since man is composed of matter, he is very much a part of a mechanistic and chemical process. "With a gloomy eye," Dreiser wrote, "I began to watch how the chemical—and their children, the mechanical forces operated through man and outside him." [11] Man was a part of a bitter struggle, of which he had no real understanding. Life fed on life—the animals lived off each other and men lived off the animals—and Dreiser never abandoned his belief in this "law of life," even though he wavered on whether or not this happened by accident or by design, whether the force had or did not have an intelligence behind it.

Dreiser's early free-lance writing documents his belief that life is based upon combat. In a newspaper article on sword fishing (July 24, 1904), he talked of the fisherman to whom "the sea is a vast opposing force," wherein swordfish "so eagerly and relentlessly pursued by men, in turn are savagely and relentlessly pursuing other fish, and these are in turn pursuing others, until the smallest is reached, and the evidence of the strife becomes indiscernible." [12] He used the same metaphor in an essay for *Tom Watson's Magazine*, "A Lesson from the Aquarium" (January, 1906) and, of course, used it once again at the beginning of *The Financier*. If we are not aware that life feeds on life, Dreiser maintained, it is because the big meat producers do the slaughtering. In "Our Red Slayer," he described a man in tarpaulin, stabbing animals in the throat so they would bleed to death as they came along a conveyor belt. "We have been flattering ourselves," Dreiser concluded, "that our civilization has somehow got away from this old-time law of life living on death, but here . . . stands our salaried red man who murders our victims for us." [13]

Like Spencer, Dreiser came to believe in the law of conflicting forces. His world was a realm of forces at war, a realm of opposites. One thing is known by its opposite, and opposites set the limits of human conduct. Life becomes a tug-of-war, and all matter is in a process of action and reaction. Man finds himself caught in a mechanistic process where he is both pulling and being pulled from a fixed center of energy—fixed to the extent that the balance of power (once it has been established) is never destroyed. This is Spencer's theory of the "suspended equation." Dreiser directly acknowledged Spencer when he discussed this principle in *A Book About Myself*,[14] and he indirectly acknowledged Spencer in his early writings. In one of his *Ev'ry Month* essays, for example, he described a major New York social event, the Bradley Martin Ball, where "representatives of half the wealth of New York were on the floor" and where glamorous personalities arrived, amidst "the throng of gay carriages . . . the swish of silk, and the sound of music."

At this point, however, Dreiser began to question the imbalance of wealth and wondered why so many were "without and miserable." He concluded with an idea straight from Spencer—that one extreme would and should (Dreiser here became exhortative) engender its opposite: "There is a general feeling," he warned, "that life should be equally balanced. Nearly everyone feels that such wide contrasts between extreme luxury and extreme poverty are a little bit odd." [15]

The language here reveals that Dreiser was talking for the "people." He goes on, in this issue of *Ev'ry Month*, to suggest that the people, represented by Clarence Lexow, would seriously limit the power, wealth, and privileges of both Tammany Hall and the Trusts, that a counter-influence was finally being asserted, and that Lexow's struggle would bring the very rich (of which there were few) and the very poor (of which there were many) into a realm of greater "balance." [16] Like many of his contemporaries, Dreiser applied Spencer's law of conflicting forces to social as well as natural processes. The great men of economic and political power reached a certain point at which they brought into operation a series of counter-forces that arrested their advancement. Dreiser believed that extreme wealth was a corollary to extreme poverty, that the rich could not exist without the poor. As some men became wealthy, other men by necessity became poor. Money, like energy, had fixed limits, and the rich and the poor lived in an inverse ratio to each other. Forces within nature and society were in furious combat. All matter was in constant motion, setting its own limits through a process of action and reaction. "Great forces are at work," Dreiser said, "strong ones, and our little lives are but a shadow of something that wills activity." [17] Even the box cars that fascinated Dreiser as they went streaming into the night were a part of this process, held together in fact by atoms— with "a central spicule of positive energy about which revolve at great speed lesser spicules of negative energy"—so that the cars are "as alive as life," "their journeys" a proper symbol of man's "equally restless" nature.[18]

Man's restlessness reflected the flux of life itself. Man was never at one with himself or with his environment. His desires were always one step ahead of his achievements—desires that were limited only by the reality of death. Like àll matter, man had limits, was caught in the flux of growth and decay, and lived in a world of change. Change, in fact, proved that life was in motion, that opposites canceled each other out, that the new replaced the old. Sensitive to beauty in the commonplace, Dreiser saw a flock of pigeons in flight as a symbol of life in perpetual motion—hence perpetual change:

> I have seen them [the pigeons] at morning, when the sky was like silver. . . . I have seen them again at evening, wheeling and turning. . . . [I have seen them] in the sunset, against the . . . storm clouds, when the turn of a wing made them look like a handful of snowflakes . . . I have watched them soaring . . . running like children, laughing down the wind.[19]

The churn of the sea also became a symbol of life in flux, man caught in the process of change. Dreiser would stare out from the New York docks, watch ocean liners move into the Atlantic, and see in the scene both life's beauty and "the tang of change and decay . . . the gradual passing of all things—yourself—myself—all." [20]

Dreiser was obviously riding the high crest of romanticism. The impermanence of man, his insignificance in the face of time, his inability to arrest the moment—all of these themes run through romantic poetry, and Dreiser was just as overcome by nostalgia—by the passage of time—as a Keats or a Shelley. We can see this in an essay like "A Vanished Seaside Resort." We can see it again in the *Ev'ry Month* article in which Dreiser, echoing Shelley's "Ozymandias," pondered the mutability of man.

> You see a great temple stand, and it looks permanent. . . . But . . . when it crumbles you realize it is only frail stonework after all.[21]

A Hoosier Holiday is, of course, an exercise in nostalgia, Dreiser visiting the Indiana of his youth; and so, in part, is *A Traveller at Forty*, particularly the moving scene in which Dreiser visits the medieval town of Mayen, Germany, his father's birthplace. Dreiser also wrote a long essay, never published to my knowledge, in which he contrasted old and new New York—and regretted the change. "There was a time (1896 to 1910) when New York seemed to put its best foot forward. It had a smart air. The principal streets were trim and elegant. Today it has a sloppy and down-at-the-heels look." [22]

Since man is limited by time, success becomes a tenuous matter. Not only does the energy used in attaining it feed upon itself, leaving one vulnerable in a world where life destroys life, but even at the moment of greatest success the skull is still just beneath the skin. One seemingly rises to fall. The pattern of rise and fall, the journey from success to failure, obsessed Dreiser from his very earliest days. In one of his early essays, "Whence the Song" (December, 1900), Dreiser described a young song writer's climb to the top and then his descent, until at last "a black boat steaming northward along the East River to a barren island and a field of weeds carries the last of all that was so gay . . . of him who was the greatest in his world." [23]

A Potter's Field burial, like that of Hurstwood's, horrified Dreiser; and he saw in Hurstwood a man whose fate could have been his own father's, his brother Rome's, his brother-in-law Hopkins', or his own. Hurstwood was a projection of his secret and unexpressed fear of what might yet await him. No one was safe from a sudden reversal of fate. In another essay, Dreiser again charted the career of a young man—a millionaire piano manufacturer named Weber—who arose "from obscurity, through gilded and flittering resorts, into the asylum and the Potter's field." His concern was again with those "unnamed" buried in Potter's Field, which he described as "the driftwood from the wrecks upon the surging sea of yonder metropolitan life." [24] If the city was a place of wonder and opportunity, it was also a place of fear and failure.

Since Dreiser was obsessed with the theme of man's limits —of energy as fixed matter and of failure as something built into the pursuit of success—it is not surprising that he worked this theme into his first novel, *Sister Carrie*. The story of Carrie is a necessary corollary to the story of George Hurstwood: the energy that Carrie used in driving to the top is in inverse relation to the momentum Hurstwood lost in his fall to the gutter. Dreiser carefully leaves Carrie's fate undisclosed: she had not yet reached the limits that will reverse the pendulum swing of her career. Carrie embodies the spirit of youthful aspiration, Hurstwood the spirit of middle-aged desperation: their two stories together reveal the pattern of all life.

Even the superman has limits. While he may try to rise above the ordinary man—may lust for inordinate wealth and power, may feel he is beyond good and evil—the masses will restrain him with their more ordinary lives and with their rigid moral values. Whether one is as seemingly self-sufficient as Frank Algernon Cowperwood or as seemingly helpless as George Hurstwood, he functions within the limits of these dynamics. All men live within circumscribed contexts, contexts which are the result of antithetical forces at work.

Just as the swing of two pendulums may be different—the arc of one higher than the other—the very swing of the pendulum away from its center produces in both an equal force in the opposite direction. Both Cowperwood and Hurstwood broke conventions in their pursuit after money and pleasure, and both became the victim of rigid conventionality. While their lives are vastly different, while the pendulum swing of their careers follows a different arc, their fates prove a common principle is at work when they both become the victims of Spencer's "equivalence of forces."

What went up had to come down, and Dreiser came to believe that some day in America there would be social and economic "equity" (an important word in his lexicon). And what was generally was also individually true. One had only so much energy, and at some point even the rich and powerful reached a limit in their upward drive and began the downward trip that ended in death. This is the reason that Dreiser told the complete story of Frank Algernon Cowperwood's life —from birth to death, from the moment he started to acquire his fortune to the time the fortune was dissipated after his death.

Dreiser's characters were the victims of the romantic dilemma: they yearned after the infinite while they were restrained by the physical; their genius was negated in the play of forces; their aspirations were in conflict with time; and their ideals were in conflict with society. Once Dreiser accepted Spencer's theory that man was mere matter, the motives of his characters became conditioned impulses and their dreams were negated on the lowest level of chemical play. Once the artist accepted the values of the tycoon, he became schizophrenic. Shelley and Babbitt, Thoreau and Yerkes, warred inside Dreiser, while cosmic and social forces warred outside.

Out of Dreiser's romantic dilemma came the displaced hero: the man who has a place in the world but cannot find it. He lives in a world where men prey on each other, where strength and subtlety are all important, and where law and justice are often used by selfish men to restrain those who oppose them. He unwittingly aspires to goals that are transient and beyond his grasp. He is never satisfied with his origins—his family or his present position—and struggles for wealth and recognition. In more sensitive moments, he intuits the beauty of life, but this only makes him more discontent with himself and his materialistic society. He is concerned with mutability, with birds in flight, water in motion, and crowded cities where men sweep by like rivers to the sea. He longs for stability but is caught in flux. He is a step behind himself, restless and yet with nowhere to go, duped by his own aspirations. He is, in a word, a victim: a victim of his temperament, a victim of time, a victim of a society that he cannot fully accept or totally reject, a victim of a world that is in constant struggle. Most of all, he is the victim of his romantic illusions: his belief in the possibility of self-fulfillment and purpose when life, in reality, is moving in a furious circle, the center holding all in balance, like a raging whirlpool going nowhere.

5

"Sister Carrie"

The world of *Sister Carrie* is one that Dreiser knew firsthand and had treated in his journalism and hackwriting—a world of factories where men toil for long hours and little money, of tenements, of railroad yards and tracks stretching away from and toward the city, of Broadway crowds and of Tin Pan Alley music, of breadlines and poverty, and of both cheap and expensive restaurants as well as shabby and luxurious hotels. We see both the poor and the rich in this novel, and we see them mostly in public—in the streets, at work, at the theater, or in restaurants or hotels.

The world of *Sister Carrie* is so close to that of Dreiser's journalism and hackwriting that Dreiser actually used some of his published essays in the novel. In November of 1899, for example, he had published "Curious Shifts of the Poor" in *Demorest's Family Magazine*. Part of the article (*pp. 22–24*) described how a number of New York tramps were housed each night by a Fifth Avenue "Captain," who petitioned passersby for money, each tramp lining up as someone gave the Captain the price of a night's bed. In *Sister Carrie*,[1] Dreiser used this article almost verbatim in Chapter 45 (*pp. 424–27*), which he also entitled "Curious Shifts of the Poor," Hurstwood becoming the tramp in the article who is "the earliest arrival."[2] Dreiser did not use his article in Chapter 46 of the novel where Drouet calls upon Carrie in her dressing room. He began, however, Chapter 47 of the novel (*pp. 439–40*) with another section from "Curious Shifts of the Poor," the section describing the Sisters of Mercy mission-house on Fifteenth Street (*p. 24 of the article*) and continued Chapter 47 (*pp. 440–43*) with a description of a breadline from his essay (*pp. 25–26 and part of p. 24 in this reverse order*). Dreiser then moved once again away from his article—described Hurstwood unsuccessfully trying to see Carrie at the Casino Company, Drouet making plans to take some girls to dinner, and Mrs. Hurstwood and family arriving in New York on their way to Europe—before he returned to an earlier section of "Curious Shifts of the Poor" and used his description of a flop house (*pp. 449–51 of the novel, pp. 24–25 of the article*). This becomes the house in which Hurstwood turns on the gas and dies.

Since "Curious Shifts of the Poor" was published at the end of 1899, it is impossible to say whether Dreiser had written it for sale and later included it in *Sister Carrie* or whether he had written it for his novel and later sold it to *Demorest's Family Magazine*. This section of the holograph (Chapter 48), however, is heavily revised and gives the appearance that Dreiser was writing this material directly for the novel.

Dreiser never made as much use in his novels of any other essay as he did "Curious Shifts of the Poor," but many of the other essays he wrote at this time have scenes in common with *Sister Carrie*—such as "Whence the Song,"[3] which describes Broadway, and "The River of the Nameless Dead,"[4] which describes a Hurstwood-like Potter's Field ending.

Dreiser's use of Broadway and the theater world is more detailed in the holograph of *Sister Carrie* than in the novel itself. Dreiser deleted from Chapter 30, for example, a discussion of Augustin Daly, the Frohmans, and Lester Walker as well as a discussion of New York financiers (Vanderbilt, Gould, Russel Sage), political life (Tammany Hall), authors and painters (Howells, G. A. Ward, John La Farge), and inventors (such as Edison), men in several instances whom he had interviewed for *Success Magazine*. In order to get *Sister Carrie* published, Doubleday insisted that he omit most specific names and places (he fought to keep Sherry's and Delmonico's in the novel), and this loss of detail makes the novel less realistic than Dreiser had intended. Yet there still is a sense of immediacy, a sense of the nineties.

Life seems to flow through this novel, to sweep by. Carrie sits depressed on Hanson's stoop and watches the workers trudge to and from their dreary tasks; Drouet takes her to a restaurant and they sit by a window and watch "the busy rout of the street"; and Hurstwood in decline retreats to hotel lobbies away from the cold and watches the rich come and go.

"With every expression came increased conception," says Dreiser of Hurstwood, who was writing a love letter to Carrie. In many ways, this summarizes what was happening to Dreiser as he was writing *Sister Carrie*. As much as in any novel that he ever wrote, Dreiser revealed that he knew himself. He was beginning to make up his mind about the meaning of the family, the city, and moral conventions; was coming to conclusions that would dominate his thinking for the rest of his life.

The story of Carrie and Hurstwood is both personal and representative: personal to Dreiser because he was telling the story of Emma and L. A. Hopkins; representative because it was the story of longing and desire, of weakness and strength, of struggle and ambition, success and defeat. Carrie's story covers eight years and parallels the crucial events in his sister's life. The novel begins in August of 1889 when Carrie arrives in Chicago from Columbia City, Wisconsin (in the holograph Green Bay, Wisconsin). In the summer of 1890, she leaves Chicago with Hurstwood, who has just robbed the Fitzgerald and Moy's safe (Hannah and Hoggs in Dreiser's original draft of the novel), and they arrive in Montreal and then leave for New York. They live more or less uneventfully in New York for the next three years, Hurstwood getting by with his one-third interest in the Warren Street saloon, bought with the thousand dollars he held out when he returned the rest of the stolen money. In the fall of 1893, Hurstwood learns, however, that the lease on the saloon will not be renewed, and he loses the saloon altogether in the winter of that year. On February 2, 1894, he pays the rent on their flat, the first money that goes out with no promise of more coming in. By June of that year, Hurstwood has either spent or lost at cards all but one hundred of the seven hundred dollars he managed to recoup from the saloon. By August of 1894, his money is totally gone, he has run up bills with the grocer, and he is asking Carrie to support them both with the twelve dollars a week that she is getting as a chorus girl. By the winter of 1894, Hurstwood is desperate enough to take a job as a strike-breaker, driving the trolley car through Brooklyn until he quits in fear after being shot at. By the summer of 1895, Carrie has left Hurstwood and is making one hundred and fifty dollars a week while Hurstwood is living in a fifteen-cent-a-night flop house in the Bowery. The next winter, Hurstwood is doing scullery work in the Broadway Central Hotel, where he comes down with pneumonia in February and is in the hospital until May of 1896. That summer Carrie takes her play to London, returning in the winter of 1896. By early January of 1897, Hurstwood is so desperate that he contemplates the suicide which he later commits.

In August of 1894, eight years after Emma eloped with L. A. Hopkins, Dreiser visited his sister and brother-in-law in New York. While the novel also covers eight years, from August of 1889 to January of 1897, the dates of Emma's story are different from Carrie's. In 1886, Hopkins, who was fifteen years older than Emma, deserted his wife and children, after stealing (contrary to the $15,000 figure Dreiser gives us in the manuscript of *Newspaper Days*) $3,500 from the safe of Chapin & Gore (most of which he later returned), taking Emma first to Montreal and then to New York where they ran a house of prostitution. While the details are different (Hurstwood is twenty years older than Carrie; he stole ten thousand dollars; Emma had no stage success; and Hopkins did not commit suicide), Dreiser was obviously using the essential elements of

Emma's story in his novel, and his visit to the Hopkins's Fifteenth Street flat gave him first-hand insight into the kind of life Hurstwood and Carrie would be living in their Thirteenth Street flat.

Dreiser's first novel was a strangely personal matter. He identified with both Carrie and Hurstwood. Carrie is eighteen when she comes to Chicago in 1889 and was thus born in 1871, the same year as Dreiser himself. Carrie's rise was a fantasy projection of Dreiser's own Horatio Alger dreams. Carrie's rise on the Broadway stage also paralleled Paul Dresser's rise in the Broadway world of music and, to some extent, Dreiser was fusing the story of his sister with that of his brother.

Hurstwood's fate was an equally personal matter. His decline after one fatal mistake paralleled that of Dreiser's own father, who was never able to start over when his wool mill burned to the ground. Hurstwood also embodied Dreiser's own experiences with poverty in Chicago, St. Louis, and especially in New York when he was free-lancing after he left *The World*. Over and over, Dreiser wrote in the late nineties freelance essays about New York breadlines, about tramps walking the streets, about the loneliness of the city, about the psychological effects of poverty, about suicide, and about homeless dead who are buried in Potter's Field graves—some of these essays (as we have seen) he included almost verbatim in *Sister Carrie*. When Dreiser was writing this novel at the end of the century, he was still having doubts about his ability to succeed, and his future was uncertain, if not bleak. Hurstwood was the imaginative product of those doubts, of Dreiser's own fear of failure, and of his obsession with poverty, an obsession which lingered from childhood.

Dreiser identified with Hurstwood in still another way. He saw the saloon manager as someone who broke conventions and escaped from a loveless marriage, impulsively to be sure, Hurstwood's desire being greater than his prudence. In Hurstwood and Carrie, Dreiser anticipated in a remarkable way his own experience ten years later with Thelma Cudlipp, which cost him his job at Butterick. Like Hurstwood, Dreiser would risk security to play the game of love.

While Dreiser used the story of his own family in *Sister*

Carrie, he was really writing a novel in which the family is superfluous. All the main characters are without family. Drouet has no family; Carrie breaks with her family—first when she leaves Wisconsin and then when she moves away from her sister; and Hurstwood breaks from his wife and children, whom he merely tolerates "by force of habit, by force of conventional opinion" (85). These characters are held in a grip larger than the family, the grip of the city, a secular realm to which all dreamers are attracted as if by an essential self.

When Carrie arrives in Chicago at night, she brings with her the sense of youth, expectation, and hope that characterizes F. Scott Fitzgerald's romantic dreamers. As Nick Carraway tells us, "the city seen from Queensboro Bridge is always the city seen for the first time, in its first wild promise of all the mystery and the beauty in the world," [5] so Dreiser tells us that "the approach to the great city for the first time is a wonderful thing" (9). Carrie embodies these feelings and gives consent to "the promise of the night" (9).

The promise of the night is always illusory. While some pursue it more successfully than others, most of Dreiser's characters have to leave the family to begin such a pursuit, primarily because a Carrie, coming from poverty, would not be accepted by an established family and thus must struggle for success in an amoral public realm at the expense of a home. In this context, it is significant that John L. Sullivan can be found in Hurstwood's saloon, "surrounded by a company of loudly dressed sports" (149). Dreiser had been most impressed with Sullivan when he interviewed him for the St. Louis *Globe-Democrat.*[6] Like Sullivan, and like the Negro today, Carrie has a better chance of fighting her way out of poverty in the public world of entertainment or sports, a more fluid world where talent is more important than influence and proper connections.

Yet the moral differences between the public and family realm are more apparent than real. Mrs. Hurstwood, for example, exhibits Jessica in the hope of marrying her "to a man of means" (129), a purpose not very different from Carrie's who also is willing to sell herself to the highest bidder.

The prime mover for both Mrs. Hurstwood and Carrie is

money. "Ah, money, money, money! What a thing it is to have" (*63*), Carrie thinks when Drouet takes her to an expensive restaurant and then gives her twenty dollars for clothes. Drouet pays her to live with him, and their relationship is completely financial. When Carrie sees that Hurstwood can offer her more, she quickly tires of Drouet. Her moral scruples are inchoate and confused. While she appears to be angry that Drouet would get her involved with a married man, she is even more angry at Hurstwood for being married—not because she respects the rights of marriage but because Hurstwood has compromised his ability to support her. While she seems to be reluctant to run away with a married man, she finally lets this happen, Dreiser not making it clear how Carrie can believe that Hurstwood has deserted rather than divorced his first wife. Most revealingly, when Hurstwood loses the means to support Carrie, he also loses the right to sleep with her, sex being something Carrie believes should be paid for and, unlike the grocer, she is dubious of Hurstwood's credit (*see p. 322*).

Carrie has one thing to sell—and that is her body. She is a twentieth-century Moll Flanders, and Dreiser had difficulty in keeping the reader sympathetic to her plight, especially his morally timid readers, while showing her kept by men. In the case of the Doubledays, he did not succeed.

Yet, if one looks at the holograph and early typescripts of the novel, one can see that Dreiser toned down Carrie's character and that she is more maidenly and virginal in the novel than she was in manuscript. Dreiser foresaw that he would have difficulty getting *Sister Carrie* published if he did not alter the Carrie—far more vamp than innocent country girl— that he had originally created. Dreiser changed Carrie's character by deleting a number of expository passages which depicted her as cunning and shrewd. He also deleted a number of passages in which she is motivated purely by money. In Chapter 17 of the novel (*p. 156, line 8*) (Chapter 18 of the holograph), Dreiser, for example, deleted a passage in which Hurstwood pulls "a thin clean roll of new $100.00 bills out of his vest" and gives one to Carrie. In the holograph, she hesitates and then takes it: "Carrie could hardly refuse the offer he was so tactful about it. He put it in her little green leather purse and closed it up." This scene would have turned Hurstwood into a higher-class Drouet and suggested once and for all that Carrie was a kept woman.

Perhaps the most substantial change Dreiser made in Carrie's character came in Chapter 26, the scene in which Drouet leaves her after their argument. Dreiser deleted here (*cf. the novel, p. 221, line 15*) the agony this caused Carrie, her fear of once again being alone and "what would happen if she were again thus rudely thrown upon her resources." Dreiser only briefly mentions in the novel that Carrie needed a job, striking from the manuscript several long paragraphs in which she once again trudges the city, is leered at by shop owners and managers ("He smiled at her as she went out in a most covert manner, and Carrie knew well enough why he did it"), is offered a job by a lustful manager of a crooked portrait painting firm who will pay her five dollars a week if she will also be his mistress: "He had an eye to cheapness and service in most of his employees. . . . In short he tacitly conveyed to her one of the most brazen propositions imaginable—seeking to buy her services and favors for five dollars a week." Interestingly enough, Carrie is tempted. "Five dollars was five dollars," she thinks as she worries about her dwindling reserve of money.

Throughout Chapter 26, Dreiser deleted or changed the manuscript to make Carrie appear less promiscuous, more self-assured and confident in her destiny, and less reliant upon Drouet. She is supposedly no longer a girl of the streets and seems less likely to repeat her experience with Drouet. Dreiser was able to reinforce this idea by having Hurstwood kidnap her—a scene which rescues Carrie from her past before it can once again engulf her and makes it appear that she was not merely running off with another man.

In order to make the "kidnap" scene reasonably convincing, Dreiser had to change Hurstwood's character from what it was in the first drafts of the novel, where he was depicted as more lustful and conniving. In Chapter 11, for example, Dreiser deleted a passage in which he had told us that Hurstwood "was worse than Drouet. He more deliberately set aside the canons of right as he understood them." Not only would this passage have linked Hurstwood with Drouet, but it would also have suggested that Hurstwood deserved his final punishment and that it did not stem from an accident which generated physical forces beyond his control.

In Chapter 25 of the novel, Dreiser deleted from the holograph much of Hurstwood's feelings about his wife. As Dreiser originally wrote this scene, Hurstwood is confronted by a dilemma. If he divorces his wife "it would affect his standing with the firm and perhaps cost him his place." Yet he no longer loves his wife and longs to be rid of her. "Whichever way he might move," Dreiser wrote, "he would not gain anything." Dreiser removed this dilemma by making Hurstwood less insistent upon divorcing his wife and by making Hurstwood's stealing the money the irrevocable act which separates him from his family. This scene becomes a more dramatic way of achieving Dreiser's narrative end, a more effective way of tying Hurstwood's fate to an accident which, as Dreiser refers to it in a deleted passage, produces a "ring of sequence."

In the first draft of the novel, Hurstwood is far more weak than in later drafts, far more indecisive and will-less *before* he steals the money. In his revisions, Dreiser altered this aspect of Hurstwood's character and put the emphasis on the safe clicking shut—that is, upon an accident which brings about the mental condition that leads to Hurstwood's decline. Thus Hurstwood becomes both the victim of his own innate weakness and of a sequence of chance events and environmental causes which ultimately determine and shape his temperament. His weaknesses are a part of him all along, of course, but they lie dormant until the safe clicks shut and he is an outcast. Dreiser documented this point in a letter he wrote in 1928 to John Howard Lawson, who was trying to adapt *Sister Carrie* to the stage. Dreiser here reduced the key reasons in Hurstwood's "mental and social decay" to three: "First, a sense of folly or mistake"; second, Hurstwood's sense of social disgrace; and third, Hurstwood's failure to grasp Carrie's true nature: "her charm betrayed him." Once Hurstwood was outside society, Dreiser continued, Carrie drifted from him, and he realized his mistake: "a mistake which ate into his energy and force. It was no doubt finally the worm at the heart of his life. And without the power to destroy it he was doomed." [7]

The novel thus pivots on Chapter 27, the scene with Hurstwood at the safe of Fitzgerald and Moy's. This scene is very much like the one on the beach in Albert Camus' *L'Étranger,* a "chance" event creating a new context within which a main character is newly defined (Dreiser) or newly defines himself (Camus). In order to put a chance event at the heart of the novel, Dreiser revised the safe scene several times. Even when the scene was firmly in his mind, he revised it again, getting the exact effect that he wanted. In both the early drafts and in the novel itself, Hurstwood takes the money out of the safe and becomes frightened. He puts it back in the wrong boxes and then takes it out again—and "now the terror had gone." Dreiser then deleted the following passage, a passage which makes Hurstwood much more complicit in the crime.

> Could he get away? What would be the use of remaining? He would never get such a chance again. He emptied the good money into the satchel. There was something fascinating about the soft green stack—the loose silver and gold. He felt sure now that he could not leave that. No, no. He would do it. He would lock the safe before he had time to change his mind.
>
> He went over and restored the empty boxes. Then he pushed the door the sixth time. He wavered, thinking, putting his hand to his brow.
>
> Suddenly the lock clicked.

The lock still clicks accidentally, but Hurstwood has made up his mind to steal before it clicks. By leaving this passage out of the novel, Dreiser made Hurstwood less conniving, less a willful embezzler and more the victim of a seeming accident.

Once Dreiser had worked out the details of the safe scene, he could revise Chapter 28 which, in the original manuscript, shows Carrie as a more willing companion as she leaves Chicago with Hurstwood. Dreiser, for example, specifically deleted a passage in which Carrie "looked at the [passing landscape] . . . with a feeling of awe. It seemed very good to be in a cab with a man for a companion." Dreiser also cut out a passage in which Hurstwood seems to be persuading Carrie with offers of money and gifts, blue-pencilling " 'I'll give you a good home' " and later " 'Oh you can have anything you want.' " He also made Carrie less impressed with this experience, more a victim and less an adventurer, deleting "Carrie looked about her at the luxurious furnishings. It was the second time she had ever been in a Pullman car in her life." While Carrie is willing to use Hurstwood, to use any man for that matter, Dreiser tries to conceal this fact and cuts a passage in an early draft which inadvertently revealed the true Carrie: "Here was offered her chance for a decent life in another city. She would be away from all past associations, she would be in a new world."

Thus, once Dreiser found in Chapter 27 how to make Hurstwood the victim of an "accidental" robbery, he returned to Chapter 26 and deleted the job-seeking scenes which revealed that Carrie was still a woman of the streets. He then moved to Chapter 28 and made her—unconvincingly to be sure—the innocent companion of the fleeing Hurstwood. Dreiser leagued Carrie with Hurstwood's chance act, and he made her more innocent in the published work than she was in narrative conception.

Chapter 27 is thus the key chapter in the novel, the *sine qua non*. Carrie here becomes "innocently" bound to Hurstwood, who is in turn a victim of an accident, an accident that propels Carrie forward at the same time as it moves Hurstwood toward final defeat and death, an accident that moves both Carrie and Hurstwood to New York without making Carrie appear too coarse and promiscuous. Dreiser's narrative ruse, however, was not completely successful. He expected us to believe that Carrie never doubted that she was legally married to Hurstwood, even though she knew that he had not divorced his wife, an explanation that makes Carrie incredibly stupid. Dreiser knew that his audience, particularly those readers in the salon, would never accept a wanton woman, knew that Carrie would have to be more inept than kept.

Once Dreiser so changed Carrie's character, he had to make other changes. In Chapter 31, for example, he made the same kind of revision with Mrs. Vance that he had made with Carrie, the Mrs. Vance who introduces Carrie into a more heightened New York world. In the manuscript, Mrs. Vance is taken from a small town in Ohio to Cleveland by a student and then runs off with her present lover, "the secretary of a large tobacco company." Her life would have thus strangely paralleled and duplicated Carrie's, which probably explains why Dreiser removed these details, allowing Carrie to enter a world more respectable and distinguished than her own.

Dreiser also changed the character of Bob Ames, Mrs. Vance's cousin. In the holograph, Ames has invented a new kind of electric light and is a kind of Thomas Edison. Also in the holograph, he is more lustful and makes advances at Carrie. When he tells her he is coming to see her on the stage, Carrie responds, " 'Perhaps you won't like the play." Ames answers: " 'Oh it isn't the play that I care about. . . . It's you.' " In the typescript, as in the novel, Ames is not so forward. He has seen Carrie's play, liked it moderately well, and suggests that she try for more serious roles. Ames takes Carrie's talent seriously, and the effect of this revision is to make Carrie's phenomenal rise on the stage more a matter of pluck and luck than of her sexual power over men. Moll Flanders here gives way to a feminine Horatio Alger. The effect of this revision is also to make Ames less like Drouet, less the seducer and more the sincere adviser. Carrie is now encouraged to climb even higher, and Ames "unlocked the door to new desire."

In Chapter 39, Dreiser tried once again to erase the impression that money held Carrie to Hurstwood, deleting passages such as the following: "When a man, however passively becomes an obstacle to the fulfillment of a woman's desires, he becomes an odious thing in her eyes." As Dreiser made Carrie less a scheming and ruthless woman, motivated only by money, he also made her less hard-hearted. Dreiser had begun Chapter 43 of the novel, for example, with a seven hundred to a thousand word passage (much of it written in what appears to be Arthur Henry's hand) describing Hurstwood waking up after Carrie has left him and going about selling his furniture, getting into a series of arguments with used-furniture dealers. Dreiser then switched (his own handwriting picks up here) to Carrie at her breakfast, "installed in her comfortable room" (see p. 396). Dreiser cut out an immediate contrast between Carrie in her new splendour and Hurstwood down-at-the-heels and built more slowly toward this conclusion, a revision that makes the end of the novel seem more inevitable and Carrie seem less cruel.

Dreiser created a purely physical world in *Sister Carrie,* a world in which the individual is sensitive to outside stimuli which in turn produces a state of mind. Dreiser's whole discussion of anastates and katastates is an awkward attempt to reduce all action to completely physical motives.

> Now, it has been shown experimentally that a constantly subdued frame of mind produces certain poisons in the blood called katastates, just as virtuous feelings of pleasure and delight produce helpful chemicals called anastates. The poisons generated by remorse inveigh against the system, and eventually produce marked physical deterioration. To these Hurstwood was subject. (297)

Dreiser got his idea of anastates and katastates from Elmer Gates, who ran the Elmer Gates Laboratory of Psychology and Psychurgy in Chevy Chase, Maryland (which according to the masthead of Gates's letters was "an institution devoted to the science of mind and its practical application"). When Dreiser was working on *Sister Carrie,* Gates had sent him a manuscript explaining Gates's theory of anastates and katastates. From a letter Dreiser wrote Gates, dated March 3, 1900 (written, that is, as Dreiser was completing his novel), we know that Dreiser had read most of Gates's manuscript and that he wanted a list of more authorities for future reading. Gates recommended Gustave Le Bon's *The Psychology of Peoples* and *The Psychology of the Crowd.* "Before you read *The Psychology of Socialism,*" Gates wrote, "read Boris Sidis' *The Psychology of Suggestion.* If you wish to take up experimental psychology," Gates continued, "by all means begin with Wundt's *Animal and Human Psychology.* Then take up Titchener's *Outline of Psychology,* and therein you will find a bibliography." Dreiser returned Gates's manuscript on April 27, 1900, enclosing a letter of glowing praise for Gates's work. Dreiser himself began at this time an article entitled "Experiments with Nine Sensory Capacities" in which he used Gates's theories of the mind. Dreiser retitled this article "The Limits of the Senses" and sent it in July of 1900 to Arthur Henry for comment. Henry responded on July 14, 1900: "It seems to me . . . you have made a mistake in clothing this article in the language of Mr. Gates." Henry told Dreiser that the "ideas are great" but that they should be handled "in a simple manner." He urged Dreiser to avoid "semi-scientific expressions" and to simplify his syntax. While Henry later cooled on Gates's theory, Dreiser did not. In December of 1901, Dreiser wrote Gates and once again asked him to summarize his ideas. On December 11, 1901, Gates answered in a style that justifies Henry's concern, discussing anastates and katastates at length, and his remarks are important to anyone interested in *Sister Carrie*.

> An evil emotion engenders the poisonous katastates which slowly destroy the structure in which memory is enregistered, whilst a good emotion augments the nutritive processes which tend to perpetuate it; the same is true of intellections: a false image, concept or idea is a structural embodiment which prevents normal and sane judgments and consequently prevents successful adaptation to environment and therefore tends to destroy or limit the life of the organism in which it is embodied.

The stories of Carrie and Hurstwood depict the polarities of life, the "positives and negatives of energy" as Dreiser put it in "Notes on Life," the systole and diastole of experience. Hurstwood's decline is a necessary corollary to Carrie's rise, and in *Sister Carrie* Dreiser was treating a theme that would fascinate him for almost fifty years.

Thus another way of talking about anastates and katastates is in terms of youth and age, youth with its burning sense of expectation and age with its declining sense of hope. This is an important theme in *Sister Carrie*. In fact, an essential difference between Carrie and Hurstwood is their age, not so much their physical ages (Carrie is eighteen at the beginning of the novel and twenty-six at the end; Hurstwood is thirty-eight at the beginning of the novel and forty-six when he dies at the end) but their mental attitude toward their age. Carrie is excited by the possibilities of the future (the "burning desire of youth"), while Hurstwood is overawed by the past ("such an atmosphere could not incite in him the cravings of a boy of eighteen, but in so far as they were excited, the lack of hope made them proportionately bitter") (266). After he loses his New York saloon, Hurstwood begins acting like an old man who has nothing to live for or look forward to. This theme is even more obvious in the typescript of *Sister Carrie*. Dreiser deleted from Chapter 21 the following passage:

> He [Hurstwood] was no longer young. He was no longer youthful in spirit, but he carried in his memory some old fancies which were of the day of his love-time. . . . His love . . . of youth [was] intense.
>
> In Carrie he saw the embodiment of old experiences and old dreams. . . . he had been in love and . . . feelings of that old time came back [when he was with Carrie].

Time, for Dreiser, was change. Time, as he said in "Notes on Life," was "matter in motion . . . the sensory record of the duration of something from star to spark, from mountain to grain of dust, from sun to atom." All matter, he believed, was limited. All growth was part of death. Each individual was so much energy, energy that was expended, the individual returning to the earth and a more primal form of energy; this in part is what Dreiser meant by the "equation inevitable" in "Notes on Life."

Hurstwood's decline partakes of the running down of all matter, of life itself. His age contrasts with Carrie's youth, his depleted vitality with her boundless energy. Moved as he always was by the contrast between the strong and the weak, the healthy and the sick, the rich and the poor, Dreiser worked all these elements into *Sister Carrie* and into the character of Hurstwood, who so pathetically portrays man's even greater struggle against the levelling forces of time and change.

Carrie's rise and Hurstwood's decline partake of the cycles of nature itself. To this extent, Carrie's rise anticipates her own decline, although Dreiser chose to stop his novel short of this point. The story of Carrie and Hurstwood is thus the story of insignificant men, caught in the river of time, struggling for fulfillment while the current sweeps them toward some unknown shore.

While all men are caught in this eternal flux of life, this

levelling process, each man responds variously—and it is on this level that the drama of life takes place. For Dreiser, there was only action and reaction, flux and change, which led to the contrasts that made up life. One element in life engendered and was known by its opposite—good by evil, beauty by ugliness, strength by weakness.

Carrie is very much aware of life's contrasts and learns from them. When, for example, she sees Mrs. Vance, elegant in a dark blue dress, "this woman pained her by contrast" (*279*). Dreiser established a series of contrasts throughout *Sister Carrie*. He sets up other characters to serve as stepping stones in Carrie's progress from rags to riches, her journey from an inchoate response to the city's bright lights to a more informed appreciation of the beautiful. We first see Carrie—bright, imaginative, full of energy, in search of a good time and heightening experience—in contrast to her sister and especially Hanson—dull, plodding, lifeless, caught in a meaningless and empty routine, dead before they are in the grave. Drouet's boisterous lack of sensitivity contrasts sharply with Hurstwood's more polished manners and his intuitive grasp of Carrie's feelings (*cf. p. 155*); and Hurstwood's intellectual emptiness and shallow materialism contrasts with Ames's wide learning and poetic grasp of life (or so Dreiser would like us to believe). Carrie is intuitively attracted toward the beautiful, a point the critics of *Sister Carrie* miss, and the personification of this higher kind of ideal is Ames, a "genius" from Indiana, who Dreiser obviously models, at least in part, on himself. Ames "was a strong man and clean . . . much stronger and better than Hurstwood and Drouet . . . the difference was painful" (*304*). As Carrie becomes more attracted to Ames, Hurstwood begins to seem more like Drouet.

In fact, Dreiser established a mechanical relationship among his characters; the other characters seem to be measured against Drouet, who is the one static and unchanging person in the novel. As Hurstwood begins to decline, for example, he applies unsuccessfully to a wholesale liquor company for a job as a travelling salesman (*315*), a job that parallel's Drouet's. Like Drouet, he is now forever hoping to swing a big deal—a point of comparison that is not lost upon Carrie:

For all her acquiescence, there was something about the way that Hurstwood spoke which reminded Carrie of Drouet and his little deal which he was always about to put through. It was only the thought of a second, but it was a beginning. It was something new in her thinking of Hurstwood. (270)

Both Hurstwood and Carrie are dreamers, pursue the big deal like Drouet; and all of Dreiser's characters are at odds with themselves, are disappointed with the moment. This state of mind is a trademark of Dreiser's fiction. Dreiser believed that modern man suffered from displacement. He was no longer at one with himself, not at home in nature or the city. He was "scarcely beast," as Dreiser put it, because he no longer was totally guided by instinct; yet he was "scarcely human" because he was not completely guided by reason (70). Man was not totally formed: he was more than mere animal, motivated by more than base appetites; yet he was less than completely civilized, motivated by less than enlightened sense of selflessness and a knowledge of universal good. Man wants to fulfill both his physical needs and his esthetic ideals. As a result, he is in a kind of no-man's land because a residue of animality taints his esthetic ideals. Dreiser showed in *Sister Carrie* how the individual was inexorably subject to both biological and environmental conditions. Man was in motion, in a half-way house between what he was and what he might become, dissatisfied with his condition, no longer at one with himself.

Forces larger than the individual work throughout *Sister Carrie* and create a sense of the inevitable. Dreiser revealed a determining force, a shaping influence, working beyond the will of Carrie in particular. Each scene extends Carrie's appetite for experience and fulfillment. The first chapter, particularly, establishes her sense of hope and her longing for a better life. Drouet created a sense of excitement when he told her about Chicago, its stores full of beautiful clothes, its tall new buildings, its wide streets, its bright nights resplendent with handsome people in luxurious restaurants and crowded theaters. As he talked, "there was a little ache in her fancy of all he described" (7). Even Minnie's grim flat could not destroy Carrie's new-found excitement and sense of expectation.

"The life of the streets continued for a long time to interest Carrie. She never wearied of wondering where the people in the cars were going or what their enjoyments were" (*49, cf. also 66, 113–14*). Carrie, like all of Dreiser's characters, has a sense of place and is sensitive to her environment. Scene, in fact, becomes part of the motives in Dreiser's fiction, arousing desire and awakening characters to social worlds beyond. When Drouet first took Carrie to a good restaurant, "the great room soothed her" and increased her desire to participate in Drouet's way of life—this "splendid" realm with its "well-dressed throng" (*57*). The meal that Drouet bought Carrie cost more than half of what she made in a week of hard work; Carrie would have to save every penny of her $4.50-a-week salary for two months to get the clothes that Drouet buys her —something that she could not very well do, since she was paying her sister $4.00-a-week for board. In these early scenes, Dreiser created an overwhelming sense of inevitability; he completely negated the dimension of will and showed Carrie a helpless victim of her environment and her appetite.

Over and over, Dreiser showed that there was a one-to-one relationship between his characters and the world that contained them—that they were merely an extension of their surrounding, that the mood of a place could and did become a matter of mind. Like litmus paper, the mind absorbed what was outside it. As winter approached, for example, Carrie's mood turned grayer with December gray: "There seems to be something in the chill breezes," Dreiser wrote, "productive of rueful thoughts" (*88*). As spring brought a softening of air, so also it brought "an infinite delicacy of feeling to the flesh as well as to the soul." Carrie "was ripened by it in spirit for many suggestions" (*107*). Carrie responded in exactly the same way to the splendid houses in Chicago's North Shore with their richly carved entrance-ways, their globed and crystalled lamps, their panelled doors and stained glass windows. "She gazed and gazed . . . longings, and all the while the siren voice of the unrestful was whispering in her ear" (*107*).

When Hurstwood was kidnapping Carrie, taking her away from Chicago, Carrie struggles and then succumbs, relaxed by the pounding of the rails and a steady gale of rain outside

—quieted by the speeding wheels which have already carried her far away, excited by the thought of such new and strange places that Hurstwood may take her. While Hurstwood feels insignificant in New York, a condition which produces a state of mind that makes him less self-reliant just when he most needs self-confidence, Carrie is overwhelmed by "the wonder of it," its infinite sense of possibility, an "atmosphere [which was] easily and quickly felt . . . like a chemical reagent" (*265*).

Each character has a kind of essence, an essential self, which he is trying to realize. New York becomes a catalyst, both releasing and intensifying the qualities of mind and character that differentiate Carrie and Hurstwood. New York becomes the wedge that separated them, and the split widens in keeping with the novel's sense of inevitability. The pattern of Carrie's life is centrifugal as she moves further and further away from her provincial background, while the pattern of Hurstwood's life is centripetal as he moves more and more into a realm of isolation and total loneliness away from his old society of established friends and celebrities. Carrie's vision expands as she responds to the "possibilities" of Broadway and high society while Hurstwood's vision diminishes. When she is having dinner at Sherry's, even Carrie is aware of how far she has moved beyond Drouet and her first good restaurant dinner. When Hurstwood sits in the hotels off of Madison Square, gray of mood in gray December, even he forlornly realizes that life has passed him by (*314*). A character's growth in Dreiser's novels is always measured against what money can buy in public places—measured, that is, against the only kind of wealth that Dreiser had known up to this time. Setting created mood and mood created motives. Since a character is determined by his environment, time becomes a physical matter, and even something as intangible as personality is caught in the changing process of time, caught in Dreiser's chain of inevitability.

Despite the sense of inevitability, despite the mechanistic assumptions Dreiser brings to *Sister Carrie,* an overwhelming sense of chance seems to dominate this novel. When Carrie is first hunting for a job in Chicago, for example, she is encouraged by an offer from a firm she applies to after she reads an ad in a newspaper that blew around her leg. Carrie meets Drouet by chance—in fact, twice by chance: once on the train bringing her from Wisconsin to Chicago and then again on the street, at a moment when she happens to be depressed by her recent illness, the loss of her job, the nagging of her brother-in-law, and the impending threat of having to return to Columbia City, Wisconsin. Her first stage experience is in a play that Drouet forgot about and then remembered that the director needed a girl for the part. Carrie breaks with Drouet when the chambermaid tells him that Hurstwood is a constant visitor, and Mrs. Hurstwood accidentally learns about her husband's infidelity from Dr. Beale who sees Hurstwood riding in the park with Carrie and from George, Jr., who sees him with her at the theater (although it is inevitable that Hurstwood would be eventually observed by others with Carrie). Hurstwood meets Carrie at the moment he has fallen out of love with his wife. Hurstwood pursues Carrie more fervently when he happens to see Drouet living alone at the Palmer House and thus realizes that Drouet has left Carrie. Hurstwood finds himself in an impossible situation because he has by chance left the property in his wife's name.

As we have seen, the central incident in the novel also happens by chance: Hurstwood fails to find Carrie at home one night, becomes depressed, happens to meet some friends, drinks too much, chances to find the safe of Fitzgerald and Moy open, and steals the money from the safe which accidentally springs shut. Chance follows both Hurstwood and Carrie to New York: Carrie meets the Vances by chance, when they move into the next door flat; through them she meets Robert Ames; thus by chance she is exposed to a heightened way of life that makes her all the more disappointed with Hurstwood. Hurstwood loses his original investment as well as the steady income from his saloon when the man who owns the land chances to sell it. Hurstwood loses a large portion of his remaining money in two card games—that is, in games of chance—the second of which he goes to after a chance argument with Carrie has driven him from the house. Carrie gets her first speaking part as an actress when the lead happens to speak to her ("it might as well have been any of the others, so far as he was concerned") and her reply gets a big laugh. Carrie's greatest success in her early career comes by chance when the director whimsically orders her to frown in her small part and Carrie delights the audience. Even the review of the play, which applauds Carrie, points to the "perversity" of her success and to "the vagaries of fortune."

The world of *Sister Carrie*, however, is not totally a realm of gratuity. Chance is "only another name for our ignorance of causes," Dreiser says in his "Notes on Life." Behind what appears to be a series of disconnected and random events in the novel is a realm of causality. While much happens or seems to happen by chance, there is also a larger context, a realm of cause and effect events. The individual may be subject to the accidents of fate, but he is also subject to the inexorable laws of both human and physical nature, laws he cannot escape even though he may not fully understand them. Given their respective temperaments, given the setting and situation they find themselves in, what occurs to characters in *Sister Carrie* happens with an inevitability, with a predictability, beyond their control. Man is only partially a creature of chance: chance works only on the level of the individual while laws work on the level of human nature and society. The catalyst may be a random one, but the sequence of events put into operation reveals a mechanistic universe—a cause and effect relationship between events on a higher and abstract level of reality.

One can easily see the sequential pattern of *Sister Carrie*. Reverse any one of the scenes and it disrupts the flow of action. For example, if Carrie had met Hurstwood, not Drouet, on the train from Wisconsin, there would have been no story. Hurstwood would not have been attracted to Carrie, who was at that time too plain for his more heightened and sophisticated tastes. Carrie, on the other hand, would not have agreed to live with Drouet if she had not lived first with her sister. Hurstwood would not have robbed the safe before he met Carrie, and Carrie would not have gone to New York at this point unless a Hurstwood forced her. Hurstwood would not have settled for such a low-class saloon in New York if he had not been so desperate, and Carrie would not have sought out a stage career if Hurstwood could have supported her.

Dreiser's concern with the proper sequential pattern of *Sister Carrie* is evident from the changes he made in the holograph and typescript of the novel. In Chapter 11, for example, Dreiser reversed two scenes. In the original draft, he put the scene (*pp. 99–101 in the novel*) in which Hurstwood sees Drouet with another woman *before* the scene (*pp. 95–99*) in which Drouet returns to their flat, insensitively misreads Carrie's mood, and begins to fall out of favor with Carrie. This change is neither subtle nor meaningless because, directly following, is the scene in which Carrie begins to fall in love with Hurstwood at the theater; and the order of the two preceding scenes affects the meaning of the third. In the revision, Carrie tires of Drouet *before* Hurstwood sees Drouet with another woman. The scene with Drouet and the girl thus functions to clear the way for Hurstwood and does not suggest—as it did in the original version—that Carrie went to Hurstwood because Drouet was tiring of her or in love with another woman. In an early draft of Chapter 11, Dreiser also had Drouet take Carrie for a drive by the expensive Chicago homes of Armour, Pullman, Palmer, and Marshall Field. Dreiser took this scene out of Chapter 11 and moved it to Chapter 12 where Mrs. Hale takes Carrie for this drive (*pp. 106–7*)—at a point, in other words, in which Carrie has lost interest in Drouet. This drive whets Carrie's desires ("When she came to her rooms, Carrie saw their comparative insignificance"); she longs even harder for a more heightened life; and in the revision she is totally dissatisfied with her present life. The seed is planted, the *fleur de mal*, and soon after she enters her rooms "the house-servant brought up the intelligence that Mr. Hurstwood was in the parlour" (*108*).

Behind the appearance of chance in this novel is a necessary relationship between scenes, a realm of causality, a river running from its source to a destined end. Carrie, Hurstwood, and Drouet are compelled to act as they do. As Dreiser says, Drouet "had his future fixed for him beyond peradventure. He could not help what he was going to do. He could not see clearly enough to wish to do differently. He was drawn by his innate desire to act the old pursuing part. He would need to delight himself with Carrie as surely as he would need to eat his heavy breakfast" (72).

An appreciation of *Sister Carrie* seems to depend upon the direction from which one approaches it. Those who come upon the novel after reading twentieth-century fiction find the story trite, labored, hopelessly melodramatic, and unconvincing (certainly Carrie's sudden rise to stardom, merely because she frowned at the proper moment, taxes credulity). Yet those who come upon the novel after reading nineteenth-century fiction can see that Dreiser was making vital use of his own immediate world and that he was extending the subject matter of the novel in asking us not to look harshly at this Victorian vamp (although much less a vamp in the final draft of the novel than in the first ones). Dreiser was working within the Horatio Alger tradition of the novel; but instead of taking a virtuous young man who succeeds by diligently pursuing a principled life, he took an ambitious young woman and allowed her to fare remarkably well by pursuing a life of dubious virtue. Dreiser took the conventions of a Horatio Alger story and turned it morally upside down.

Neither Carrie nor Hurstwood are subject to the "laws" of morality. While they both "sin," one profits and the other suffers from the course of events. There is absolutely no relationship in this novel between what one does against society and what happens to him. In fact, Carrie rightfully scorns the girls who remain virtuous in the sweat shops that she has left behind, and Hurstwood almost made another start in New York until he ran out of energy and drive. The laws at work in *Sister Carrie* are those of mechanistic and not conventional morality.

Dreiser, in fact, deleted from the end of Chapter 9 of the holograph the suggestion that all life—either inside or outside the family—moves "on in conventional manner to old age and dissolution." Yet, while money is the prime motive for all of Dreiser's characters, what befalls a character outside the family seems to be of more consequence than what befalls him inside the family. This was the closest Dreiser came to suggesting the danger that lies in violating Christian morals which, he believed, have no relationship to anything in nature ("For all the liberal analysis of Spencer and our modern naturalistic philosophers, we have but an infantile perception of morals") (85). Dreiser finally negated Christian morality as an absolute by contrasting Carrie's and Hurstwood's final fate. Once outside the family, Carrie subjected herself to "the forces which sweep and play throughout the universe" (70), just as Hurstwood subjected himself to these forces when he deserts his family and runs away with Carrie. Yet, while Hurstwood falls victim to these forces, Carrie rises above them, and Dreiser created an amoral world where there was no relationship between the virtuous life and earthly reward. As Dreiser said at the very end of the novel, Carrie's story gives the lie to conventions which say " 'You shall not better your situation save by honest labor' " (453).

In *Sister Carrie*, Dreiser first expressed his belief in blind and insignificant man, continuously struggling for fulfillment in the face of death. The end of Hurstwood anticipates the end of Carrie, at least in essence, for his story is the story of all men. That Carrie cannot realize this is one of the many ironies of the novel—an irony that stems here, as in all of Dreiser's novels, from the characters' lack of knowledge, from their inability to see themselves fully, and from their blurred vision. Throughout this novel, there is a gulf between what is happening and what the characters believe or know is happening, just as Dreiser believed that there was a gulf between modern man's pride in his achievement and man's ultimate insignificance in the face of the gigantic universe. When Carrie, for example, is most depressed with her sister and Hanson, Drouet is speaking of her most enthusiastically to Hurstwood, an event which anticipates the rise of Carrie's career when she feels that it is at lowest ebb.

> Thus was Carrie's name bandied in the most frivolous and gay places, and that also when the little toiler was bemoaning her narrow lot, which was almost inseparable from the early stages of this, her unfolding fate. (47)

And as Hurstwood plots to steal Carrie away, Drouet feels the most friendly toward Hurstwood.

"There's a nice fellow," Drouet thought to himself as he turned the corner towards Madison.

"Drouet is a good fellow," Hurstwood thought to himself as he went back into his office, "but he's no man for Carrie." (*123*)

Moreover, Drouet is willing to marry Carrie at just the moment that he loses her (*172*). Hurstwood feels most "relieved" about what his wife will do at just the moment she is plotting the divorce that will ruin him (*211*).

At the play, Drouet has contempt for the insensitive husband who loses his wife to another man at just the moment when Drouet is losing Carrie to Hurstwood because he is insensitive to Carrie's feelings.

"Served him right," said Drouet afterward. . . . "I haven't any pity for a man who would be such a chump as that."

"Well, you never can tell," returned Hurstwood gently. "He probably thought he was right."

"Well, a man ought to be more attentive than that to his wife if he wants to keep her." (*127*)

As they leave the theater, Hurstwood pays no attention to a desperate tramp begging "the price of a bed," completely unaware that the same fate will ultimately befall him (*127*).

The play Carrie acts in, Augustin Daly's *Under the Gaslight*, also adds an ironic dimension to Carrie's own story. Daly's play described how Laura, a virtuous young girl, is cast out of established society when it is suspected that she is of poor birth. Ironically, it is not Laura but Pearl, supposedly her sister, who is the orphan—the play testifying, much like Mark Twain's *Pudd'nhead Wilson*, to the meaninglessness of values that underpin society. Moreover, Laura's expulsion from established society ironically parallels what happens to Hurstwood once he leaves Fitzgerald and Moy's. Furthermore, Carrie's first success comes in a play that expounds the rewards which come with the virtuous life while her own life proves the opposite. Dreiser must also have been aware of the ironic parallels between Daly's play and his own novel. The kidnapping and robbery scenes in *Under the Gaslight*, for example, foreshadow the story of Hurstwood and Carrie. And the situation between Hurstwood and Drouet fighting over Carrie parallels that of Laura and Pearl fighting over Ray.

Carrie never makes the connection between *Under the Gaslight* and her own life—but this is typical. Throughout *Sister Carrie* there is no connection between what is really happening and what the characters believe is happening. Carrie and her roommate, Laura, laugh at a man who falls into the snow, Carrie not realizing that it is Hurstwood (*447*). Carrie, who has been reading Balzac ("'Oh, dear,' said Carrie, with whom the sufferings of Father Goriot were still keen. . . . 'Aren't you sorry for the people who haven't anything tonight?'"), would like to relieve general suffering at exactly the same moment that Hurstwood, to whom she is now almost indifferent, commits suicide. The final scene in the novel is also ironic. Carrie, like all of Dreiser's characters, feels that time will bring complete fulfillment while in reality it will bring only death. A second voice is heard here, as we hear it often in this novel, a voice of cruel irony that reveals the gulf between what Carrie expects to happen and what will really happen.

The omniscient point of view, the overseeing eye of the author brooding over what his characters cannot see, is technically proper and extremely effective in Dreiser's fiction. Like a whisper, too faint for Carrie and perhaps even for the reader to hear, he tells us what Dreiser believed was an indisputable human truth: the blind will strive after beauty, dream and long for pleasure, but for everyone there "is neither surfeit nor content" (*454*).

Throughout the novel, characters rock in their chairs, a detail which suggests the flux of life: Carrie's drift toward an unobtainable fulfillment, and Hurstwood's toward death and dissolution. Carrie at the end of the novel rocks away, completely unaware, still aspiring. Dreiser suggests that all life is in motion, that man is a mere drop in the ocean of life (sea imagery predominates in this novel). In the world of *Sister Carrie*, man will never find a moment of restful contentment; and the tides of life will not spare him in their rush toward unknown shores.

6

"Jennie Gerhardt"

One of Jennie Gerhardt's favorite books is Nathaniel Hawthorne's *Twice Told Tales. The Scarlet Letter* would be more appropriate reading for her because Jennie Gerhardt and Hester Prynne have much in common: both have had illegitimate children, both suffer from violating established convention, and both are or become separated from the men they truly love. Jennie and Hester live in closed societies, ruled by conventions, the violation of which brings destructive consequences, a fact that connects colonial Boston in *The Scarlet Letter* to the equally moral and highly restrictive realm of high society in *Jennie Gerhardt*. Jennie and Hester live by the dictates of their hearts, are generous and unselfish, and their weakness is that they care too much and are faithful to those they love. They are, in many ways, too good for the world in which they live. Both Vesta and Pearl, the daughters of Jennie and Hester, are ironically a source of consolation in bitter moments. As Hester tries to reestablish Pearl's good name, so Jennie feels that "Vesta must not be an outcast any longer." [1] Both Vesta and Pearl are bright and gay spirits in a drab world —only in Hawthorne, Pearl's natural brightness seems to be a prelapsarian throwback to a pre-Christian world; in Dreiser, Vesta's happy spirit merely stands in contrast to the sombre religious world that condemns natural innocence.

Here, of course, the similarity ends. In *The Scarlet Letter*, Hawthorne created a moral realm where sin can be redeemed. Hester, in fact, is strengthened by the process in contrast to Dimmesdale who is weakened and dissipated by the hidden sin and by his guilt. As Hawthorne says of Hester, "the torture of her daily shame would at length purge her soul, and work out another purity than that which she had lost; more saint-like, because the result of martyrdom." [2] In contrast, Jennie can find no way back. Her "sin" starts a chain of events which leads inevitably to the abandoned life, a lonely and empty end.

The endings of both novels are significant. In *The Scarlet Letter*, Hester and Pearl have brought Dimmesdale to the scaffold; he has made his public confession and defeated the demonic Chillingworth; Pearl's good name has been restored; and Hester returns from England to live out her days knowing that Pearl is happily married abroad. Although Dreiser had originally ended *Jennie Gerhardt* with Jennie and Lester serenely married, he revised that happy ending and Jennie and Lester go their separate ways; Lester marries Letty Gerald; Vesta dies of typhoid fever; Lester dies soon after; and Jennie is left alone, counting empty days and waiting for the release that only death can bring. There is no way back in Dreiser's world—a completely materialistic realm where one is a victim of forces beyond his control.

Both Hawthorne and Dreiser were in their forties when they finished writing their novels: Dreiser had just turned forty, Hawthorne forty-five. Dreiser, however, had begun his novel when he was not yet thirty. In the top left-hand corner of the holograph of *Jennie Gerhardt,* he wrote on Chapter 1 "Sunday January 6, 1901, 11 p.m.," which appears to be the date he finished the first chapter. From the dates on the following chapters of the holograph, Dreiser seems to have gotten off to a good start with his second novel. He had written ten chapters (over one hundred pages of printed text) by "Sunday February 3, 1901, 9:30 a.m." After this, however, the writing went more slowly, until by mid-December he had bogged down. Yet Dreiser believed that he would finish the novel the next year. On April 12, 1902, he wrote J. F. Taylor, who had contracted to publish the novel, that he thought he might finish it by June. Taylor at this time set up a few pages in "dummy," Dreiser entitling the novel *The Transgressor*, and these sheets are among Dreiser's papers at the University of Pennsylvania. By June of 1902, Dreiser was far from finished. In fact, he was on the verge of his nervous breakdown, and he gave up altogether on the novel. In 1904, once he had overcome his depression, Dreiser returned to *Jennie Gerhardt* and wrote to Chapter 41, at which time he abandoned the manuscript. This section of the novel was written on half-sheets. In 1910, Dreiser returned once again to his novel, this time writing on 8 × 11 inch paper. He left the opening pages more or less as they were in the original draft, beginning with Chapter 14 of the holograph (Chapter 16 of the novel) and rewriting from this point on. When he reached Chapter 30 of his new draft, he used two chapters (Chapters 37 and 38) that he had written in 1904. In fact, at the top of what had been Chapter 38, Dreiser wrote "1904 work."

Since J. F. Taylor was no longer a prospective publisher, Dreiser sent the manuscript to Harper's, which accepted it for publication in April of 1911. Dreiser had revised his work by June, and the novel was published on October 19, 1911. By December 31, 1911, *Jennie Gerhardt* had sold 7,712 copies, netting $1,330.42 in royalties. In the next six months, the book sold another 4,713 copies, netting an additional $915.85 royalties.

Dreiser had carried *Jennie Gerhardt* a long time in his mind. In one sense, he had been carrying the novel there for most of his life because, once again, he was writing out of deep personal experience. Mr. Gerhardt is an exact duplicate of Dreiser's father (he escaped German conscription, came to America in 1844, married a Mennonite girl, had a severe accident from which he never fully recovered, became "unstrung by his misfortunes," and saw his family break up after the death of his wife) just as Mrs. Gerhardt is modeled on Dreiser's mother. As we have already seen, Jennie's story is the composite story of Dreiser's sisters, Mame and Sylvia, even to the extent that Mr. Gerhardt dies in the care of Jennie just as Mr. Dreiser died in the care of Mame. Like Jennie, Mame became pregnant during her affair with an influential Terre Haute lawyer and politican who gave her money and who helped get Paul out of jail for check-forging (just as Senator Brander gets Bass out of jail). As in the novel, these events take place in 1879–80 when Mame, like Jennie, is eighteen years old. To these incidents Dreiser added the story of Sylvia which roughly parallels the Jennie-Lester Kane plot. Like Jennie, Sylvia had had an affair with Don Ashley, from one of the best Warsaw families, who left her (even though she was pregnant) when his family (like Lester Kane's) objected. Unlike Sylvia, who abandoned her child to her mother, Jennie is a loving mother who dotes on Vesta.

Like *Sister Carrie, Jennie Gerhardt* presupposes a public world. The Columbus hotel is significantly the starting point for both Jennie and the novel. The hotel exposes her to a larger kind of life ("the glamor of the great world was having its effect upon her senses") (20–21). Like Carrie on the train to Chicago or later in the restaurant with Drouet, or like Clyde Griffiths in the Green-Davidson hotel, Jennie sees the limitations of her life more fully when she is in public places that reveal what money can buy. Her brother, Bass, modelled upon Paul Dresser, is also attracted to the Columbus House. A poorman's dandy, Bass is tiring of the family, and he wants the heightened life that goes with money and success. As Paul Dresser seemed to know intuitively that one could best escape from poverty in a "public" occupation—entertainment, sports, or politics—Bass also seems to know that his best chance for quick success is in public life, and he spends his evenings in the lobby of the Columbus House trying to make the right contacts: "It seemed to him that this hotel was the center and circumference of all that was worthwhile in the social sense" (23).

In some ways, Dreiser was rewriting *Sister Carrie* in his

second novel. This is even more obvious in the first draft of the novel in which both Senator Brander and Jennie are more knowing of what is happening. Dreiser had trouble, particularly with Brander, deciding whether to make him a blue beard ("He had had his relationships with women and knew the sex fairly well," Dreiser wrote—and later deleted from Chapter 3 of his first draft) or to make him timid and shy with women. In the first draft, Brander takes Jennie on his knee and fondles her. In this draft (*p. 80 of the holograph*), when Bass is arrested, Mr. Gerhardt goes to Colonel Haven, who gives him the bail-money. Senator Brander reads about Bass in the newspaper and sends Mrs. Gerhardt twenty dollars. When Dreiser rewrote this scene almost ten years later, Colonel Haven is out of town when Mr. Gerhardt calls, and Jennie goes to Senator Brander, who seduces her after he gets Bass out of jail. Dreiser later rewrote this scene once again because he had depicted Brander taking conscious advantage of Jennie's situation. In his third version, Brander is even more well-meaning, more the victim of insuppressible passions, Dreiser deleting such sentences as "At this moment he [Senator Brander] knew that Jennie was in his hands."

Also in the holograph—that is, the 1901 version of the novel —Dreiser made Bass a more central character. Like Dreiser himself, Bass becomes a bill collector and meets men "from cities far and near." A gambler at heart, he loves cards. When he loses sixty dollars of his employer's money, he sends Jennie to Brander for the money, and this—not his arrest for stealing coal—leads to the seduction scene. Dreiser's revision makes Bass the victim of a railroad policeman bully and keeps the initiative with Jennie, who goes on her own—and is not sent—to Brander.

For some reason, Dreiser had great trouble making his women virginal in the early drafts of his novels. Both Carrie and Jennie are more coarse and lascivious in the early manuscripts than in the novels themselves, perhaps because he was writing so close to his own views of his sisters. At any rate, like Carrie, Jennie becomes much more innocent and virginal in the revised version of the novel. In the holograph, Jennie practically gives herself to Brander, throwing her arms around him so that he can carry her to a couch. In the original version, Jennie is equally unrestrained with Lester Kane, who, after her father's accident, takes her to Bezenah's Hotel, orders an impressive dinner (the scene almost duplicates the one with Carrie and Drouet), and gives her money. Not only was Dreiser writing the same kind of scene between novels, he duplicated scenes within the novels. Senator Brander tells Jennie "You are mine," and Lester Kane repeats the words exactly. Senator Brander (in an early version) "presses" money into Jennie's hand and Lester does the same.

In the holograph, Lester is also a very different kind of character, more lustful and cunning than in the final version. In fact, Dreiser began Chapter 28 of the holograph by calling Lester a Machiavellian lover.

> The Machiavellian manner in which Lester thus complicated Jennie's sense of consideration for her mother with the need of yielding to him, while at the same time destroying any illusion as to the nature of his feeling for her, was calculated to upset and undo that little wanderer—to make her feel the helplessness of her position.

In the final version of the novel, Dreiser also played down the effect New York has upon Jennie, which is the same effect it had upon him (when he visited New York in 1894) and upon Carrie. He deleted scenes in which Lester and Jennie "stroll up Broadway [and] Fifth Avenue" as if they were in a "true paradise," scenes in which Jennie is in awe of fine hotel rooms swollen with "soft carpets," bright with lights, "elegant" with draperies and furniture, and "incrusted" with gilt.

As a result of these revisions, Jennie is motivated far less by the good life than any of Dreiser's earlier characters. Unlike Carrie, Jennie is more sensitive to life's "song," is more moved by "nature's fine curves," more happy in the garden or forest where "color was not lost upon her" or where "every sound and every sigh were welcome to her because of their beauty" (29). She is a selfless and idealistic girl in a selfish and materialistic world. She longs to be one with nature, to respond to its beauty, to "incline her head and listen" to the birds in the field until "the whole spiritual quality" of what she saw and heard beat with "her own great heart" (29). Jennie has a "poetic soul," to use Dreiser's own words, and in one sense she begins where Carrie leaves off, becomes what Carrie aspires to become. She tries to release the spirit from the flesh (Double, Page almost entitled his first novel *The Spirit and the Flesh*), and *Jennie Gerhardt* looks back to *Sister Carrie* and forward to *The Bulwark*. The materialistic and idealistic motives that competed with in Dreiser himself also competed within his characters. Jennie is too poor to take money for granted; but unlike most of Dreiser's earlier characters, she never lets her desire for money destroy her sense of the beautiful.

In this context, the conversation between Robert Ames and Carrie in the holograph of *Sister Carrie* (Dreiser deleted these passages from Chapter 46 of the novel) is interesting. At Ames's suggestion, Carrie has been reading Balzac's *The Great Man from the Provinces* (one of Dreiser's favorite novels). In discussing the novel with Ames, "Carrie expressed something about the sadness of the failures of Lucien de Rubempré," Carrie identifying with the man of ambition and desire. Ames responds: " 'If a man doesn't make knowledge his object he's likely to fail . . . [and] it's the man who fails in his mind who fails completely.' " Ames (whom Dreiser modelled upon himself) tells her of his impoverished childhood and then advises her to develop her artistic talents, which will bring "as much satisfaction as you will ever get." Ames then outlines his theory of art. As in the novel, where it is only briefly mentioned, he tells Carrie that the artist is aware of the beauty in life to which less sensitive men cannot respond. A higher and larger force is working in nature and " 'you and I,' " Ames insists " 'are but mediums through which something is expressing itself. Now our duty [like that of the writer, the artist, and the composer] is to make ourselves ready mediums.' " Ames's words move Carrie ("Curiously all he said appealed to her as absolutely true"), but when Ames is no longer with her—no longer a physical presence—his ideas lose their force, and she once again becomes "the old mournful Carrie, the desireful Carrie, Carrie unsatisfied."

Carrie and Jennie represent two different states within

Dreiser's own psyche and perhaps within the American psyche itself. It is not mere coincidence that Dreiser was attracted to both Charles Yerkes and Henry David Thoreau. If a Yerkes or a Benjamin Franklin—with their rags-to-riches careers and their overpowering sense of materialism—represents one extreme of the American consciousness, and if a Thoreau—with his belief in a higher reality that negated man-made laws and material goals—represents another state of consciousness, then Carrie and Jennie taken together embody the indwelling values of American culture. Jennie sacrifices herself for those she loves —for something beyond her—in a way that would seem foolish to Carrie.

In making Jennie so unselfish Dreiser seems to be creating a fantasy character, an ideal woman, one who will remain faithful to a man without making any demands upon him. To this extent, Jennie is exactly what Sara White was not—in fact, what any conventional woman could or would not be. " 'I wouldn't expect to be all in all to one man' " (*303*), Jennie tells Lester, giving him the sexual license that Dreiser believed every woman should grant a man—particularly himself.

Yet, despite her willingness to defy conventions, Jennie, unlike Carrie, never really leaves the family. She wants most, in fact, to be a wife and a mother, and the years she spends living out of wedlock with Lester Kane are ironically the most conventional years of her life, for here she finds the home and family that she most desires. She is condemned by a society more faithful to the letter than the spirit of the law.

If Dreiser reiterates one idea, it is that society tries to make man into something that he is not. Underneath the respectable surface of social conventions, there is a realm of life—vital, forceful, chemical, and crude—that the most civilized minds cannot and will not entertain. This is one of the key themes in Dreiser's fiction—a theme that he will develop at greater length and with subtler variation in the Cowperwood trilogy. Dreiser's world has a vital center, a realm that lies beneath layer after layer of social pretense and religious clichés, a center to which Dreiser's most vital characters—Carrie, Jennie, Eugene Witla, Cowperwood, and even Clyde Griffiths—intuit and respond. These characters have an essential self, a temperament and physical nature that is fixed at all stages of their development, and which is realized by circumstance—and often chance circumstance. This is why these characters perform the same act over and over, why Carrie is continuously selfish and Jennie perpetually self-sacrificing. Man is an impersonal machine, a product of his temperament and of his bodily nature.

While Dreiser does not over-emphasize the chemical nature of motives in *Jennie Gerhardt,* he makes it perfectly clear that the source of conflict stems from the disharmony between man's instincts and moral conventions which try to destroy these instincts:

> Although the whole earth, not we alone, is moved by passions hymeneal, and everything terrestrial has come into being by the one common road, yet there is that ridiculous tendency to close the eyes and turn away the head as if there was something unclean in nature itself. "Conceived in iniquity and born in sin," is the natural interpretation put upon the process by the extreme religionist, and the world, by its silence, gives assent to a judgment so marvelously warped.
>
> Surely there is something radically wrong in this attitude. The teachings of philosophy and the deductions of biology should find more practical application in the daily reasoning of man. No process is vile, no condition is unnatural. The accidental variation from a given social practice does not necessarily entail sin. No poor little earthling, caught in the enormous grip of chance, and so swerved from the established customs of men, could possibly be guilty of that depth of vileness which the attitude of the world would seem to predicate so inevitably. (*104–5*)

As in *Sister Carrie,* Dreiser suggests in *Jennie Gerhardt* that man exists in a no-man's land. While Lester Kane was, for example, "an essentially animal-man," he was also "pleasantly veneered by education and environment" (*138*). Because he is no longer at one with himself, Lester, like man in general, is no longer mere animal and far from perfectly civilized. He is trapped: his animal passions are in conflict with the restraints of conventional morality. "He would not wear the social shackles," says Dreiser of Lester, "if it were possible to satisfy the needs of his heart and nature and still remain free" (*140*). It is, of course, impossible to be morally restrained and temperamentally unrestrained; and the conflict is between convention and instinct.

Man in Dreiser's fiction exists in two contexts: a natural one in which he is moved by animal appetites and instincts, and a social one in which he is moved by a desire for position and respectability. Since man did not make himself, and since he does not know for what purpose he was made, he can do nothing to change his nature. Man is, however, responsible for conventions. The tragedy of Jennie Gerhardt is made more pathetic because it need not have been. Man is not only blind; he is also the victim of his blindness when he creates a world that is at odds with his own nature. Man is unique, for he is the only animal that is able to defy his natural condition and to circumscribe himself within a system of law that is of his own creation, just as if the fish in the sea decided arbitrarily that they preferred to live in the skies. And once this "moral environment" is established its laws take on the force of nature itself. "So well defined is the sphere of social activity," Dreiser wrote, "that he who departs from it is doomed. Born and bred in this environment, the individual is practically unfitted for any other state. He is like a bird accustomed to a certain . . . atmosphere, and which cannot live comfortably at either higher or lower level" (*237*).

Once he has become divorced from nature, man tries to fulfill two opposing selves, tries to be true to both a natural and social self. In some cases, the natural impulses of Dreiser's characters are in conflict with established morality. In other cases, his characters have an ideal image of themselves that they cannot realize in society. In both cases, they are socially displaced, at odds with themselves and their environment. They are doomed before they begin, displaced by their own natures, destined always to be in conflict with themselves and the world that contains them.

While the story of Jennie is the story of Mame and Sylvia, Dreiser's own sisters, Jennie's story is meant to be representative, to show what befalls a character who is true to her innate nature, especially when that nature is in conflict with a Puritan society. As long as Christian laws prevail, what happens to Jennie is inevitable. The individual is just as much subject to his environment (and moral laws are a part of man's environment) as are the birds in the air and the fish in the sea. Yet all conventions are relative to the conditions that dictate them, at best man's blind attempt to regulate his own nature and condition. Dreiser suggests that Western man has never really come to terms with his nature—and thus has never come to terms with the moral laws which regulate that nature. When Lester and Jennie travel to Europe, Dreiser has a chance to put their story in a larger context—that of "decayed Greece, of fallen Rome, or forgotten Egypt," thereby suggesting that each culture is only a variable part of a larger, mechanistic continuum, the laws of which the human mind has never completely understood: "Lester liked to point out how small conventions bulked in this, the larger world, and vaguely she began to see." If Jennie had "sinned," it was only from the limited point of view of her immediate culture. "In the sum of civilization, in the sum of the big forces, what did it all amount to? . . . Did anything matter except goodness—goodness of heart? What else was there that was real?" (298–99).

Dreiser gives the screw another turn when he suggests that modern religion is merely a part of the dead vestiges of the past, that there is little or no relationship between the teachings of the modern Christian Church and twentieth-century life. The baptism of Vesta, whose birth out of wedlock disgraces Jennie, is full of cruel ironies, especially the minister's supplication "that she may prove an honor and comfort to her parents and friends" (128). If anything, the forces of religion compound Jennie's trouble. Senator Brander would have married Jennie at the very beginning had not Mr. Gerhardt's religious scruples prevented it (*cf.* 83). Pious in the face of opportunity, Gerhardt's religion makes him his own worst enemy, a quality of character that Dreiser saw in his own father. While all of Dreiser's characters are blind, lacking self-understanding and unable to anticipate the future, the religious characters are the blindest and the source of the most obvious irony. Mr. Gerhardt turns Jennie from his house when he discovers that she is pregnant.

"She shall get out!" he said electrically. "She shall not stay under my roof . . . Let her get out now. We will see how the world treats her." (*96*)

The world treats the "sinning" Jennie much better than it does the pious Gerhardt; and of all his children, it is only Jennie, the one he sent from his own house, who will give Gerhardt a home when he needs one:

"Now, papa!" she pleaded, "it isn't as bad as that. You will always have a home—you know that—as long as I have anything. You come with me." (*187*)

The war that goes on between self and society is the source of Jennie's and Lester's dilemma and their loss of free will. Outside forces negate volition. Jennie is the height of social irrespectability and Lester of respectability. By working within such extremes, Dreiser negated the dimension of will because Lester does not really have a choice at all when he finds himself caught between the irreconcilable desires of wanting Jennie and also wanting his father's money, of living out of wedlock and of being socially respectable. The two objects of desire are not of equal weight; one is more attractive than the other; one exerts itself over the other (Jonathan Edwards also used this argument to disprove the possibility of free will). The objects of desire in themselves negate volition by influencing the choice beforehand. One's course of action is determined from the outside by the objects to be chosen between and not from the inside by the chooser deciding freely which way to move.

Dreiser's characters thus become the victims of alternatives that are really not alternatives at all—that is, the victims of "choices" that are really illusions. Since each situation will present one alternative more compelling than another, his characters become victims of that situation, victims of their condition, which was the way that Dreiser looked at man in general. While Jennie has reservations about taking Brander's money and about living with Lester Kane, given her desire to help her family and her need of money, she has no choice in what she does. While Lester is attracted to Jennie, given his inability to live within a modest income, he has no choice but to leave

Jennie if he is to escape being disinherited. Dreiser's theory of "weighted alternatives"—that is, his belief in determined action—is central to every one of his novels.

Since all events in *Jennie Gerhardt* are determined, these events have a mechanistic continuity, and chance—like free will—is a matter of illusion. This is true even though chance seems to predominate in this novel. If Mr. Gerhardt had not been "unstrung by his misfortunes," Jennie would not have gone to work at the hotel where she meets Senator Brander. As Dreiser explicitly states, "If she had not gone to the hotel all this . . . would never have come [to pass]" (*74*). Even then Jennie's relationship with Senator Brander might have been a harmless one if, by chance, Bass had not been caught at exactly this moment stealing coal and arrested. When Jennie goes to Brander for help, she conceives Vesta. She would have been saved from the embarrassing consequences of this if Senator Brander had not died before he could marry her. Once more the family might have struggled along if chance had not struck with Mr. Gerhardt burning his hands seriously in a factory accident. Jennie feels obliged to "sacrifice herself" (*159*) a second time and, in a clandestine meeting, agrees to live with Lester Kane in return for his financial help. Undoubtedly this relationship could not long be kept secret; but it might have turned out differently if Lester had not been reluctant to marry Jennie after he chances to discover that she has an illegitimate child (*cf. 202–6*). It might have also turned out differently if Louise, Lester's sister, had discovered that Lester and Jennie were living together after—and not before—their father died, and thus not given Archibald Kane reason to change his will: " 'a devilish trick of fortune,' " Lester says, describing these turns of events. Lester loses part of his capital in an investment that fails because a meatpacking firm happens to move, spoiling his real-estate deal. At this moment, he meets Letty Pace Gerald, an old admirer, who happens to be widowed, her husband dying of pneumonia four years after they were married, leaving her a fortune amassed in banking and the stock market. These events lead up to Lester's leaving Jennie, an unhappy event that is compounded by the loss of Vesta, who dies of typhoid fever.

While chance is an element in each of these events, it assumes secondary importance because something in each of the characters' makeup determines how he will respond to such chance events. Chance occurrences in Dreiser's fiction create situations which reveal the essential nature of each character. Each character carries his fate within him. If one specific event did not shape a character's end, another such event would affect his fate: it would only be a matter of time. Given Lester's love of the good life, he would abandon Jennie when their relationship threatened his expensive comforts. Like George Hurstwood, Lester is a victim of his temperament. He "drifts" through the novel, drifts into his relationship with Jennie, drifts out of it, even drifts into death: "drift[s] into a physical state in which a slight malady might prove dangerous. The result was inevitable, and it came" (*401*). Mr. Gerhardt is also a victim of his temperament. Given his innate weaknesses, it is only a matter of time before he will "unstring himself" (*74*). Jennie is equally a victim of temperament. Given her generosity, it is inevitable that she will sacrifice herself first for her family and then for Lester.

Chance is thus a catalyst in Dreiser's fiction, revealing what is quintessential and abiding in each character, which in turn accounts for their fate. Thus beneath the appearance of gratuity is a realm of causality. Chance may throw Jennie and Lester together, may create the extenuating circumstance; but once given this circumstance and once given the residual quality of each character's temperament, what happens is inevitable. Dreiser made this even clearer in the holograph of *Jennie Gerhardt* when he wrote: "I have read a story in my time, wherein a row of dominoes was used to illustrate the dependency of one thing upon another, and how the toppling of one meant the tumbling of all, but I know of no better instance than that which happened in this family. Jennie was as the next domino. Her father and mother the forces arrayed behind her." While Dreiser deleted this passage from the novel, he worked the idea into another context. After Vesta's death, Lester tells Jennie: " 'all of us are more or less pawns. We're moved about like chessmen by circumstances over which we have no control' " (*386*). While the metaphor is far from original, it does reveal

Dreiser's belief in a "mover," a mechanistic force that works beyond man's ken. As he put it himself, everything can "be brought back to its chemical constituents. . . . something else [was] back of the superficial appearance of things" (266).

Dreiser's characters realize an essential self, and the end for them is in their beginning. The outcome is inherent in the character and in the situation. Given their temperament and the circumstances that befall them, they are destined to act as they do, to remain true to their primary nature, to the chemic pull of temperament, and to the laws of probability that govern such temperaments in their given society. And this is true whether they succeed or fail. Dreiser negated the will of his characters and made them dupes of their temperament, of circumstance, and of time.

The cruelest irony within this process of events is that the most generous and unselfish character in the novel, Jennie Gerhardt, is the one who suffers the most. She is a victim of the poverty into which she is born and of her moral transgressions; over both she really has no control. As in *Sister Carrie*, there is no relationship between punishment and character. Jennie was who she was, and she did what she had to do: she deserved better. She is a victim of her culture and of the inexorable workings of time.

Descriptive detail in this novel provides an important thematic context, and the story is projected against the flow of life and time. The city particularly reveals the flow of life and, like most of Dreiser's characters, Jennie and Lester are a part of "the great mass of trucks and vehicles, the counterstreams of hurrying pedestrians [which pass like] shadows . . . in a dream" (386). Twenty-five years pass in this novel. Jennie moves from a beautiful eighteen to a matronly forty-three. "After the first heedless flights of youth have passed," says Dreiser, "there is a deadening thought of uselessness which creeps into men's minds—the thought which has been best expressed by the Preacher in Ecclesiastes" (192).

Through descriptive detail, Dreiser equates sex with the very workings of nature. After Jennie becomes pregnant with the senator's child, Dreiser breaks into a long, lyric passage in which he compares the spirit of youth and the spirit of nature. As nature realizes itself in the spring and summer of the year, so youth realizes itself through sex. Part of the power of *Jennie Gerhardt* comes from the sense of time in flux, the movement from youth to age, from life to death, from the lyric description of the physical moments that only the young can realize: "The few sprigs of green that sometimes invade the barrenness of your materialism, the few glimpses of summer which flash past the eye of the wintry soul, the half hours off during the long tedium of burrowing, these reveal to the hardened earth-seeker the universe which the youthful mind has with it always" (89). One of the compelling reasons that Senator Brander is so attracted to Jennie—he is fifty-two and she is eighteen when they first meet—is that Jennie brings the last hope of renewed youth: "he felt exceedingly young as he talked to this girl" (36); she was "all beauty" passing before him as "the world slipped away" (85).

Opposed to the spirit of youth, which is equated with natural impulse, is the spirit of age, which is equated with the old morality. Opposed to Jennie is Mr. Gerhardt, the personification of the old morality. Like Dreiser's own father, he is obsessed with sin, driven by the fear of hell and the desire of heaven. To him, Jennie, and even his wife, are sinners, Jennie damned forever for living out of wedlock and his wife for taking tainted money. Opposed to Lester is Archibald Kane, who, again like Dreiser's father, is a rigid Catholic. He is less motivated by religious impulses, however, than he is by a desire to protect his good name and to remain respectable. Behind him, of course, is the power of his money, which is the real mover in this as well as all other Dreiser novels.

As Senator Brander is attracted to Jennie because she holds out the promise of lost youth, so also is Lester ("her youth . . . made him feel young") (266). Both of their deaths anticipate hers, and the sweep of time in this novel is grand testimony to the final insignificance and temporality of man caught in a rush of time over which he has no control and no understanding. Dreiser ends the novel on this note, emphasizing the theme of time, suggesting that Jennie, like all of us, will pass "days and days in endless reiteration, and then—?" (*414*). We move in *Jennie Gerhardt* from the level of the individual, to the level of society, to the level of metaphysics, seeing man in one larger vortex after another, spinning like chips of wood in a whirlpool toward a center that can best be described with a question mark.

7

"The Financier," "The Titan," and "The Stoic"

Dreiser begins *The Financier* with a description of Philadelphia in its infancy, waiting to be developed, waiting for a Frank Algernon Cowperwood who would fulfill his personal destiny as America fulfilled its social destiny. At the end of this novel, Dreiser continues to emphasize Cowperwood's stoic sense of purpose, his belief in an essential self, his commitment to "the greatness that was inherent in him." [1] In his story of Cowperwood, Dreiser was looking at life through the other end of the telescope, not through the eyes of Sister Carrie or Jennie Gerhardt with their limited view, but through the eyes of a maker and shaper with an expanded range of focus.

In *Sister Carrie* and *Jennie Gerhardt*, Dreiser could write directly out of known experience—either his own or a member of his family's. In his *Trilogy of Desire*, he had moved to a larger public world, and he researched these novels in a way that he had never done before. Among Dreiser's papers are lengthy notes on Charles T. Yerkes, on the brokerage business in Philadelphia, on Chicago tycoons and their ages in relationship to Yerkes, on the National Banks of Chicago, on Chicago hotels, on the earnings of the West Chicago Street Railway Company from 1892 to 1893, on Bathhouse John Coughlin and Michael "Hinky Dink" Kenna (the Chicago aldermen who are the models for Michael Tiernan and Patrick Kerrigan), and on traction stock that (after Yerkes' Chicago defeat) Ryan, Whitney, Widener, and Elkins (the Hand, Schryhart, and Merrill of the novel) sold to the public for four times its worth, this group pocketing $70 million from these watered shares.

Dreiser read well over a dozen books treating the history and the operation of the stock market;[2] he went to Philadelphia and worked at length with the files of the *Public Ledger* getting information on James McManes (the Henry A. Mollenhauer in the novel), the political leader of the Philadelphia "gas ring," and on the Republican Party in Philadelphia under Mayor Fox (Jacob Borchardt in the novel) and City Treasurer Marcer (the George W. Stener of the novel); he read novels about big business (particularly Frank Norris' *The Pit*) and journalistic essays (especially the writing of David Graham Phillips); he had clipped an article by Charles Edward Russell which treated the rise of Yerkes in Philadelphia and Chicago[3] and an article by Edward Lefèvre which described Yerkes' final days;[4] he took the account of Yerkes' attempt to bribe Governor Altgeld from Chicago newspapers[5] and the story of Yerkes' final combat with Mayor Carter W. Harrison and the citizens' committee (in favor of municipal control of the streetcar lines) from the December 12, 1898 issue of *The World*; and he visited Chicago in December of 1912 (staying until February 10, 1913) getting Edgar Lee Masters to introduce him to those who were involved in or knew about Chicago business and politics—including Mayor Harrison. Even when he had returned to New York, Dreiser continued to write Masters for information, particularly (on August 13, 1913) for information about the Van Buren Street tunnel. Dreiser may not have known Zola's work at firsthand, but he never doubted the methods of the experimental novel.

While *The Trilogy of Desire* was a thoroughly researched

piece of work, the story of Yerkes-Cowperwood was as personal a matter for Dreiser as were the previous stories of his sisters. First, both Dreiser and Yerkes were ambitious, driven by a lust for success. Yerkes was another Horatio Alger hero, another man who had moved from humble circumstances to wealth and power, and Dreiser came to his life with the same excitement that he brought to his interview with famous men for Orison Swett Marden's *Success*. Second, Yerkes was a materialist who also seemed to appreciate beauty and good art, the two impulses warring within him, although not as strongly as they did within Dreiser himself. Third, Yerkes, again like Dreiser, was a man with a strong sexual nature, who was discontent with one woman, who lived the heightened life beyond conventional middle-class restraints, and who remained forever young (or so Dreiser tells us) as long as he could attract beautiful women. Fourth, Yerkes loved splendor and tended to identify beautiful women with the beauty of art, his final sense of beauty stemming (as it did for Dreiser) from acquisitive and sexual sources. Fifth, Yerkes was a man of the city: he grew up in the city, and he made his fortune in the city. *The Financier* is the story of Philadelphia, *The Titan* of Chicago, and *The Stoic* of London. Fascinated and in awe of the man with energy and drive, Dreiser saw how Yerkes manipulated modern forms of power at their very source. Sixth, Yerkes lived in a corrupt world where money brought power and where power brought more money in return. Dreiser had moved beyond the realm of the hotel and the Broadway stage of *Sister Carrie* and *Jennie Gerhardt* to the larger public world of bought elections, crooked city treasurers, bribed city councils, controlled newspapers, city bosses, and civic corruption—to the vested interests that moved and shaped life in the nineteenth century. We see in these novels a man who wanted money because it was power (*cf. The Financier*, 227), and we see power in conflict with power, Yerkes-Cowperwood pushing and his enemies pushing back, a process that Dreiser believed was consistent with Spencer's laws of force. While Dreiser admired Yerkes' rugged individualism, he disliked his contempt for the poor, who ultimately paid for his ruthless and corrupt control over city and state government. These novels reveal that Dreiser could never reconcile the selfish and altruistic motives that fought within himself. This personal conflict, in fact, became the basis for the narrative conflict: Dreiser both extolled the rugged individualist and attacked the vested interests of the robber barons, just as he had sung their praises in *Success* and attacked them in *Ev'ry Month* and later in *The Call*. Better than any other American novelist, Dreiser in these works revealed the dynamics of American political and social life—not only the battle between tycoon and tycoon, but also between the tycoon and the public, a battle that warred within his own heart.

Dreiser not only could but did believe that he and Yerkes were temperamentally alike. Strangely enough, even their lives had taken parallel turns. Like Dreiser, Yerkes had married an older woman, his marriage also failing. Like Dreiser, who had reached a kind of success when Doubleday accepted *Sister Carrie* only to lose everything the next year, Yerkes had reached financial success in Philadelphia only to be imprisoned for mishandling public funds. Like Dreiser, who had become a high-paid and successful editor only to lose his Butterick job because of sexual indiscretions, Yerkes became a leading Chicago industrialist only to lose his hold there when, in great part, his affairs antagonized others. To be sure, Yerkes was handsome, Dreiser ugly; Yerkes came from a closely-knit Quaker family, Dreiser from a quarreling almost fatherless Catholic one; Yerkes was self-confident, Dreiser more stumbling. Yet they both felt in different ways "destined" to succeed, that fate had chosen them. Dreiser was merely revealing his own sense of self when he took flight into fancy and identified himself with Yerkes. He had, after all, written in *A Book About Myself* that "To be president or vice-president or something, some great thrashing business of some kind. Great God, how sublime it seemed!"[6] Yerkes embodied Dreiser's concept of the great man: he had risen beyond the common element; he defied moral conventions; he brought turmoil to society as the very forces of nature seemed to work through him when he went beyond the limits—in both his business and personal life—of the past; and he in turn was defeated by his enemies and finally by the larger forces of time and decay, others taking his place and the battle going on without him.

Among the Dreiser papers at the University of Pennsylvania is a newspaper clipping pasted on an eight-by-eleven inch piece of paper and dated (in Dreiser's hand) February 4, 1906. The clipping is titled "The Materials of a Great Novel" and summarizes the life of Charles Yerkes from his Philadelphia days to the aftermath of his death. The article concludes:

> We could not expect Mr. Howells to deal with such a story. It is hardly for the young person. We shudder to think what might happen if Mr. James undertook it. The tale is too intricate and various and melodramatic for any kind of living novelist. . . . By divine right it is the property of Balzac, with Daudet as residuary legatee. Both are dead.

Dreiser did not begin writing the story of Charles Yerkes until 1910, but this clipping, dated four years earlier, may have been the germ of his Cowperwood novels—*The Financier* (1912), *The Titan* (1914), *The Stoic* (1947)—entitled *A Trilogy of Desire.*

Using 915 pages of eight-by-eleven inch paper, Dreiser wrote at the top-center of each page the important dates in Yerkes' life, including relevant dates after his death. Whenever he found pertinent information in newspapers, magazines, books, court records or other sources, he entered it, usually verbatim, on these pages. Dreiser has as many as twenty and thirty pages of notes for some days in Yerkes' life. The notes themselves have the same kind of sweep and range as the novels, reveal the power and drive of this man, and depict the open-ended and fiercely combative world in which he ruthlessly made his way. They end on the same anti-climactic and poignant note as *The Stoic*: Yerkes dead, his fortune plucked to the bone by "legal vultures," his whole world come to ashes, a truer testimony to the final insignificance of man than the $50,000 mausoleum in which he was buried in Brooklyn's Greenwood Cemetery.

Yerkes' career can easily be summarized from Dreiser's notes. He was born on June 25, 1837, went to Central High

School in Philadelphia, and clerked for a flour and grain company. In 1858, he opened his own brokerage firm at Third Street and soon after bought a banking house on 20 South Third. A schemer from the start, he profited greatly from the Civil War and later from a deal in which he manipulated city bonds—the deal that led to his conviction and imprisonment. After seven months in prison (Dreiser kept Cowperwood in jail for thirteen months), he was pardoned on September 27, 1872, at which time he returned to the business world and, on September 18, 1873, made a fortune on the failure of Jay Cooke and Company. He increased this capital with shrewd investments in the Philadelphia Transportation System, and then left Philadelphia in 1880 (Cowperwood left soon after his 1873 success), going first to Fargo, North Dakota, where he made money on a real-estate deal, and then in 1881 to Chicago, the new and vital center of the postwar economy. In Chicago, he lived near the lake, in a mansion at 3201 Michigan Avenue, began a grain and stock commission house on the corner of LaSalle and Madison Streets, and was successful in establishing a Chicago gas trust. Along with three other men from Philadelphia—Widener, Elkins, and Dolan—he turned his attention between 1884 and 1886 to the Chicago public transportation system, acquiring the franchise for the whole north side. At this point, he was one of the most powerful industrialists in America. When Moore Brothers collapsed in 1896, the big Chicago bankers failed in their attempt to ruin Yerkes by buoying up the market with Yerkes' outstanding loans and stock, which they held in large quantity. The incident that Dreiser describes in *The Titan* in which Mr. Arneel calls the Chicago investors to a meeting at his home is based on such a meeting held at Philip D. Armour's house, Yerkes actually saying the words Dreiser attributes to Cowperwood: "I must say I never saw so many straw hats at a funeral before." To prevent Yerkes from gutting the market at this time, the stock exchange was closed for him—testimony to his power and influence. This, however, is really a turning point in Yerkes' Chicago career, for he is finally defeated when he is unable to renew the transportation franchise.

During his last days in Chicago, Yerkes was building an expensive house in New York, on the corner of Fifth Avenue and 68th Street. Here he housed his world-famous art collection: three Rembrandts, a Franz Hals, a Van Dyck, a Hobbema, a Tyron, a Jan Van Beers, several Turners as well as pieces by Corot, Claude Lorrain, Bouguereau, Delacroix, and Millet, among others. From here also he manipulated his new interests in the London subway system, living in Savoy Court when he needed to be in London. While still in the middle of his London speculation scheme, Yerkes became seriously ill as he returned to America, was taken by ambulance to a suite at the Waldorf-Astoria, where he died on December 28, 1905, of Bright's disease. He was buried from his Fifth Avenue home, but only four carriages followed the casket to its fifty thousand dollar tomb, and one was filled with hired detectives.

Of the estate valued at fifteen million dollars, Yerkes left two hundred thousand dollars to his first wife, and the same sum to her stepson and his stepdaughter. His second wife was to receive an income from half the estate, and the rest was to go to his children. Upon his wife's death, the house and gallery were to go to the city of New York, to be kept as a public museum. Yerkes also left provisions for a hospital in the Bronx, to be built especially for the poor (whom he cared little about in life), everyone admitted regardless of race, creed, or color.

None of this came to pass. Primarily through the finagling of one Louis S. Owsley, an executor for the estate, only eight million of the original estate was accounted for and debts of five million dollars were set against this. The fight for the money was prolonged by years of legal red tape until, finally, the London Underground Railway system attached all of Yerkes' property, Mrs. Yerkes losing the house, the paintings sold at auction. Mrs. Yerkes moved to 871 Madison Avenue, where she died of heart disease on April 2, 1911. A clipping in *The Evening World* (June 14, 1913), an important source for much of this information, appends the moral to Yerkes' story: "the millions which seem never to have given any one any real pleasure faded away like an evil dream." [7]

Dreiser deviated radically from the record only once, when he described Cowperwood being buried amidst sad throngs, while in reality Yerkes—much like a Jay Gatsby—was deserted in death by those who pursued him in life. Dreiser, for some reason, chose not to use this sad contrast between Yerkes living and Yerkes dead. Instead, he sustained the heroic image of Cowperwood after his death, and emphasized how quickly his fortune disappeared when he was not there to protect it. Cowperwood's achievement seemed, as a result, even more impressive: his strength is highlighted by Aileen's weakness, his own shrewd and devious ways contrasted with the way that Aileen is tricked and ruined by vicious and money-hungry manipulators.

While Dreiser stuck fairly close to the public facts of Yerkes' life, he was less faithful to the private facts, especially Yerkes' marriages and affairs, which he modeled more on his own far-ranging experience. Dreiser, however, was faithful to his sources in portraying Yerkes' first wife, Mrs. Gamble—whom he called Mrs. Semple—a woman five years older than Yerkes whom he married when he was twenty-one. While Yerkes had six children by Mrs. Gamble, Dreiser changed the number to two, reducing the years they had to stay married, and making Cowperwood into more of a man about town than the dutiful father of six children.

The most obvious change in Dreiser's use of source came in his handling of Aileen Butler, who is modeled on Mary (Mollie) Adelaide Moore, one of nine children of a chemist employed by a drug firm. Dreiser made her the daughter of Edward Butler, modeled on a city politician Dreiser interviewed in St. Louis, and connects the two plots by establishing a relationship between Cowperwood's business life and his love life, the events of one affecting the other. For the same reason, Dreiser made most of Cowperwood's mistresses related to men of social standing, who can do him real harm: Stephanie Platow is the daughter of a rich furrier; Cecily Haguenin the daughter of an important editor; Florence Cochrane the daughter of the president of the Chicago West Division Company; and Carolyn Hand the wife of one of the three or four men who control Chicago financial and social life. Cowperwood had a highly sexual nature and was easily motivated by feminine beauty. By connecting the business and love plots in these novels, Dreiser made Cowperwood the victim of his temperament, reduced the main motives to chemical reactions, and made his central character the instrument or tool of a force beyond his control. The winds of life blow upon Cowperwood, as they do upon Shelley's lyre. Cowperwood continuously desires power, youth, love, and beauty. When Mrs. Semple loses her youth and beauty, Cowperwood must put her aside for Aileen. When Aileen in turn falls victim to the ravages of time, he must put her aside for Berenice Fleming.

These narrative elements—which dominate the novels—are cut from the cloth of Dreiser's experience. Dreiser deviated from biographical sources, although Yerkes' promiscuity was a happy fact with which he could work. He made the fading Aileen, contrary to anything in the sources, alcoholic and suicidal, beaten by life. While in reality Mollie Moore Yerkes drove herself about New York in a carriage drawn by four coal-black horses, Aileen is driven about in a "sedate brougham." Although Mollie Moore was certainly embittered, Dreiser intensified her hate for Yerkes: Aileen refused to visit Cowperwood on his deathbed, while Mollie actually gave in when entreated by her stepson. Aileen loses her fortune and dies a lonely death, whereas Mollie Moore married Wilson Mizner of San Francisco a month after Yerkes' death, when she was near fifty and Mizner twenty-five. Mizner was a roustabout with many interests. He co-authored with Paul Armstrong the play *The Deep Purple* and with Bronson Howard *The Only Law*, and he wrote by himself *The Greyhound* and *A Loyal Deception*. Before he died on April 4, 1933, Mizner also managed Stanley Ketchel, the prize-fighter.

While Dreiser made radical changes in his use of Mollie Moore as the model for Aileen Butler, he remained much more faithful to the real-life model of Berenice Fleming, a girl named Emily Grigsby, the daughter of a Confederate soldier from Louisville, Kentucky. Emily's mother, who later became a prostitute, took her and her brother to Cincinnati. From there the brother was sent to a private school, and Emilie (she changed the spelling) went to a convent. The mother then brought the daughter to New York, where she met Yerkes (although some reports maintain they met in Cincinnati). Yerkes fell in love with her and paid handsomely to keep her as his mistress, even adopting her to put up a respectable front. Like Berenice, Emilie lives on the very edge of society. As Berenice was courted and then dropped by Lawrence Braxmar, so Emilie was courted by Spencer Trask, from a good Southern (Sarasota) family, and then never invited again to his house in Washington Square when Trash discovers her relation with Yerkes. After Yerkes' death, Emilie sold her New York home and moved to London, where she moved in high society and was influential enough to make it difficult for Dreiser to publish *The Titan*. One of Dreiser's clippings, dated September 5, 1911, describes Miss Grigsby returning for an American visit aboard the Olympic of the White Star line, declaring over eight hundred thousand dollars in jewelry at customs.

If Dreiser planned to use these events, it would have been in the last pages of *The Stoic*, the last of the Cowperwood trilogy. Dreiser obviously chose at this point in his life, just before his death in 1945, to drop Emilie as the model for Berenice. Trying to reconcile the tug in his own personality between selfishness and compassion, materialism and idealism, Dreiser moved directly away from his source. While Emilie in real life kept her money, Berenice gives her wealth to a hospital (perhaps Dreiser was remembering Yerkes' provision in his will) and works among the poor. Although the tension between greed and altruism had been in the novel from the beginning, Dreiser ended his trilogy of "desire" on a far different note from that on which he began it.

While the scope is far different, the pattern of the Cowperwood novels is similar to Dreiser's earlier novels. There is the same emphasis upon youth as a moment of splendid possibility and hope. The city—especially Chicago—encourages the ambitious and the young—in fact, the city partakes of youth, intensifying the very spirit of hope and success in the young. When Cowperwood arrives in Chicago—the new man in the new city —Dreiser describes it this way:

> Here was life; he saw it at a flash. Here was a seething city in the making. There was something dynamic in the very air which appealed to his fancy . . . [Chicago] was more youthful, more hopeful. . . . The world was young here. (*The Titan*, 23–24)

Cowperwood struggles to keep this spirit of youth alive. "He must always have youth," Dreiser says of him, "the illusion of beauty," (*The Titan, 208; cf. also, 352, 357, 390, 541*). Cowperwood's continual pursuit of beautiful women stems, Dreiser tells us, from this desire to stay young, to keep the world in perpetual bloom, to stay the cold hand of age and death (*cf. The Titan, 461*). In a strange way, Cowperwood secretly feels that he can triumph over others—even over the universe itself —with the power that money can bring. He is materialistic and mundane and reduces values to what money can buy. His love of both women and fine art shares the same context. He thinks of paintings in terms of their worth, and he thinks of women in terms of painting: "He had little faith in the ability of women aside from their value as objects of art" (*The Titan, 131*). By the time we get to *The Stoic*, this force has become a creative energy which "expresses itself" through the artist, so that Cowperwood's sexual longings and appreciation of fine art are really a "constant search for beauty in every form . . . nothing more than a search for the Divine design beyond all forms" (*The Stoic, 305*).

The spirit of beauty which so moves Cowperwood is embodied in the new and vital city, in the artist, and in the universe itself. Dreiser, through such associational leaps, equated youth, the city, sex, beauty, art, and the creative energy of the universe. Since Cowperwood's financial and sexual natures are closely related—are in many ways one and the same—Dreiser moved back and forth between the business plot and the love plot, back and forth between the board room and the bedroom. And since the very flux of life—the spirit of youth, beauty, and art—is at the source of Cowperwood's many compulsions, the very source of his motives, Cowperwood—like Dreiser's other characters—is moved to actions over which he has no control. He is "caught at last by the drug of a personality he could not gainsay" (*The Titan, 552*). Once again, Dreiser removes the dimension of will from his novel by giving his characters an essential self, a being not of their own making.

Frank Cowperwood becomes a financier for the same reason that Eugene Witla will become a painter; they are attracted by instinct to their respective vocations. Cowperwood's financial instinct and "knowledge . . . [was] as natural to him as the emotions and subtleties of life are to the poet" (*The Financier*, 26). In both *The Financier* and *The Titan* there is a continued sense of Cowperwood's manifest destiny—a sense that he carries greatness within him, that his future success is guaranteed, and that his final fate resides within him just as the oak tree is contained by the acorn. At the end of *The Financier*, when Cowperwood is still in prison, he looks into the sky and ponders whether or not he is significant in the face of this gigantic and mysterious universe. He decides that he is, that he has been given a nature and a temperament that distinguish him from the throngs of lesser men, that he has been chosen for greatness.

> It was not given all men to see far or to do brilliantly; but to him it was given, and he must be what he was cut out to be. There was no more escaping the greatness that was inherent in him than there was for so many others the littleness that was in them. (*The Financier, 506*)

Even in Cowperwood's darkest hour, when his prison sentence has cut his career in two, he still has an overwhelming sense of self-confidence, a burning optimism and self-assurance that goes beyond hope; he felt "within himself," as Dreiser goes on to tell us, "that the whole world was still before him" (*The Financier*, 511). Greatness "was inherent in him." He could feel it "within himself." The phrasing is important. Dreiser's conception of character is an exercise in the verb "to be": his characters *are what they are*. They are machines, and their natures are fixed, just as the nature of a machine is fixed. The product of their own temperament, driven by inner necessity, Dreiser's characters are governed by physical compulsions that make their motives as instinctual and mechanistic as those of a cat when he sees a bird. Just as Dreiser concluded *The Financier* on this theme, he also worked it into the ending of *The Titan*. Berenice Fleming looks at Cowperwood and realizes he is "a kind of superman" whose power comes from beyond him, that he is driven, that he is "impelled by some blazing internal force which harried him on and on" (*The Titan*, 459).

Dreiser developed this theme in other ways besides just

stating it. Throughout the novels, everyone immediately recognizes Cowperwood's worth, his heightened nature, just as he recognizes their essential temperament. His uncle, a successful Cuban planter, lays his hands on Frank's shoulder in an almost (for Dreiser) symbolic ritual, and predicts he will become a financier (*The Financier*, 30). Henry Waterman, head of a large import and export company, also recognizes Cowperwood's worth "after only three or four minutes of conversation with the boy" (*The Financier*, 42). Even in prison, the guards and warden feel they are in the presence of a superior person. Their response is no different from the financial giants of Chicago who are awed by him before he even begins to realize success (*cf. The Titan*, 27 and 32).

The other characters in these novels also have an inner, essential reality. Cowperwood recognizes Stener's (the city treasurer's) inherent weakness at the same moment Stener recognizes Cowperwood's inherent strength: Cowperwood "realizing at once that he had a financial baby to deal with," Stener realizing "that he had found some one on whom he could lean" (*The Financier*, 120 and 122). Their relationship is static and fixed, Dreiser creating a mechanical relationship between characters that is consistent with his belief in a mechanistic world. The Cowperwood-Stener relationship does not change. Even when they are on the verge of being indicted for misuse of city money, Cowperwood remains supremely confident of the future, while Stener quivers before the threats of the city bosses (*cf. The Financier*, 254).

When Dreiser introduces a character, he delimits his personality and the character always remains true to this essential self. There is no existential realm in Dreiser's novels, no character over-leaping himself, having limitless possibility. McKenty, the Chicago politician, is "forceful" with an "animal coarseness" and a "temperamental pull [that drew] to him that vast pathetic life of the underworld in which his soul found its solution" (*The Titan*, 99). Harold Sohlberg, an ineffectual artist, was destined to be ineffectual because of his "erratic emotional temperament" (*The Titan*, 128). Aileen Butler cannot escape her "innate sensuousness" and "sense of grandeur," which drives her toward a heightened world of color and passion at the same time that it makes her the victim of her own intellectual inabilities as well as her lack of taste and refinement.

While all the critics are quick to maintain that Aileen is the only woman in these novels who comes alive, they never tell us why this is so. Aileen, in many ways, anticipates a character like Clyde Griffiths: she is the victim of contradictory qualities within her own self. She is driven by her passionate nature and held back by a kind of coarseness. On fire with the desire for adventure and love, insensitive to the subtleties of life, she is driven to be what she cannot become. Her tragedy is in her being. She is born to suffer.

Dreiser's characters have a fixed nature, and their strength and weaknesses are a matter of physical and temperamental makeup. Chance events bring momentary reversals: the Chicago fire happens just when Cowperwood cannot cover his loans, at just the moment when Stener is out of town and beyond Cowperwood's control, and at just the moment when Cowperwood has confided his financial troubles to Edward Butler—all leading, in a sequential way, to Cowperwood's financial fall. Yet such a reversal is only temporary. Cowperwood is larger than any one chance defeat, and he is there to ride the waves of another chance event—the collapse of Jay Cooke and Company—to financial fortune and to the start of a new and even more successful career.

As in Dreiser's other novels, behind the appearance of chance is a realm of determined being. Cowperwood rises and falls and then rises again. Unlike Hurstwood, who is too weak to begin over when he loses first his social position and then Carrie's love, Cowperwood is strong enough to make his way against the severest kind of adversity. When Hurstwood is at the peak of his career in Chicago, he has within him the capacity for defeat which chance (the closing of the safe) will soon realize. When Cowperwood is at the bottom of his career in the Philadelphia prison, he has within him the capacity for success which chance (the bear market of 1873) will soon realize. One of the differences between Cowperwood and Hurstwood (as with Hawthorne's Chillingworth and Hollingsworth, Dreiser's use of similar names for opposite characters may be

intentional) is that Hurstwood's fate turns upon almost inconsequential happenings of chance, while Cowperwood's fate
turns only with catastrophic happenings: the Chicago fire and
panic of 1873, the rise of the outraged Chicago citizenry
against his streetcar company, and finally death itself. Unlike
Hurstwood, Cowperwood never gives up even in the face of
defeat, valiantly fighting against all three of these adversities—
even the ravages of time, as he conquers one beautiful, young
girl after another.

"No least inkling of [the] storms and terrors [of life] is ever
discovered except through accident," Dreiser wrote in *The
Financier* (268). The romance between Cowperwood and
Aileen Butler is even a chance event, "a foreign chemical agent
introduced into a delicate chemical formula," and like all
chance events in Dreiser's fiction it starts a chain or sequence
of events. Chance is only a catalyst, bringing out the quintessential quality of a character, whether it be Carrie's ambition,
Hurstwood's defeatism, Jennie's fidelity, Eugene Witla's artistic
genius, or Cowperwood's financial prowess. In every one of
Dreiser's novels, an accident or a series of accidents—the closing of the safe in *Sister Carrie*, the death of Senator Brander in
Jennie Gerhardt, the Chicago fire in *The Financier*, the pregnancy and then the "accidental" death of Roberta Alden in
An American Tragedy, and the death of Psyche in *The Bulwark*—create the circumstance which either immediately or
eventually brings out the main character's essential nature. As
important as chance and circumstance may be in Dreiser's fiction, as often as they may bring about a fortunate or an un-
fortunate sequence of events, one can only evaluate Dreiser's
characters at the novel's end. Here one can see that behind the
realm of chance is a realm of causality, of destiny, that whether
a character be as rich as the mighty Cowperwood or as poor
as the inept Hurstwood, as successful as the cunning Carrie or
as unsuccessful as the bungling Clyde, he becomes what he
was meant, conditioned, and (in the case of Hurstwood) had
the capacity to be. All of Dreiser's characters carry the seed of
victory or defeat within themselves.

While Dreiser's characters carry the principle of their destiny within them, they are not, of course, the primary source

of their own strength or weakness. As a mechanist, Dreiser believed that their ultimate being was outside them—that they were the products of a creative impulse and that they were being used in a way that they did not have the intelligence to understand. Dreiser never deviated from this belief which he expresses in his early essays for *Ev'ry Month* as well as his "Notes on Life." In 1934, he put the idea this way:

> I am convinced that I am not so much an individual force but a mechanism for the mind . . . of some exterior and mental process which has constructed me. . . . I am not wholly and individually living—but being lived by something else that . . . is using me.[8]

Man, in other words, is a tool, an instrument, an agent of a higher force, although Dreiser is vague about the nature of this higher force and in what way and for what purpose man is being used. In Dreiser's world of correspondences, men also use other men just as they are being used by a cosmic power. In fact, the difference between the great and the small, the successful and the unsuccessful, is the ability of the mentally and physically strong to use other people. This is one of Cowperwood's primary beliefs, something that he learned young and never forgot.

> A man, a real man, must never be an agent, a tool, or a gambler —acting for himself or for others—he must employ such. A real man—a financier—was never a tool. He used tools. He created. He led.
> Clearly, very clearly, at nineteen, twenty, and twenty-one years of age, he saw all this, but was not quite ready to do anything about it. He was certain, however, that his day would come. (*The Financier*, 62–63)

His day comes, indeed. Very soon Cowperwood is manipulating people and institutions in this world of "factotums," to use Dreiser's word. He works his will with Stener, with Stephen Wingate (his "cat's paw" while he is in prison) (*The Financier*, 426), with Peter Laughlin (the Chicago grain broker who was "no more than a tool in Cowperwood's strong hands") (*The Financier*, 36), with Francis Kennedy (a Chicago reporter whom Cowperwood saw as "a possible useful tool")

Dreiser at age of twenty-two.

Dreiser in 1909 at the age of thirty-eight, just before he left The Delineator *to begin writing* Jennie Gerhardt.

Dreiser, right, on the Riviera in 1912 when he was forty-one. The other two men are Grant Richards, center, who helped to arrange Dreiser's 1912 trip to Europe, and Sir Hugh Lane, at the left, who was director of the Municipal Art Gallery, Dublin.

Taken from a portrait of Dreiser, painted in 1927.

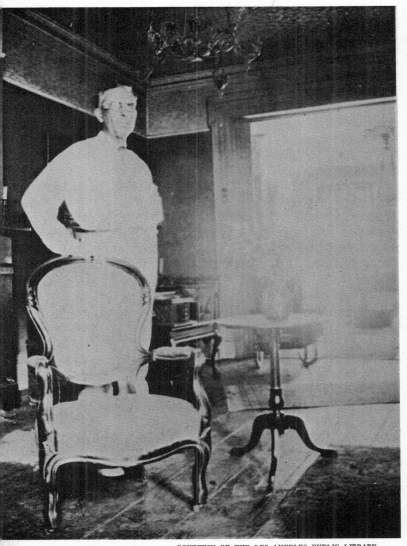

Dreiser, while he was living in St. Luke's Place in Greenwich Village, New York, before the publication of An American Tragedy.

Dreiser in his Greenwich Village apartment. This photograph was used in the publicity campaign to sell An American Tragedy.

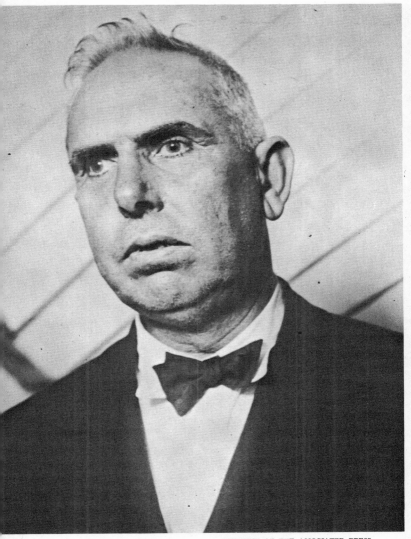

Dreiser in October of 1929, when he was being considered for the Nobel Prize. He was fifty-eight.

Dreiser on his sixty-first birthday, August 28, 1931, in his apartment in New York. When interviewed, he said that he looked forward to a "few more rows." He had just emerged from such rows with Sinclair Lewis and the movie producers.

Dreiser on November 8, 1931 outside the miners' soup kitchen at Wallins Creek, Kentucky where, as chairman of the National Committee for the Protection of Political Prisoners, he led a three day investigation into charges of political terrorism in the southeastern Kentucky coal field area. Shown with him is Captain Frank McAuliffe of the Kentucky National Guard.

FROM LEFT TO RIGHT: *John Dos Passos, Dreiser, and Samuel Ornitz, November 12, 1931 shortly after their return from Harlan, Kentucky where they had gone to investigate labor conditions in the coal fields.*

Dreiser with one of h
secretaries, October 1,
1934, at the murder
trial of Bobby Edwar
in Wilkes-Barre, Pa.
Edwards was accused
murdering his sweeth
Miss McKenchnie, wh
they were swimming.
Dreiser was covering
trial for a news servic
because of the similar
between the Edwards
and that of Clyde G
in An American Tra

Dreiser in Paris in July of 1938, delivering a speech at an
international peace conference.

Dreiser as he was seen leaving for Paris, July 13, 1938, on board the Normandie.

Dreiser on his return from Spain in August of 1938, at the age of sixty-seven.

Dreiser and artist Boris Chaliapin, who painted Dreiser's portrait in 1939.

Dreiser, January 20, 1941, in San Francisco for the 150th anniversary of the incorporation of the Bill of Rights into the Constitution. From left to right: Dreiser, Dalton Trumbo, Ella Winter, and Donald Ogden Stewart.

Dreiser and Helen outside their home at 1015 North King Road in Hollywood, where they lived from the end of 1940 to Dreiser's death at the end of 1945.

Dreiser, taken before his death in December 1945.

(*The Titan, 239*), with John J. McKenty (the Chicago alderman), and even with the Chicago city council, which in turn
controls the mayor (*The Titan, 109*).

The main source of conflict in both *The Financier* and
The Titan stems from Cowperwood and his enemies trying to
manipulate the same people and institutions for similar reasons. In both Philadelphia and Chicago, Cowperwood's antag-
onists, or the corporations they represent, control the judges
(*cf. The Financier, 316, 351, 352, 428, 456, 459*), the newspaper (*cf. The Financier, 112 and The Titan, 108*), the governor of Pennsylvania (*The Financier, 521*), and a Chicago
mayor (*The Titan, 305, 330*). Once again, Dreiser comes close
to a theme he will develop at greater length in *An American
Tragedy*. Despite their many differences, Frank Cowperwood
and Clyde Griffiths have one important experience in common: they both at one point in their lives become the scape-
goats for the Republican Party, for the ambitious politicians
and citizens who are willing to sacrifice them in order to save
the party or heighten themselves.

Life is combat. Beneath the calm appearance of civilized
life is a struggle as deadly as that in the jungle. The metaphor
of animals at war runs throughout both novels. Dreiser even
begins *The Financier* with the famous description of the lobster devouring the squid. Men, of course, devour the lobster
in turn. And who preys on men? Cowperwood puzzles. The
answer soon comes: they prey on each other. Self-interest and
self-aggrandizement is the prime law of life. The idea of law
and justice is sham: the laws are devised by the strong to
manipulate the weak. Beneath the "illusion" of democracy—
beneath the idea that all men are created equal in a just and
equitable society—is the truth of life: the battle is to the
cunning and the strong, and Christian morality and Puritan
conventions are a distortion of man's very nature.

As Dreiser begins *The Financier* with a metaphor, he also
ends it with one, describing the Black Grouper, a fish of 250
pounds which can perfectly adapt to its surrounding, change
its color, and prey upon the unsuspecting. If the Black Grouper
reveals anything about the nature of creation, it is that not
only strength but "subtlety, chicanery, [and] trickery [are] at

work" (*The Financier, 540*)—are indeed the principles upon which all life rests.

Because Cowperwood believed so firmly in the power of strength and cunning, because he believed that all men were selfish and ambitious and that corruption lay beneath all levels of government, Cowperwood has both contempt and awe for Governor Swanson, the idealist who turns down Cowperwood's bribe of one hundred thousand dollars because he feels that the people should control public transportation. Cowperwood at this point in his life believes that idealists are destined for defeat in a materialistic world, that they do more harm than good by creating ideals which are really illusions, that Swanson is inadvertently cooperating with Cowperwood's equally ruthless opponents, and that these other financiers will destroy Swanson when they find that they cannot use him.

> "I am a scoundrel [Cowperwood tells Swanson] because I am selfish and ambitious—a materialist. You are not a scoundrel, but a dangerous person because you are an idealist. Whether you veto this bill or not, you will never be elected Governor of Illinois if the people who are fighting me succeed, as they will succeed, in fighting you." (*The Titan, 480*)

The idealist will find it hard to be at home in a materialistic world, a fact that Dreiser will try to reconcile in *The Bulwark* and *The Stoic*.

In *The Financier* and *The Titan*, Dreiser defined more clearly than ever before his concept of man, of society, and of the universe. Man is a machine. A creative force talks through him in the form of "temperament." He lives by his strength and cunning in a society of illusions, which upholds absolute justice and Christian restraint while the forces of greed, trickery, and self-interest work corruptingly, and in deadly combat, beneath view.

Cowperwood thought of himself as a superior man, a genius, a "perfect mechanism" (*The Titan, 195*). He had absolute contempt for the masses who "were so dull. They were rather like animals, patient, inartistic, hopeless" (*The Titan, 195*). He was willing to give them "decent living wages . . . nothing more" (*The Titan, 196*). They were his to be used.

With this idea, Dreiser was moving toward the key theme of *The Financier* and *The Titan*—the theme of the "equation inevitable," which he was to develop at chapter length in *Hey Rub-A-Dub-Dub* and "Notes on Life." Dreiser, in fact, even ends *The Titan* on this theme, and the ending is always thematically the most important part of his novels.

Cowperwood has just been defeated by the outraged Chicago citizenry. The struggle all along had been not only between tycoon and tycoon, but also between the rugged individualist and the people, between the idealists (like Governor Swanson and Mayor Lucas) and a "daring manipulator who [was] . . . to seize upon other and larger phases of American natural development for his own aggrandizement" (*The Financier,* 179). The people win, at least for the moment. Cowperwood's ruthless and reckless ways bring into play the counter-forces that destroy him, one force in nature engendering its opposite.

> In the end [of all struggle] a balance is invariably struck wherein the mass subdues the individual or the individual the mass— for the time being. For, behold, the sea is ever dancing or raging. (*The Titan,* 540)

Dreiser continues: "A balance must be struck. The strong must not be too strong, the weak not too weak" (he used the same words in "Notes on Life" over twenty years later) (*cf. The Titan,* 540). While Dreiser came to believe in a creative intelligence which absorbed life's contradictions, he did not deviate from his belief that antagonistic forces canceled each other out; that all matter was limited and fixed; that (as he wrote between 1914 and 1919 and filed in "Notes on Life") "one force constantly balanced or off-set another in order apparently that there might be both variety and unity"; that there was no cosmic or social progress because all matter is held together in chemical balance, which leads to change (one force counteracting its opposite), which leads to contrast, which leads finally to the variety and drama of life.[9]

Like all men, weak or strong, Cowperwood demonstrated the nature of man in motion—a fury of activity, struggling, plotting, tricking—and going nowhere. And yet—hungry for experience, for power, for love, for beauty—he lived. Life may have no purpose; the mad race may go in a strange circle; life may be its own blind justification; and to have lived may be both nothing and all. At the end of *The Financier*, the Weird Sisters speak. Those voices which predict Macbeth's rise and fall—his ambitious struggle which came to nothing—speak also to Cowperwood.

> "Hail to you, Frank Cowperwood, master and no master, prince of a world of dreams whose reality was disillusion!" (*The Financier*, 541–42)

At the end of *The Titan*, the same sisters speak again, Dreiser counterpoints their words of inevitable doom with his own words which justify the Frank Algernon Cowperwoods: "Thou hast lived" (*The Titan*, 542).

In Yerkes' story, Dreiser found the means to illustrate that man's nature is fixed, that he contains his destiny within him, that life feeds on life, that the strong and the sly win for a time, that all combat is eventually destructive, that life cancels itself out and then begins again—and that this mysterious process is its own justification.

8

"The 'Genius'"

In a letter to H. L. Mencken dated February 24, 1911, Dreiser said that he had finished *Jennie Gerhardt* and was half way through another novel—*The "Genius."* On April 10, 1911, he wrote Mencken that he expected to finish his novel by the first of May, and on April 17, 1911, he claimed that *The "Genius"* "draws to a close. It's grim, I'm sorry to state, but life like."

The "Genius" is the most autobiographical of Dreiser's novels. In *Sister Carrie*, Dreiser had written the story of his sister Emma; in *Jennie Gerhardt*, he had written the story of Mame and Sylvia; in *The "Genius"* he wrote unblushingly about his own frantic and erotic career: his restless beginnings in a small town, his "call" to the city, his pursuit of success, his physical breakdown, his new success in the publishing world, and particularly about his torrid romances which ended his hapless marriage and editorial career. Dreiser treated much of this material in his autobiographical *Dawn*, written while he was working on *The "Genius"* but not published until 1931, and in *Newspaper Days* or *A Book About Myself* (1922), changing some of the details but sticking to the main outline of his own life, even using passages from *Dawn* in his novel. The difference between *Dawn* and *The "Genius"* is that Eugene Witla has a more substantial background than Dreiser himself: his sisters are not promiscuous; his father is not a helpless failure; and his mother is less a suffering soul than Dreiser's own mother.

While Dreiser expected to finish his novel by May of 1911, he did not complete it until August of that year, shelving it at that time to work on the Cowperwood trilogy when Harper's thought it too frank an account of personal matters. Dreiser was able to move so easily from *The "Genius"* to the Cowperwood trilogy because *The Financier* and *The Titan* are merely less personal accounts of the same kind of story. Dreiser was working in each case within the Horatio Alger tradition of the novel, the rags-to-riches story which he could now understand in personal terms since he was writing these novels after his rise to a $15,000-a-year job with Butterick. Frank Algernon Cowperwood and Eugene Witla have, in fact, much in common with each other—and with Dreiser himself: all are men of energy; all are driven by the desire for success ("He was *making good*," Dreiser writes of Eugene, italicizing the words); all have to break with their family in order to pursue success; all feel the need of the big city; and all are over-sexed— their enormous sense of desire making them restless, as dissatisfied with one woman as they are dissatisfied with their place in the community.

Like Cowperwood, Eugene Witla wants power, and he is in awe of the railroad executive who sits "as an engineer at a switch board directing so large a machine." [1] He is equally in awe of Daniel C. Summerfield who, like so many of the Horatio Alger characters in Dreiser's fiction, clawed his way to the top, moved from a family of Georgian sharecroppers to the head of a successful advertising firm, using others to increase his own power and bringing to his office the "order—one might almost say beauty" of the machine (407).

In *The "Genius,"* Dreiser clearly showed that the desire for money and sex had their common source in the desire for power, in an ego that needed to transcend others, to conquer the very secrets and mysteries of life, including those locked in a woman's heart. In an extraordinary passage, Dreiser described both Eugene's sexual motives and perhaps the origin of his own promiscuity: "The excitement [of sex], of adventure, of intrigue in a sense, of discovering the secrets of feminine personality—these were really what had constituted the charm, if not the compelling urge, of his romances. To *conquer was beautiful*" (245, italics mine).

"To conquer was beautiful," a most revealing statement. Elsewhere in *The "Genius,"* Dreiser wrote: "power, however displayed, is fascinating" (385). And still elsewhere he talked of Eugene's interest in "the hierarchies of power in the universe" (326). Ever since he had read Spencer, Dreiser was fascinated with the nature of and the means to power—on all levels of being. On the most immediate level, he saw that the moment of seduction was a form of power, saw that money most easily secured other kinds of power, and saw that women could often be a source of money, so that a victory in the battle of love was often a double victory—a triumph over the woman herself and a means to wealth. Eugene, for example, saw Suzanne Dale in this double context—saw her as a beautiful woman who also offered him a "vision of empire" (656).

Since money and sex are the prime movers for Dreiser, we move in *The "Genius,"* as we moved in *The Financier* and *The Titan,* back and forth between the pursuit of each. An unsatisfactory sex life, Dreiser went on, could "rob talent of its finest flavor," "discolor" reality, limit the powers of the imagination, destroy "a perfect art," and "make all striving hopeless . . . and death a relief" (246). Dreiser thus added art to this string of desires, and he once again equated striving (that is, success) with sex and sex with art. The frustration with any one of these three desires leads to the destruction of the others, so that the desire for fame, sexual power, and artistic recognition become the primary reasons for living. As fantastic as this may sound, Dreiser shrilly told us that beyond this terrain was the void called death.

While the desire for money and beauty (feminine and artistic) stem from the same source, Eugene finds it difficult to reconcile his artistic temperament with a philistine society. Like Dreiser himself, Eugene becomes the victim of the romantic dilemma: he finds the ideal is never real, and the real is never ideal. In a tedious philosophical discussion at the end of the novel, Dreiser pursues this problem: Eugene is in search of a higher reality, a larger "I," a universal mind to which his ideas and ideals can correspond so that he can identify with something outside himself in a way that he cannot identify with society. In this hope, Eugene has much in common with Shelley's poet. In his "A Defense of Poetry," Shelley maintained that the poet "is an instrument over which a series of external and internal impressions are driven, like the alterations of an ever-changing wind over an Aeolian lyre." Since the artist is sensitive to the presence of the spiritual in nature, he "participates in the eternal, the infinite, and the one." He "lifts the veil from the hidden beauty of the world." [2] These ideas also dominate Dreiser's esthetic. In *The "Genius,"* for example, Eugene is a kind of Aeolian lyre, "the medium," as Dreiser puts it, "for some noble and superhuman purpose" (238). Like Shelley's poet, Dreiser's artist never reasons to the Beautiful. The artist is a man of moods and temperament, a man of sensitive response. Eugene has an essential self, a residual emotional nature, and he tries to find persons and places which will help him best realize his moods. As Dreiser says in *The "Genius,"* "we take on so naturally the material habiliments of our temperaments, necessities and opportunities" (308). Dreiser means this literally, and Eugene can even find beauty in the city, where it is an inextricable part of industrial and commercial life.

Places as well as characters thus have a dominating mood, a temperamental or emotional nature—and in Dreiser's world the artist tries to capture the essence of a place, the quality of mood it inspires. Eugene, for example, paints Greeley Square in a drizzling rain and "by some mystery of his art had caught the exact texture of seeping water on gray stones . . . the values of various kinds of lights, those in cabs, those in cable cars . . . shop windows . . . street lights—relieving by

them the black shadows of the crowds and of the sky" (228).
As the artist responds to the mood of a situation or place—a
mood perhaps which is latent within him—he tries to embody
the spirit of that mood, and his art then becomes a catalyst,
just as the city itself is a catalyst, creating an emotion in a
particular viewer. This is why Dreiser believed, wrongly perhaps, that art was life and that life was art. If one accepts
Dreiser's concept of temperament and mood, if one believes
that emotions and feelings are embodied in art as well as life,
then art becomes as important as life, the means of awakening
one emotionally. Eugene, for example, brings Christina Chan-
ning a copy of Villon's poems, "chosen according to his most
recent mood" and thus "sad in their poetic texture" because at
this point in his career he believed in "the nothingness of
life, its sadness, albeit the perfection of its beauty" (156).

There is a direct relationship, then, between Dreiser's
esthetics and his concept of character and place. Some men
are chosen, have "art within them," are sensitive to both their
own nature and spirit of place, can grasp the essence of these
realities in art, and awaken those with rougher natures to the
beauty of the universe. Dreiser's artist is very much Shelley's
seer, the romantic prophet. In *The "Genius,"* Dreiser divides
his characters into the privileged ones with artistic temperaments, who are above the restraints of philistine law and convention, and those who are not so privileged. The simplicity
of characterization stems from the principles of romantic esthetics—principles that Dreiser carried one step further when
he equated Eugene's love for the beautiful with his appreciation of women and his need for sex.

This idea, interestingly enough, is also latent in romantic
writing. Shelley, for example, says that "The great secret of
morals is love; or a going out of our nature, and an identifica-
tion of ourselves with the beautiful which exists in thought,
action, or *person,* not our own." [3] Shelley believed that a natural empathy existed between the artist and all objects of
beautiful contemplation. Dreiser extended this idea, equating
the artistic temperament with sex, a magnificent kind of ration-
alization which allowed him to justify his passionate nature in
the sacred name of Art.

Bringing these abiding ideas and preoccupations to his novel, Dreiser used the same essential pattern in *The "Genius"* that he had used in his earlier novels. Eugene becomes discontent with the small town, feels an "essential self" (the artist in him) is being thwarted, ventures to the city which is both exciting (the city "put vitality into almost every wavering heart: it made the beginner dream dreams") and cruel ("underneath, of course, was struggle"), finds a release for his passions in work and art and love, is ultimately defeated by philistine values, and ends alone and abandoned, still faithful to his ideals but a social outcast. Every one of Dreiser's earlier novels—*Sister Carrie, Jennie Gerhardt, The Financier,* and *The Titan*—has some if not all of these narrative elements.

Like Carrie and Frank Cowperwood, Eugene has an "essential self," a potential being that is waiting to be realized. Eugene's story, in fact, is written in the stars, or so Dreiser would like us to believe when a fortune teller predicts the catastrophic events in his life, her words hanging over him as they do the heroes of Greek tragedy (*see 253 and 676*). Dreiser tells us that one event in a person's life can start a sequence of events which is predictable. The most important event for Eugene is the break with his family, which was the first and hardest step in his development. Even when he has moved beyond the easy demands of the small town, he cannot completely reject the family, still has "a profound reverence for a home" (*161*). The family, however, retards the ambitious young man in his drive for success (*cf. 60*), and Eugene sees that he must break with his home if he is to realize his "second self," the "genius" within him. "He really had art in him," Dreiser says at the outset (*71*). The logic of the novel is to show him becoming aware of this dormant self (he is described at first as only "half-awake"), and Eugene's expanding sense of self is paralleled by an expanding scene as he moves from Alexandria to New York, from where he takes a trip to London and Paris. Dreiser once again equated the spirit of youth with the spirit of the city. The city "was running with a tide of people which represented youth, the illusions, the untrained aspirations, of millions of souls" (*39*). The city is still a catalyst, stimulating the dreamer as well as introducing him to a heightened world. To this extent, the people that Eugene meets in the city seem to embody the spirit and values of the city, so that the journey from town to city is also a journey from one kind of mentality to a completely different one. Women, in particular, embody his feeling about the city, and Dreiser equates the two in this world of emotional correspondences. When Eugene loses Suzanne, for example, the city seems to fade before his eyes: the "buildings were high and silent— receding from him in a way. . . . A mirage dissolved into native nothingness" (678). When Eugene meets Ruby Kenny (the Alice Kane of *A Book About Myself*), she is modeling in the nude. In both works, the girl represents the spirit of the city—of youth, of new found experience, of a vital beauty. We see this from the way Dreiser introduces us to Ruby Kenny.

> The young Irish girl had gone behind the screen. Eugene could see partially, from where he was sitting, that she was disrobing. It shocked him a little. . . . Suddenly he saw the girl divest herself of a thin, gauze shirt, and the next moment she came out, naked and composed. . . . It seemed a wonderful thing for him to be . . . in this room, to see this girl posing so; in short, to be an art student. So this was what it was, a world absolutely different from anything he had ever known. And he was self-called to be a member of it. (55–56)

Ruby Kenny makes Eugene feel privileged, just as Dreiser felt that the artist was privileged—that he lived more fully, observed more carefully, and captured through his craft the beauty which less sensitive and talented men failed to see. As a result, Eugene comes to feel that he is beyond good and evil, beyond conventions, subject only to his own temperament.

As Dreiser came to identify the city with certain kinds of women, he also equated women with the artistic experience —an equation that becomes even more clear in *A Gallery of Women* where the experiences of the city, the experiences of the women, and the experiences of art become one and the same. We can see that these connections were in Dreiser's mind when he was working on *The "Genius"* by comparing the way he handled these matters in *Dawn* and in his novel. In *Dawn*, he described the "beauty" of the Chicago railroad yard, in which he briefly worked: the many-colored switch lights "winking and glowing like flowers, the suggestion of distant cities, and the chemic shift and play of things in general." [4] In *The "Genius,"* Ruby Kenny lives near the railroad yards, and Dreiser uses almost the exact words to describe the scene —with one significant addition: he moves from the image of the lights as flowers ("At night the switch lights in these great masses of yards bloomed *like flowers*") to Ruby Kenny as a flower ("this raw *flowering girl* lived near something like this") (*76*, italics mine). The use of detail here can hardly be accidental. Dreiser took a passage out of one book, used it in a different context in another, and established an inextricable relationship between the exciting "raw" and uncouth beauty of Ruby and the same raw vitality ("the suggestion of distant cities and the chemic shift . . . of things") of the railroad yards where the slick trains move like "shadows" in the rain—Ruby personifying the spirit of the city, of love, and of beauty, Dreiser equating her with the metropolis, sex, and art.

Dreiser's world is one of correspondences—correspondences created by the similarity between things and by the similarity of mood that various objects can stimulate. Dreiser used the image of the flower here in much the same way that Hart Crane used the sea anemone at the end of *The Bridge*—to suggest an ultimate monism, that man and machine are really one, that both are part of a cosmic machine, a part of nature's beauty. Crane's bridge is like a flower rising from the sea, healing the iron-dealt cleavage. Dreiser's Ruby is as exciting to Eugene as the new city of which he is a part. The symbols establish emotional connections which, after all, are the connections that the artist perceives and by which he lives.

Along with the image of the sea and the rocking chair, Dreiser used the image of the flower over and over to suggest life in "chemic shift," in flux, in growth. In *Dawn,* for example, he described his early days in Chicago, how he sat "in a rocking chair" on the porch before leaving for work, and how he thought "of the mystery of life and my future. Like the rest of the *flora and fauna* of the world *I was growing toward fruition or bloom* without knowledge of the process involved . . . all moving, soothing, beautiful." [5] Dreiser then described the flux of life below the porch, how he was taken with the "accidental experiences of individuals," how he yet believed that behind the realm of chance was an order of coherent being, "inviolate [and] perfect in itself," and how "this perfection was not static." All life, he believed, was forever moving, youth giving way to age, birth to death, growth to decay. The rose brought death to its bloom. Yet the transiency of the individual flower could not be divorced from the permanency of the type. Life went on, a mysterious and inexplicable force at work, seemingly a force of which he was a part.

If Ruby is an important influence on Eugene's growth, she is a chance influence, a means and not an end; and when Eugene has used her, he grows beyond her, and she is dismissed. When self-fulfillment is at stake, Dreiser's characters have no compassion, consider their careers privileged and destined, and are as ruthless as any robber baron. Dreiser's characters outgrow their lovers—Carrie, Hurstwood; Lester Kane, Jennie; Cowperwood, Aileen; and Eugene, Ruby Kenny. Eugene feels that he is being carried to a way of life beyond Ruby, and he outgrows her as he outgrows Chicago, leaving her when he goes to New York. This is not a matter of will, but of destiny, a matter of realizing a larger life, of developing a heightened self: "it was necessary for him to leave," Dreiser says in a revealing passage, "to come where the greatest possibilities were" (*104*).

An irony in both Dreiser's and Eugene's life is that they meet the girl they marry at this point. In *A Book About Myself*, Dreiser described Sara White, a schoolteacher from a small town outside St. Louis, whom he met on the train to Chicago where he was covering the World's Fair for the St. Louis *Republic*. In *The "Genius,"* Sara White becomes Angela Blue, whom he meets in his home town of Alexandria when both happen to be there on a visit—she from Blackwood, Wisconsin, he from his newspaper job in Chicago. Sara was two years older than Dreiser, Angela five years older than Eugene. Conservative, conventional, timid, restrained, and parochial, these girls represent everything the young artist is trying to grow beyond.

In *A Book About Myself*, Dreiser tells us that marrying

Sara White was the mistake of his life: "I can imagine no greater error of mind or temperament than that which drew me to her." [6] "Drew me to her"—these are the key words, suggesting the inoperative will and suggesting also that behind the veil of chance events is a purpose which the mind cannot fathom. Even unhappy events may help realize and develop one's potentiality, one's final growth and destiny, one's essential self. In a passage that is central to his concept of character, Dreiser explicitly develops this idea: "It is quite possible that this [marrying Sara White] was all a part of my *essential destiny* or development, one of those storms—breeding mistakes by which one grows." [7] The *"Genius"* ends on this note, Eugene hardened by his experience, ready to get on with his work, "intellectually and emotionally" larger than he was before his disastrous experience with Angela, reading Spencer, Schopenhauer, and Nietzsche and pondering "the mystery of things" (*734*).

Like many of Dreiser's novels, The *"Genius"* divides into three books: Book I is called "Youth" (*9–195*); Book II, "Struggle" (*197–497*); Book III, "Revolt" (*499–736*). Book I begins with Eugene's growing beyond the small town and ends with his marrying Angela. Book II begins with his establishing his name as a painter, treats his nervous breakdown and recovery, and ends with Eugene at the height of his career as general editor of the United Magazine Corporation. Book III begins with Eugene meeting Mrs. Dale, treats his falling in love with her daughter Suzanne, and concludes with the consequences of all this: Suzanne spirited out of the country and Eugene losing his job.

In The *"Genius,"* Dreiser faithfully rendered his love affair with Thelma Cudlipp, even to the extent of using the same letters he wrote Thelma, describing the dances to which he took her, and portraying Angela ill with rheumatic fever from which Sara White is known to have suffered. As Mrs. Dale kidnaps Suzanne, taking her to Canada, Mrs. Cudlipp kidnapped Thelma, taking her to Saluda, North Carolina. When the jealous Erman J. Ridgway played upon George Wilder's fears of a scandal, Wilder fired Dreiser as editor of the *Delineator* (which was part of the Butterick chain of magazines

that included the *Designer* and *New Idea Woman's Magazine*)
—just as Eugene is fired when the jealous Florence J. White
plays upon the same fears of Hiram Colfax. The only change
Dreiser made in his own story was with the ending of this
fateful romance. In one version of the novel, Eugene and
Suzanne are happily reconciled. Suzanne returns "and with
that old time cry that brought back a lost paradise to him,
she yielded herself to his eager . . . love." In this version,
Eugene has it both ways: Angela is swirling around in space
and Suzanne in his arms.

> "Somewhere in that—in *this*," he corrected himself thinking
> of space, "is Angela—an idea in this universal, circumambient in-
> telligent control. She is as safe as I am—no more so, no less so."
>
> . . . .
>
> "Eugene," called Suzanne.
> "Yes, I'm coming, sweet."

While this "happy" ending leaves a lot to be desired, the revised—and final—ending of the novel is not much better.
Suzanne does not come to him but falls out of love and forgets
him. Angela (contrary to the actual events in Dreiser's life)
dies in childbirth and leaves Eugene alone with a baby girl.
Striving for a poignant touch, Dreiser hopelessly overreached
and ended the novel melodramatically, making Eugene's final
loneliness part of the cruel punishment he suffers from dis-
obeying convention.

Both endings of *The "Genius"* were bound to be melodramatic. The reason is obvious: Dreiser created two worlds in
this novel—the world of art (temperament) and the world of
society (conventions)—and then eliminated any ambiguity
between them, making the realm of art totally privileged, an
extension of natural impulse, and making the realm of conventions totally evil, the source of all frustration. Dreiser
pushed his characters toward extremes, creating a world
of heroes and villains, of oppressed and oppressors, of enlightened minds in combat with philistines. Such extremes destroy ambiguity: Eugene is too good for the world that contains him; he is Dreiser's innocent man in a corrupt world.
As a result, *The "Genius"* totally lacks irony. Dreiser, unwilling
to test Eugene's values against characters who could sympa-

thetically and credibly oppose them, refused to establish a double view in this novel—to use a character torn simultaneously between different realms of value, an Isabel Archer or Nick Carraway attracted and repulsed at the same moment. Dreiser's imagination worked with extremes, and he pulled us emotionally in two separate directions (in sympathy for Eugene and in scorn against those who opposed him), failing to see that the issues were not as simple as this: for Eugene treats Ruby Kenny as cruelly as Mrs. Dale treats him. Eugene has only a passing moment of concern for Ruby; yet he expects unqualified sympathy for himself.

The trouble with Dreiser's narrative assumptions—his use of the privileged artist who feels a part of life's force and who is in deep pursuit of beauty and self-fulfillment—is that they led him toward a fantasy world, a world where the imagination supplies most of the motives. "Naturally barred [from society] by temperament," as Dreiser put it (308), Eugene retreated into his own mind. A man of ideals, disengaged from society, Eugene has a kind of Emersonian self. Emerson could handle such a notion of self in his essays because he could rely on statement. Dreiser had difficulty with these ideas because, even though his novels are full of expository passages, as a novelist he still had to create a sense of place and relate his characters to society. Dreiser never bridged the gap between self and society. His characters have ideals that cannot be socially realized. As a result, his characters function beyond society, a law unto themselves, obligated only to an esthetic ideal and an artistic desire for self-fulfillment. While Dreiser's city is in one sense real (the descriptions of Fifth Avenue and Broadway especially), Dreiser's city is in another sense unreal: the possibilities of the city are the promises that abide beyond fulfillment in the fantasy world of Eugene's mind.

Because Eugene Witla is very much the product of his own mind, he is without a conscience, has no time for regret, and lives only in the present and for the future. *The "Genius"* lacks the dimension of past time. A comparison between Theodore Dreiser and F. Scott Fitzgerald immediately reveals the absence of a meaningful past in Dreiser's fiction. There are, surprisingly, a number of similarities between Fitzgerald's and Dreiser's fiction. Fitzgerald had, in fact, great admiration for Dreiser, once saying that "my view of life . . . is the view of the Theodore Dreisers and Joseph Conrads—that life is too strong and remorseless for the sons of men." [8] Fitzgerald especially revealed the influence of Dreiser and Mencken in *The Beautiful and Damned*. The theme of youth and beauty— youth as the moment of hope and promise, youthful beauty in conflict with the ravages of time—abound in both Dreiser and Fitzgerald. Yet there are three realms of time in Fitzgerald and only two in Dreiser. Fitzgerald believed in the idealized moment, the moment of regretful nostalgia, and the moment of horror. Fitzgerald's characters—idealists in a materialistic world—look forward, often unrealistically, to a perfect moment of fulfillment, and are often frustrated in their dreams, usually by acts of the cruel rich. They desire nostalgically to return to an original moment of youth when life was splendidly full of possibility and, at the same time, they are overcome by their misuse of time, the horror of their miscommitted talent and waste of energy.

Dreiser's characters also look forward to an idealized moment, and they too put a priority on the possibilities of youth. The city in both Fitzgerald and Dreiser is resplendent with possibility. But Dreiser's characters seldom look back. They are too bent on fulfilling their destiny to ever abandon hope. They give way to self pity at times—but never to despair. Eugene Witla's love of Suzanne Dale is almost as idealized as Jay Gatsby's love for Daisy Fay. Both affairs end unhappily, and both pairs of lovers are separated for five years. Gatsby, however, yearns for Daisy, waits for the moment he can see her again, hopes unrealistically that she will leave Tom Buchanan, and expects to turn the clock back and begin all over again, as if the five years of Daisy's and Tom's marriage never existed. Eugene Witla has no such romantic longings. He does not exist in a hole in time; life goes on and he must go with it. Suzanne Dale is a beautiful woman, but there are other beautiful women, and the hunger for life demands new experience. Five years after the break-up of their affair, Eugene and Suzanne chance to meet in the street, and Dreiser significantly ends (save for "L'Envoi") *The "Genius"* with this passage:

> She was crossing Fifth Avenue at Forty-second Street. He was coming out of a jeweler's with a birthday ring for little Angela. Then the eyes of this girl, a pale look—a flash of something wonderful that he remembered and then—
>
> He stared curiously—not quite sure.
>
> "He does not even recognize me," thought Suzanne, "or he hates me now. Oh—all in five years!"
>
> "It is she, I believe," he said to himself. . . . "Well, if it is she can go to the devil!" (733)

Dreiser is very careful in *The "Genius"* to show that Eugene is only "hardened"—not defeated—by his experience with Suzanne Dale. The artist in him has been "tempered for life and work" (734). Eugene is still too hungry for life, for experience, for sex to brood over the ashes of the dead past. Unlike F. Scott Fitzgerald, Dreiser had no time to look back.

9

The Masses & the Classes

One of the most significant influences on Dreiser before the First World War was H. L. Mencken. They had met back in 1908 when the cigar-chewing, beer-drinking Mencken was contributing to *The Delineator*, which Dreiser was editing. Mencken and Dreiser had a great deal in common. Mencken's grandfather had come from Germany in 1848, just four years after Dreiser's father came to America. Both Dreiser's father and Mencken's grandfather were Catholic, although Mencken's family were half-hearted Catholics. Mencken himself attended a Methodist Sunday school and later the Lutheran church but, like Dreiser, he soon gave up religion altogether. Although Dreiser's mother died when he was nineteen, both Mencken and Dreiser were exceptionally close to their mothers—a relationship from which they never really recovered.

Like the early Dreiser, Mencken was a journalist, a drama critic, a free-lance writer, and an editor. While Mencken dabbled with socialism around 1909, he turned rigidly from radical politics and spent his time ridiculing middle- and lower-class values. He attacked moral timidity, outrageous hypocrisy, religous fanaticism, and the rigidity of the ignorant mind, especially when he found these characteristics in businessmen and Fundamentalists.

Like Dreiser, Mencken was passionately anti-English and pro-German, sentiments that got him into trouble during the First World War. He wrote Dreiser in February of 1914, for example, that "the Germans will fight their way out. My one hope is to see them in London. English pecksniffery must be crushed." He added in December of the same year, "I shall name my next child Hindenburg whether it's a boy or a girl. A pox on the English!" When America entered the war, he grumbled: "Once the world has been made safe for democracy, all that will remain will be to make democracy safe for the world."

In the spring of 1917, Dreiser wrote an essay (forty-three pages in typed manuscript) entitled, "American Idealism and German Frightfulness." Here he maintained that England caused the war by refusing "to allow Germany to have any share in the development of Mesopotamia or the spoils of Asia and Africa." England, he said, wanted to keep captured German colonies and to work out "an arrangement in the Balkans"; Italy wanted large parts of Austria and Northern Africa; and France wanted Alsace and Lorraine as well as Belgium. England, he insisted, "has no more love for democracies than she has for autocracies save only as they will benefit her." America was also a democratic fraud: it upheld the idea of liberty but kept Cuba, the Philippines, Santo Domingo, and the Canal Zone. The American government "has done little so far save allow the big dog full rein to pounce upon the little one." Dreiser complained about the lynching of Frank Little (an I.W.W. labor leader) in Butte, Montana; the fate of Sacco and Vanzetti and Tom Mooney; and the deportation of Emma Goldman and Alexander Berkman for opposing the draft. "Isn't this actually one of the most narrow, the most moralic [sic], the most Puritanic and pecksnifferic nations in the whole world barring only Puritan England?" he asked. Germany, on the other hand, had farm loan banks, old age pensions, labor regulations, revised insurance laws, workingmen's compensation, and new Federal banking laws. What is wrong with German autocracy, Dreiser asked, "that seeks to look after the masses so well?"

In June of 1917, Waldo Frank accepted "American Idealism and German Frightfulness" for publication in *The Seven Arts* but then reneged. He said that it would be interpreted as a plea for violence and added: "Your criticisms of England are based not so much on her intrinsic faults as on the fact that she is England"—a point only partly true. Dreiser then sent the manuscript to Douglas Doty of *The Century Magazine*, who rejected it on July 12, 1917 as "neither sound nor convincing." He pleaded with Dreiser not to publish it because it would do irreparable damage to Dreiser's career. The damage, however, had been done. Although Dreiser could never find a publisher for "American Idealism and German Frightfulness," his anti-English, pro-German feelings were widely known. The cruel reviews of both *The "Genius"* and *Hey Rub-A-Dub-Dub* (where he expressed the same views in "Some Aspects of our National Character") stemmed partly from Dreiser's Anglophobia. When the English office of John Lane and Company, Dreiser's publisher, read *A Hoosier Holiday*, they insisted that Dreiser delete a passage treating Canada's anti-German sentiments. When Dreiser refused to alter the text, the English did it for him—a fact he did not know until years later when David Karsner, of the New York *The Call*, brought it to his attention in a letter dated May 26, 1925:

THE ORIGINAL TEXT	THE ALTERED TEXT
"The war! The war! They were chasing German-American professors out of Canadian colleges, and making other demonstrations of hostility towards all others having pro-German leanings. I, with my German ancestry on one side and my German name and my German sym-	"Naturally there was much excitement, and on all sides were evidences of preparations being made to send armaments and men to the Mother Country. We had looked forward with greatest pleasure to a trip into Canada, but the conditions were so unfavorable that we

pathies—what might they   hesitated to chance it. We
have done to me! We didn't   didn't go." [1]
go."

While the Mencken influence on Dreiser was significant,
a more appreciable influence—and one coming from another
direction—was that of the editors on the radical journal the
Masses. Floyd Dell, who had read *The "Genius"* in manuscript, was one of the editors, along with Max Eastman, whom
Dreiser met in Greenwich Village, and John Reed. In April
of 1915, Mencken wrote Dreiser, asking him to endorse the
Smart Set. Dreiser refused, replying (April 20, 1915) that
Mencken's magazine was "as innocent as the *Ladies Home
Journal.* Really the thing is too debonair." Dreiser then added
that he wished Mencken would "take a tip" from the *Masses*
and the *International* "and do the serious critical thing in an
enlightening way." Mencken replied (April 22, 1915) with an
attack on Dell, Herts, and Benjamin DeCasseres, whom he
called "the red-ink boys." Dreiser answered (April 26, 1915)
that he held "no brief for the parlor radicals. Viereck, Rethy,
Herts, . . . but when you mix in Dell and DeCasseres . . .
you are sound asleep." Dreiser went on to say that "a man like
Max Eastman, radical though he is, lays his finger on notable
pecksnifferies, sores, and shames."

The *Masses* was suppressed in 1917 for opposing the war,
and the editors were tried under the new sedition laws. John
Reed spoke for Dell and Eastman when he compared the war
to a fight between two tigers who would eat him after one
won. He wanted to see the house (of capitalism) torn down so
that (as a worker) he could rebuild it for himself.[2] Dreiser's
view was not this radical, but it was less reserved than Menck-
en's position. Floyd Dell, in fact, would attack Mencken for his
middle-class timidity, just as years later Dell would be attacked
by the even more radical V. F. Calverton and Michael Gold.[3]

The difference between Mencken and the editors of the
Masses was a significant one. Mencken used humor to make
his points. Opposing a state tax, he said that bachelors should
be taxed a dollar a day because their freedom was worth it.
Ridiculing the evangelists, he nominated Aimée Semple Mc-

Pherson for Miss America. Challenging arrest by J. Frank
Chase, secretary of the Watch and Ward society, he went to
Boston Commons and sold him a copy of the April (1926)
American Mercury which had been banned in Boston, and
then bit the silver dollar with which Chase paid him. Dell and
Eastman, who thought that politics was serious business, had
little sympathy for such antics, and (to borrow Dreiser's
phrase) they felt that Mencken was about as radical as the
Ladies' Home Journal.

Dreiser at this time was much more interested in the
Masses' blunt position than in Mencken's satires on the middle
class. In fact, the Dreiser-Mencken friendship began to strain
at this point and finally broke (at least for a time) when
Mencken published a partly unfavorable account of Dreiser in
his 1917 *Prefaces.* While Dreiser did not write for the *Masses*
during these years, he did write for *The Call,* a New York socialist paper, whose views overlapped those of the *Masses.* In
one essay, "More Democracy or Less? An Inquiry," Dreiser
attacked the trusts, maintaining that they had created a social
breach in America and suppressed the means by which the
masses could work for an economic balance.

> In my personal judgment [Dreiser wrote], America as yet cer-
> tainly is neither a social nor a democratic success. Its original
> democratic theory does not work, or has not, and a trust—and
> a law-frightened people, to say nothing of a cowardly or suborned,
> and in any case helpless, press, prove it. Where in any coun-
> try not dominated by an autocracy has ever a people slipped about
> afraid to voice its views on war, on freedom of speech, freedom
> of the press, the trusts, religion—indeed, any honest private con-
> viction that it has? In what country even less free can a man be
> thoroughly browbeaten, arrested without trial, denied the priv-
> ilege of a hearing and held against the written words of the
> nation's Constitution guaranteeing its citizens freedom of speech,
> of public gathering, of writing and publishing what they hon-
> estly feel? In what other lands less free are whole elements held
> in a caste condition—the Negro, the foreign born, the Indian?" [4]

This attack was slight compared to what followed. Dreiser
blasted a democracy controlled by privileged families, and

corrupt, bribe-influenced legislatures and political machines, all of which work to keep the status quo while increasing the tax burdens of the masses.

> When one considers the history of American commercial development, the growth of private wealth, of its private leaders—the Rockefellers, Morgans, Vanderbilts, Goulds, Ryans, et al., indeed all the railroad, street car, land and other lords—a (until the war) practically stationary wage rate, an ever-increasing rising cost of living, cold legislative conniving and robbery, before which the people are absolutely helpless. Tammany Hall, the New York street car monopoly, 753 different kinds of trusts that tax people as efficiently and ardently as ever any monarchy or tyranny dreamed of doing—I should really like to know on what authority we base our plea for the transcendent merits of democracy, and I am as good a democrat as most Americans, if not more so.[5]

In another *Call* article, Dreiser pinpointed the political abuses in the cities: he condemned the politicians who give away the people's franchises, the gas companies that made exorbitant profits, the street railroad companies which raised the fares when prices went up but did not lower them when prices fell, the phone companies which overcharged for poor service, and the churches which—while all of this was going on—lectured the citizen on his moral and patriotic duties.[6]

While Dreiser wrote for socialist papers, he never joined the Socialist Party. The Socialist Party was formed in 1901, rose in membership in the next ten years from under 10,000 to almost 150,000 in 1912, and polled 897,000 votes in that year's presidential election. The men who most helped the Socialists' cause at this time were Eugene Victor Debs, Upton Sinclair, and Jack London. The Socialist Party capitalized on the same feelings (hatred of the railroad and trusts) which brought the Populist movement into being—and it had a powerful influence on groups as different as the Midwest farmers and the Jewish garment workers in New York.

The American Socialist Party was composed of splinter groups: to the left was a revolutionary spirit (Eugene Debs wanted to take control of the trusts); to the right was a reforming spirit (Victor Berger opposed Debs' radical views at the Socialist Party's convention in 1912). Within the left, the anarcho-syndicalists (Bill Haywood and the I.W.W. carried on the successful Lawrence, Massachusetts textile strike in 1912) warred with the Marxists (Louis Boudin and his group became the basis for the Communist Party of the United States formed in 1919).

The First World War brought a moment of unity when the Socialist Party, reflecting a minority of European Socialists, voted overwhelmingly for America to stay out of the "imperialist" war. When America entered the war, the Party was once again split by those who supported and those who opposed the war, the pro-war leaders (including Upton Sinclair) eventually leaving the movement.

Since Dreiser's political thinking was never of a piece, it is difficult to fit him into any of the radical political camps in America at this time. While he was in sympathy with the more liberal Socialists in opposing the war, he advocated reforming rather than confiscating the trusts. He believed such reform would come about through the concentrated energy of the masses against the classes. The people had to overcome the trusts and the churches—the two institutions which he believed most suppressed them. He called the people "deeply illusioned" to believe that they were economically and intellectually free when in reality they were the victims of an economic structure that exploited both the natural resources of the country and the working man—a victim also of a puritan social order that defined man in such a way as to prevent full human expression. Yet Dreiser firmly believed in individualism, gave consent to the titan, and felt that the only solution to America's economic problems rested in a systole-diastole struggle that would give the people more than they had but which would not eliminate the financier.

Only when the organized sense of the mass becomes sufficiently intelligent for it to act in concert is it possible to sweep away or even curb the individual. For the individual and the mass are interdependent facts, and one cannot escape the other, try as each may.[7]

These years from 1910 to 1919 were years of reaction for Dreiser—reaction to both American politics and established morals. He was growing more and more discontent with middle-class values and with the smug and self-satisfied people who imposed their own way of life upon others. Finding little to admire (except for his mother) within his own family, he could not understand why the family should be the basis for society. Ironically, he had married a woman who had embodied all the conventional values—the values of his own father. Dreiser even wrote a sketch of Jug's father in which he lauded the resourcefulness and the determination of the old patriarch. When Dreiser finally rejected Jug, he was rejecting a whole way of past life. He was attracted first to men like Mencken and later like Floyd Dell because they scorned the middle class. He sought also at this time the "new" woman who would live the liberated and bohemian life of artistic unconformity in the Village. He found a number of such women, who became close friends or mistresses, especially Helen Richardson with whom he lived off and on from 1919 until his death.[8]

Dreiser's short stories in particular depict over and over the agonies of a loveless and conventional marriage ("Free," "The Second Choice," "Married," "Convention," "Marriage for One," "The Shadow," and "Rella"), portray the pain of frustrated love ("Chains," also "Convention," "Typhoon," and "Marriage for One"), and reveal the desire—particularly of the artist—to go beyond the limits set by society. In the story "Fulfillment," for example, Ulrica, a young actress who is vaguely modeled on Helen Richardson, finds a soul mate in Vivian, an artist modeled upon Dreiser himself ("Beauty was his . . . a beauty of mind and dreams and of the streets and the night and the sea and the movements of life itself, but of that which was material he had nothing").[9] Ulrica climbs to the top of her profession; but before she is a complete success, Vivian dies; and Ulrica marries another man and "out of sheer weariness she endured him." Dreiser wanted both success and freedom, to be accepted by the society he in turn could reject, and Ulrica (the irony here is contrived) finds love without success and then success without love—as if the two are mutually exclusive ("Was it not a part of the routine, shabby method of life to first disappoint . . . and then lavish luxury upon one?").[10]

In *A Gallery of Women,* Dreiser portrayed in more detail a number of the "new" and liberated women who were obsessed with the desire to succeed in a man's world ("Reina," "Ellen Adams Wynn," "Ernita," "Ernestine," [11] and "Emanuela").[12] He also depicted the woman who desired to break down restricting conventions ("Olive Brand," [13] "Lucia," "Albertine," and "Esther Norm").[14] Interestingly enough, while Dreiser sympathized with those women who defied the conventional life, he was very hard on those who did it at the expense of men—especially men like himself—and his more ruthlessly ambitious women have sad endings. Even those women who may consciously want to overpower men are unconsciously looking for men who are emotionally stronger and upon whom they can rely. The case of Lucia is typical. The product of a conventional childhood, she becomes aware of her strong sexual nature and develops "a thirst for adventure" after a trip to Paris. She is torn between men who embody the artistic (with Daniello, an artist, "she could really concentrate on painting which . . . was what she truly wished") and the good life (with Frank Stafford, the manager of a Montreal bank, she was "drifting back into a worthless life of pleasure again").[15] When Daniello begins to rely upon her, she leaves him for Stafford, only to break with him in turn when she could no longer tolerate his respect for both the formal and the conventional life. She then returns to Paris where she spends the rest of her youth "dreaming of how much I might receive from the ideal one who might come but who I know is never to appear." Dreiser's new woman wants to be free, but Dreiser will not let her be so free that she goes beyond men like him. Dreiser's own sense of ego becomes the limits of his women's freedom. "I need," concludes Lucia, "a strong compelling force whom I could love—before whose strength and temperament I could be humble." [16]

Almost all of these stories are studies in frustration—the women finding it impossible to fulfill themselves, either through love or fame, in the modern society. Few of Dreiser's women reach fame; and when they do, it is at the expense of sexual fulfillment. Also, because they unconsciously long to give themselves to men (or so Dreiser tells us), these women are often used and misused—the dupes of men or of fate itself. They "draw a certain kind of success or disaster [it is interesting that Dreiser here equated success and disaster] about as plants draw a certain kind of insect." [17] While some of these stories postdate *An American Tragedy*, their concerns—with success and disaster, with imbalances of wealth, and with conventional intolerance—preoccupied Dreiser from 1910 to 1919; and the stories and essays that he wrote during these years anticipate the themes of *An American Tragedy*.

Dreiser was moving toward political commitment; yet from 1919 to 1925 he was too busy writing *An American Tragedy* to be active in politics. These were, however, politically active years. In 1919, under the import of the Russian Revolution of 1917, two communist groups—the Communist Party and the Communist Labor Party—broke with the Socialist Party. While there were slight doctrinal differences between the two factions, the source of their split was over party power. This kind of in-fighting—to Dreiser's eventual disgust—went on for the thirty-eight years (1919–57) the Communist Party lasted in America. While the two communist factions could not tolerate each other, they did have an enemy in common—the craft labor unions like the AFL. Significantly, Dreiser gave much of his political energy at this time to attacking such unions. On October 4, 1921, for example, he wrote M. W. Martin, Chairman of the Hammond Defense Fund Committee in Chicago, which was trying to raise money to prosecute the guards who shot and killed four strikers in the Standard Steel Company. Dreiser was unsympathetic to Martin's plea and insisted that labor was selfishly concerned with only higher wages and less working hours, was "prone to ally itself with the forces of predatory capital," that it did little in the fight for public control of public utilities, was indifferent to political reform (Dreiser cited abuses in governmental fixed-freight rates and utility taxes), and was callous to the plight of the clerks and the farmers.[18] In an exchange of letters with Joseph Schlossberg (October, 1921), Dreiser again attacked the narrow idealism of

the labor movement, its limited activity, and—significantly—
its failure to help Russia.

While he did not believe in progress, Dreiser did believe
in change: man was in motion, a part of the constant flux that
revealed the forces of life at work. Dreiser was looking forward
to a climactic change in American life—one as drastic as the
change that in 1917 shook Russia to its roots. As early as 1921,
Dreiser was well prepared for his 1927 visit to Russia. But before he made this trip, he wrote *An American Tragedy*, his
major achievement.

10

"An American Tragedy"

Dreiser had begun a version of *An American Tragedy* as early as 1914. The details of such a story fascinated him, probably because he could so easily identify with someone who had grown up in poverty, had fallen in love with a simple and conventional girl, and had become trapped between a sense of duty and even pity for the girl he no longer loved and a desire for a beautiful woman who represented a life of wealth and luxury. In the final version of *An American Tragedy*, Roberta Alden is two years older than Clyde Griffiths, despite the fact that Chester Gillette was two years older than Grace Brown in the actual Gillette-Brown case which was the basis for Dreiser's story. This is only one of several details that suggest that Dreiser was thinking of his own relationship with Sara White (who was two years older than Dreiser) while he was writing this novel.

When Dreiser fictionalized the famous Gillette-Brown murder case, he selected only one of a number of such cases that had caught his interest. He had, in fact, written several drafts of different stories that might have become *An American Tragedy*. Dreiser has told us of the various cases (most of which involve a young man who murders a pregnant sweetheart because he has met a richer and more beautiful woman in the meantime) that had caught his interest.[1] He had covered such a case for the St. Louis *Globe-Democrat* in 1892 when a young man murdered his girl friend with poisoned candy. He saw that pattern again in 1894 when a young medical student named Carlyle Harris (Dreiser actually knew the boy's mother) gave his pregnant girl friend some poisoned pills that were supposed to bring about a miscarriage. He saw the pattern again in 1899 when Theodore Durant lured a girl to a belfry in San Francisco and murdered her. He saw it again in 1909 in the famous William Orpet case which became the basis for his story "The Wages of Sin" (later entitled "Typhoon"). And while the details are not exactly the same, Dreiser saw the pattern again in the well-publicized Roland Molineux case of 1907, which he had decided by the end of 1914 to turn into a novel called *The Rake* (or *The Moron*). This is really the first version of *An American Tragedy*, and we know that Dreiser was working on it by at least the end of 1914 because embossed on the upper-right-hand corner of the typescript is the date—Thursday, January 14, 1915—along with Dreiser's Greenwich Village address—165 W. 10th Street. Since Dreiser did not type, he must have begun writing this version before the end of 1914.

Molineux was from a good family, which had long social standing, but which no longer had much money. He met and fell in love with Blanche Chesebrough, from a wealthy New York family, who was in love with Henry Crossman Barnet. Miss Chesebrough would probably have married Barnet, but he suddenly died, supposedly of diphtheria, and she married Molineux instead. Molineux was an expert gymnast, a member of the New York Knickerbocker Athletic Club. As a member of the club's athletic committee, Molineux became involved in a violent argument over club policies with one Harry Cornish, the club's manager. Cornish lived in a boarding house, along with Mrs. Adams and her son, John, who also worked at the club. One day Cornish received through the mail a bottle of bromo-seltzer at his home address. He thought nothing of this, put the package in the medicine cabinet, and there John Adams found it when his mother complained of a severe headache. Mrs. Adams took a tablet and died at once. An autopsy proved that she had been given cyanide. At this point, Adams recognized Molineux's handwriting on the bromo-seltzer package, and various people then remembered that Barnet had taken Kuntow powder (a stomach remedy) before he died.

Dreiser was particularly interested in this story because an accident, an element beyond man's reckoning, determined the final sequence of events. In fact, Dreiser wrote in hand at the top of the typewritten page: "*Important:* Molineux intended to provide only a lingering death. The hydrocyanic acid accidently produced instantaneous death and precipitated the murder inquiry!" By mixing the bromo-seltzer and cyanide of mercury, Molineux had unwittingly created a new and stronger poison—hydrocyanic acid. This new mixture did not produce diphtheria symptoms (as did the cyanide of mercury mixed with Kuntow powder) but killed immediately (and not, as with Barnet, after ten or twelve days).

The Rake, set in the 1890s, would have been somewhat different from the actual Molineux case. In the fragment that Dreiser left us, Ausley Bellinger of Newark, New Jersey is from an old but destitute American family. Ausley was a bit of a dandy: restless, dabbling in literature and philosophy at Columbia, and intent on living a more luxurious life than his father could afford to give him. When the money runs out, Ausley asks his father to get him a job as chemist (which anticipates the poisonings) in the Hengerer Agate Ware Company. Colonel Bellinger has a social but not financial advantage over Hengerer, who is happy to do him a favor—especially because Hengerer's own son is shiftless and irresponsible. Ausley (like Clyde Griffiths) goes to work in this factory, powered by the waters from the Passaic Falls. He is depressed by the poverty he sees around him but excited (like Clyde) by the rough beauty of the working girls. At this time, he meets Celesté Martzo, whose father successfully manufactures leather goods (he has, in fact, perfected a process of refining leather). The scene suddenly shifts from Paterson to the Solent Athletic Club, a beach resort on Long Island (Dreiser had Gravesend in the manuscript but crossed it out). Although Dreiser introduces Oakleigh Gail, who seems to be the model for Cornish, the manuscript does not get significantly beyond this point. From what we have in *The Rake*, however, it seems that Dreiser intended Ausley Bellinger to become involved with Celesté Martzo (the name itself suggesting someone from a foreign background, albeit newly rich) before he meets another girl from established society, for whom he is willing to murder—a pattern of action which is similar to but not identical with that of *An American Tragedy*.

Roland Molineux was found guilty of murder at his first trial, but he was acquitted at a subsequent trial. He died of paresis (brain disease) in November of 1914. Dreiser had a number of clippings—both about Molineux's death and the case itself—in his files when he began writing this version of *An American Tragedy*. In fact, Dreiser seems to have been writing this version of the novel at the time that Molineux's death was making news.

Dreiser shared his interest in Molineux with another murder case that occurred in the same year. Clarence Richesen, a young minister from Hyannis, Massachusetts, created a sensation when he murdered Avis Linnell, his pregnant sweetheart. When he would not marry her, Avis threatened to expose Richesen, who had left Hyannis and accepted a position in a socially prominent Cambridge, Massachusetts church and had become engaged to a society girl. Although the details are slightly different, the pattern of this case is identical to that of *An American Tragedy*; and while we do not have the fragment that he is talking about, Dreiser told us that "I planned to write this as *the* American tragedy, and I did write six chapters of it before I decided to change to Clyde Griffiths." [2]

Why Dreiser abandoned his early drafts of *An American Tragedy*, we cannot say for certain, but abandon them he did —perhaps to finish *The Titan*, revise *The "Genius,"* and to write reams of short stories. When he finally began work on a novel again, it was *The Bulwark* and not *An American Trag-*

edy. In fact, when Dreiser left New York in October of 1919 for Los Angeles, Horace Liveright was anxiously waiting for *The Bulwark* manuscript, expecting it by the end of the year. Liveright did not know that Dreiser was tiring of *The Bulwark*. Why he was tiring of it, we do not know, but what was big news at this time in Los Angeles may have led Dreiser to put *The Bulwark* aside for (as it turned out) twenty-five years.

On July 15, 1919, Harry New, son of ex-Senator Harry New of Indiana who was then postmaster general, murdered Frieda J. Lesser on Topanga Canyon Road in Los Angeles. He confessed to the crime on December 20th, 1919 and was convicted of second-degree murder on January 16, 1920. This case fascinated Dreiser, who followed it closely, perhaps because it once again repeated the familiar story with its pattern of love, desire, hate, and murder. At any rate, he dropped *The Bulwark* at exactly this time, singled out and then fixed his full attention on the story of Chester Gillette and Grace Brown, and began in earnest to write *An American Tragedy*.

The Grace Brown-Chester Gillette case began on July 12, 1906, when Grace's body was found in seven-and-a-half feet of crystal-clear water, one-hundred-and-sixty feet from the south shore of Big Moose Lake (which is four miles long and one mile wide) in the Adirondack mountains in upper-state New York. A fifteen-foot cedar rowboat had overturned. When the guides came in search of Grace and her escort, who had never returned the preceding night to the Glenmore Hotel, they found Grace's silk coat and a man's stiff straw hat (without a lining) floating near the boat. When they found Grace's body, one whole side of her face had been bashed in, there had been brain damage from a three-inch gash behind her ear, and a part of her light-brown hair had been yanked off in an oarlock. Her escort, whose body was not found, had left his own coat and Grace's hat on a clothes rack in the hotel, but he had taken with him a large suitcase, to which he had strapped a tennis racket, an umbrella, and a tripod for a camera.

When the coroner found that Grace was six months pregnant, the district attorney sent a deputy to Cortland to interview Noah Gillette, the owner of a skirt factory, for whom Grace worked. The deputy questioned Noah, and his son

Harold, who could tell him little. He then questioned the girls with whom Grace worked, and his suspicion centered on Chester Gillette—the owner's nephew, who looked very much like Harold—because Chester was known to be friendly with Grace and his initials matched the fictious names—Carl Graham and Charles Gordon—that Grace's escort had used on various hotel registers. With a search warrant, the deputy went to Gillette's boarding-house room and found a bundle of incriminating letters that Grace had recently written from her home in Otselic. The deputy then notified District Attorney Ward by telegram that "Chester Gillette is the man you are looking for." Ward received this telegram while he was talking to Albert Gross, who, coincidentally, was both a superintendent in the Gillette factory and Chester's best friend. Gross, in fact, had heard about Grace's drowning when he was on his way to Eagle Bay to bring Gillette five dollars that he had requested (by postcard) from the paymistress. Together, Ward, Undersheriff Austin B. Klock, and Gross went to Eagle Bay where they found and arrested Gillette at the Arrowhead Lodge—ironically, as it turned out, dressed for tennis.

Chester Gillette, the son of religious missionaries, had been born in Nevada in 1884, ran away from home when he was fourteen, worked his way through Oregon and Washington State to Vancouver, British Columbia, where he became a printer's devil. He then drifted down to San Francisco, and later visited, as a merchant seaman, Havana and other ports. When he gave up the sea, he became a brakeman with the Chicago, Milwaukee, and St. Paul Railroad. He left this job to to go to school, spending two years as a student at Oberlin College. Soon after, he met his uncle by accident in Zion, Illinois and came East to take a rather humble position in the Cortland factory.

There he met Grace Brown, who was one of nine children from the poor farming family of Mr. and Mrs. Frank B. Brown, of South Otselic. Grace, who was helping to support her impoverished family, lived with a married sister in Cortland. When she and Chester became lovers, she moved to a room in the home of Mrs. Wheeler, where Chester made love to her twice a week. When Grace became pregnant, Chester forced her to return to her parents and virtually forgot about her. He did not even answer her pathetic letters until, in desperation, she threatened to tell his uncle. Chester obviously wanted more than Grace Brown for a wife. He was particularly interested in one Harriet Benedict, the daughter of a rich lawyer, but she never returned his love. As Harriet Benedict later testified, she had only been out with Chester once.

When he was arrested and charged with Grace Brown's murder, Gillette's uncle and cousin deserted him, and the state had to appoint two lawyers to defend him: A. M. Mills, a former state senator, and Charles D. Thomas. Although Gillette had changed his story several times, he finally fixed upon one for the trial: he said that when Grace threatened to expose him, he had agreed to meet her at the Tabor House in De Ruyter (between Cortland and Otselic), took her to Canastota, then to Utica (each travelling in separate cars because he did not want to be seen with her on the train), and from there to Big Moose Lake. When he got off the train at Big Moose Lake, he mailed two cards, one to the paymistress at the factory requesting five dollars and a card which Grace had written her mother. Once they registered at the lodge, they planned to see the lake, first deciding on a steamboat, and then changing their mind and taking a round-bottom boat. After rowing for a time, they went to the shore, ate a light lunch, and then went back into the boat, Chester leaving his suitcase on the shore where they planned to return. Once again on the lake, Chester told Grace that he could not marry her and advised her to go back to her parents. She became despondent and, he maintained, jumped into the lake. When he bent over to find and assist her, the boat tipped over. When Grace did not surface, Gillette said that he swam to shore, changed clothes, buried the tennis racket (because it was too heavy to carry), and walked along a road and then railroad tracks (seeing three men on his way) until he had covered the two miles to Eagle Bay, where he took a steamboat to Arrowhead Lodge. He went to Seventh Lake the next day to visit Josephine Patrick, a casual friend, whom he had met on the train coming up.

All through his trial, Chester insisted that Grace Brown

committed suicide when she jumped into the lake. He maintained this even though a Dr. Edward Douglass testified that she was beaten over the head with a blunt instrument (such as a tennis racket) and that she was dead when she entered the water. Another doctor probably strengthened rather than weakened this testimony when he maintained that even if Grace Brown were not dead when she entered the water, her injuries were so serious that she would have died if they were not properly treated and that, in any case, she would have been blind for life.

After five hours of deliberation, the jury found Chester Gillette guilty of murder in the first degree. His case was unsuccessfully appealed to a higher court and then to Governor Hughes before he was executed in the electric chair at Auburn, New York.

While Dreiser obviously stuck closely to the actual facts of the Gillette-Brown case, he made some significant changes. He sentimentalized Clyde, made him less calculating and cold-blooded, more an innocent victim of his own nature and a world he does not understand. Whereas Grace Brown suffered severe and brutal injury, Dreiser changed all these details to make them consistent with an accidental death: Roberta has only a slight mark on her face (where Clyde accidentally hit her with the camera) and on her head (where she was hit by the overturning boat). Dreiser even removed from Clyde's luggage the tennis racket that was strapped to Chester Gillette's suitcase, although he left the tripod and the umbrella.

Clyde also has much less worldly experience than Chester Gillette, is much more the product of poverty and a public world of cheap hotels. Clyde's whole life, in fact, has never provided him with more than a fraudulent and unexamined glimpse of a heightened life—one that he has neither the social experience nor the intelligence to evaluate.

Unlike Chester Gillette, Clyde is also the victim of his past: his flight from the hit-and-run accident in Kansas City haunts him at the trial. Moreover, it reflects the passive quality of his character—a quality of character that leads to predictable behavior when circumstances repeat themselves.

Dreiser also intensified Chester's casual relationship with

Harriet Benedict, made Clyde and Sondra lovers, and gave Clyde every expectation of marrying her. He in turn made Clyde's relationship with Roberta more secret, made Clyde more lonely and dependent on others, and portrayed him as torn between pity for Roberta and desire for Sondra. When Chester Gillette leaves Big Moose Lake, he is not really thinking of another woman. When Clyde leaves Big Bittern, he makes his way directly to Sondra, who is never out of his thoughts. After Roberta's death, Clyde goes swimming with Sondra and her friends (paralleling the irony of Chester being dressed for tennis when he was arrested), makes love to Sondra, and unconciously awaits the arresting officers, painfully caught in a tug-of-war between an impulse to flee and a desire to remain with Sondra. The scene with Clyde in the woods—ready to run at one moment, ready to return to camp at the next—is a representative moment because it reveals the way the will is pulled in two directions and negated by counter impulses.

As Clyde is pulled in different directions from within, he is also pulled in different directions from without, and he is helplessly caught between opposing forces. Dreiser intensified the political implications of the case by having Clyde's lawyer running for a judgeship against the district attorney. District Attorney Ward was a political enemy of A. M. Mills, one of Chester's lawyers; and Ward did become a judge; but Ward and Mills were not running for office against each other as were Mason and Belknap in the novel.

Even on the most simple level of the novel, forces are at work over which Clyde has no knowledge. Whereas Chester mails the postcard Grace wrote her mother, Clyde does not know that Roberta has written such a card or that it is in her coat back at the lodge (Chester had taken Grace's coat with them) just waiting to identify her and to incriminate him. Whereas Chester's family abandons him, Clyde's uncle finances the defense. As a result, Clyde is unable to plead temporary insanity (which is closer to the truth) because his uncle does not want to besmirch the family name. Again, as a result, Clyde's lawyers invent the story that leads him to the electric chair, for Clyde is unable to explain how he has travel-folders and a map of Big Bittern—all with a Lycurgus address on them

—when he supposedly had had his change of heart in Utica and decided there—and not in Lycurgus—to come to Big Bittern. In a novel where appearance and reality are never clearly in focus, Dreiser added the ironic detail of having a lie condemn Clyde when the truth might have saved him. In a novel where chance events seem to play such an important part, Dreiser created a character with a fixed nature to whom the same kind of thing happened repeatedly so that chance events are merely catalysts which bring about the inevitable.

A number of elements in Chester Gillette's story obviously appealed to Dreiser. He could release his sympathy for the underdog, could show the agonies of desire for wealth and the heightened life, could depict sexual desire frustrated by conventions (there is a remote similarity between Clyde's entanglement with Roberta which caused him to lose Sondra and Dreiser's entanglement with Sara White which caused him to lose both Thelma Cudlipp and his job with Butterick), could once again treat the psychological and social effects of an illegitimate pregnancy (one of Dreiser's compulsive concerns dating back to the time that he was embarrassed by his sister's promiscuity), could vent his wrath on religion and small-town morality, could again express his love for the mother and sympathize with the plight of such a woman whose son was to be electrocuted for murder, and he could express his own personal fear of disaster (especially a criminal ending) and of death (a really compulsive fear) by water.

We can see by examining the first holograph of *An American Tragedy* how closely Dreiser identified himself with Chester Gillette's story. In fact, in the first version of this story, he modelled Clyde and Clyde's father primarily on himself and his own father. Asa Griffiths, for example, becomes a composite of John Dreiser and Dreiser himself. Asa, we are told, "was considerably more sensuous than either his [Asa's] father or his two elder brothers"—a quality of character Dreiser certainly saw in himself. When Asa leaves home, he becomes a dishwasher in a restaurant—just as Dreiser left home and washed dishes in John Paradiso's restaurant when he first arrived in Chicago. Like Dreiser, Asa "saw life swirling about him"; "he began more keenly to notice girls"; he was always dissatisfied, always quick to "sicken of the deadly monotony to which he was subject and [which] would stir him to seek something better—most often trying some new place." Like Dreiser, Asa is hopelessly restless—one of the many displaced characters who have rejected or been rejected by the family and in continual search for some kind of abiding satisfaction and achievement.

Although he could not subdue his own ego when he made Asa a counterpart of himself, Dreiser modelled Asa primarily upon his own father. The holograph, for example, began with a history of Clyde's father, whose family owned a prosperous hardware store from which he was disinherited because of his ineptness—just as Dreiser's own father lost his wool mill when it burned down and he was too inept to rebuild it, this event exposing his fumbling nature, his essential self (just as chance events draw out the inner man in Dreiser's fiction).

Like Dreiser's own father, Asa Griffiths moves from New York to Tonamanda, Pennsylvania, where he meets the young farm-girl who becomes his wife, primarily because she feels sorry for him: "Elvira saw in him a rather inefficient wanderer very much in need of mothering." Elvira, in fact, really takes the place of his mother ("Since last he had seen his mother there was no one who had appealed to him so much"), and Mrs. Griffith's role as the archetypal mother is established from the very beginning.

Asa goes to work in a Tonamanda ice plant so that he can be near Elvira Strunk, who comes from a family that was "more religious" than his own religious parents. He soon leaves the ice plant for a better job selling farm implements. After he has been away from home for five years, Asa's father dies, leaving him three thousand dollars, the two elder brothers getting the hardware business. He now feels secure enough to get married. Once this happens, the inept Asa loses his total inheritance in a foolish investment (once again Dreiser seems to be equating this misadventure with the burning of his own father's uninsured mill, in which he had invested his life's savings).

He moves west to Buffalo, looking for a clerkship. There his first son is born, followed by a child "every second or third year, for a period of fifteen" (paralleling Dreiser's own family).

He finally leaves Buffalo for Chicago where, with the help of Elvira's relative, he opened a small restauraunt, which soon goes out of business. In Tonamanda, they had both been influenced by a Mr. Conklin (Dreiser tells us in *Dawn* that a real estate agent by this name is a chief model for Asa Griffiths), a strong Baptist. Elvira suddenly becomes very religious and converts the weaker Asa with her enthusiasm. While living in the Chicago slums, they are helped by a missionary, John Sigurson Bard, for whom they work six years. Asa completely gives up at this point, leaning on the stronger Bard, living in abject poverty, and yet seeing in the mission "the end of his material and financial fears."

Interestingly enough, Bard is far more a mechanistic philosopher than an Evangelist, and he expresses ideas that Dreiser himself accepted when he was writing *An American Tragedy*. Bard insisted, for example, that not only the Bible but all "created aspects of life revealed God—as a mechanist or monist would see it—a moving and restless force expressing or varying itself as best it might." Dreiser believed that man was a part of this natural "expression," the current of life actually passing and working through him, as long as it was not short-circuited by the moralists or the philistines. Asa, as might be expected, cannot follow Bard's thinking. He refuses to believe that "life preys on life." For him "God was kind—Love—and he [*sic*] saved all men whole."

When Bard suddenly dies of *angina pectoris,* the Griffiths take over the mission, which soon collapses without the strength and force of Bard behind it. Mrs. Griffiths goes to work in a factory—"some wholesale tailoring establishment"—just as Roberta Alden does, and Roberta becomes her double. As things go from bad to worse, Griffiths (like Dreiser's own father) insists that "God would find a way." Mrs. Griffiths petitions various banks, manufacturers, and businessmen for help and starts another mission. The family spends much of its time in the park distributing hot coffee and sandwiches to the destitute, particularly in bitter weather. At school, Clyde (and this is something Dreiser could understand) is laughed at by even the "less well-bred children." He begins, we are told, "to develop a peculiar and yet rather well concealed sombreness or morbidity which grew directly out of the wounds inflicted upon a sensitive and decidedly responsive psyche."

The family drifts from Chicago to Kansas City. Dreiser, of course, finally began *An American Tragedy* here, perhaps because in this early version Clyde first came of age in Kansas City.

> Kansas City [was] a city which somehow took his fancy more than any he had so far seen or remembered [because] he was just beginning to experience those first traces of a nervous and sensual interest in regard to girls. . . . This larger city . . . somehow restored his very earliest childish impressions of Chicago [and] he seemed to come into a sense of his individuality and personality.

In Kansas City, he lives with his parents in a mission, on the windows of which are lettered "God is Love," and "How Long Since You Wrote to Mother?" (both ironies in terms of Clyde's final fate). He is so embarrassed by his parents and their life that he lies to a friend about where he lives. When the friend discovers the truth, he ridicules Clyde, who gets into a fight, and suffers a "psychic wound" which "festers." When Clyde's parents discover how mission work embarrassed him, they no longer insist that he do it, and for the first time in his life he has a chance to see the city on his own. He is particularly attracted to the city at night, excited by the lighted fire signs, the rush of the crowd, the many colors all in a dim and fascinating whirl. Like Sister Carrie, he is especially interested in the theater district.

Clyde gets a job in Kansas City, unloading crates in a department store for $1.50 a week. The store has the same effect on him as the Green-Davidson Hotel in the later version of the novel: it exposes him to all kinds of material items, whets his appetite, and starts him on a career of yearning and desire: "to Clyde who had never known plenty in any form these things . . . so eager is the material soul for *enough* of anything . . . held him spellbound." He meets the same kind of boys in the store that he meets in the Green-Davidson Hotel. He also meets and becomes sexually interested in a number of girls who work upstairs, girls very much like Hortense Briggs "who were to be seen too freely on the streets at night or in dance halls— or in the parks." He wonders if his sister has sexual thoughts, and he feels guilty about his own.

Clyde meets at this point a boy named Teget (to get?). Despite a "defective parentage," Teget was "vital and curious with an eye and a taste for better things"—in other words, another Clyde. Like most of Dreiser's restless characters, he is lured by a sense of a new life in a big city and wants the larger life. His main desire is "to travel and see strange cities: Chicago, San Francisco, New York—indeed anywhere except where he was." Teget is also interested in the theater and has seen *Siberia, The Blue Diamond, The Silver King,* and *The Still Alarm.* He and Clyde often go to the theater together, and Clyde soon shares with Teget the desire to see new lands and "the new city" (Dreiser's words). Teget wants to go to San Francisco by way of the Southwest and from there to the Orient. Dreiser here seems to be sticking closely to his source, since Chester Gillette slowly worked his way to San Francisco and from there to Hawaii.

At this point in the holograph, Esta, Clyde's older sister (modelled on Mame), runs away, lured on by the outer world which has upset a delicate balance and clashed with her "religious values," and by the moods of the city men who "awakened responsive moods in her—these rearranging chemisms upon which the [new] morality of the future is certain to be based." Esta has been seduced by an actor named Coutts. Like Sister Carrie, and even Jennie Gerhardt, she is carried off to New York on the promise of marriage and on Coutts' hope to make "some money and buy her many things." He abandons her, however, and Clyde's mother helps rescue her. Esta's break with the family—perhaps also her fate—anticipates Clyde's: she becomes his double in a novel where things happen in twos.

Upon Esta's return, the family leaves Kansas City to take up a new mission in Denver. Clyde goes with them because "it was a step toward that Western Paradise." The theme of the golden West dominates this holograph version of *An American Tragedy.* Dreiser, of course, was living in California when he was writing this version of the novel. He seems, however, to be using the theme of the West ironically, linking it with the American dream of success, Horace Greeley's idea of "Go West young man, go West!" "There were mountains there," Dreiser writes, "and mines of silver and gold, or so he imagined, and great unexplored vastness beyond."

As they travel to Denver in a Pullman, Clyde is jealous of the successful businessmen, "their wives and daughters . . . framed in imitation mahogany, blue plush, and seen against a dead level of changing scenery." This is a dream world, the material equivalent "of all the luxury that his mind was capable of holding." Dreiser here establishes an "equivalence," a one-to-one relationship between Clyde's mind and the scene. Clyde wants all that he sees, and the more he sees the more he dreams, and the more he dreams the more he wants. He becomes a victim of youth's hopeless desire: ("it was the Circe of youth that was investing [this scene] with perfection"); and once he has seen there is no looking away. Clyde's break with the family ("by contrast . . . how dreary and unsatisfactory his parents looked") is thus inevitable. Such scenes as this— and there are many in the final version of *An American Tragedy*—both supply and control Clyde's motives. While Dreiser would give Clyde many glimpses of a heightened existence, he would never in the final version allow the family to participate in it with him.

When the Griffiths arrive in Denver, it is dusk. Along with the scenes which extend Clyde's appetite, which give him a glimpse of a heightened life, dusk scenes predominate in both the holograph and the final version of the novel, and Clyde is at times enveloped in a world of gloom. The family goes to Samuel Yearsley's mission on Lefferts Street, where they hope to save "the immortal souls" of "the drunkard, the failure, and the bum," who are often no worse off than themselves. Yearsley sees their own hopeless condition and decided to use them in the most functionary manner.

While Clyde is disappointed with his surroundings, he is confident in his future. He finally gets work at Beardsley, Buskett, and Marsh Company, wholesale grocers. Like Dreiser in Chicago, at the wholesale hardware firm of Hibbard, Spencer, Bartlett & Company, Clyde feels superior to his fellow workers, feels destined for success—even if it is "via love or favoritism or some other freak of fortune by which he was to be lifted to some high estate." Dreiser deleted these words from the finished version of the novel so that Clyde unconsciously, not consciously, acts this way—thus becoming more the victim of his own misunderstood motives.

In this holograph version, Dreiser makes Clyde more of a dreamer than in the novel itself. The foreman dislikes Clyde (he is always "look[ing] out the window when there's plenty to do") just as the foreman at Hibbard, Spencer, Bartlett & Company disliked Dreiser for being a dreamer.[3]

At this point, the holograph abruptly ends, Dreiser abandoning this draft of the story. The reason may very well be that Dreiser had nowhere to go: he was modelling Clyde too closely upon himself, Clyde's life paralleling his own, until he reached the point where Mildred Fielding, Dreiser's old high school teacher, rescued him from a slow death—physical as well as intellectual—at Hibbard, Spencer, and Bartlett. Dreiser needed to expose Clyde more quickly to a heightened kind of life, to put him in a social situation that would increase his appetite and start him in pursuit of a life that he could never attain. At the same time as he was doing this, Dreiser also needed to keep Clyde blindly unaware of his limitations and ignorant about life. Without outside stimuli pressing in and the dream expanding under such pressure, Clyde would never become the victim of his environment, his temperament, and the accidents of life—accidents which often bring out the essential self and propel one toward a final destiny. By putting Clyde more quickly in the Green-Davidson Hotel, by cutting off his newfound sense of luxury with the hit-and-run automobile accident, and by introducing Clyde more quickly to his uncle, Dreiser more deftly—and more mechanistically—moved Clyde toward what fate had in store for him.

An American Tragedy is the study of a young man who is caught in and finally destroyed by the crush of conflicting forces. Clyde is trapped between his early poverty and a world that lures him on—first the gaudy world of the Green-Davidson Hotel ("more arresting, quite, than anything he had seen before"), then the more sedate realm of the Union League

Club in Chicago, and finally the prosperous and tasteful world of the Lycurgus rich (which "evoked a mood . . . of roses, perfumes, lights and music. The beauty! The ease!"). As Clyde moves from scene to scene, his world gets larger, more refined, and more luxurious. And as the scene heightens, Clyde's appetite expands in direct proportion to all that he sees. Yet significantly enough, directly across the river from the beautiful Lycurgus homes of his uncle and the Finchleys was "a miserable slum, the like of which, small as it was, he had not seen outside of Chicago or Kansas City." [4] Dreiser once again created a realm where the opposing forces of Herbert Spencer are in play.

Dreiser personifies these opposing forces and conditions, and Clyde is torn between people who represent vastly different ways of life. He is torn first between his sense of duty and even pity for his mother (who wants fifty dollars to help the pregnant Esta) and his passion for Hortense Briggs (who wants fifty dollars for a gaudy coat). He is caught again between a sense of duty and even pity for Roberta (who embodies his drab past) and by his desire for Sondra (who embodies his hopes for the future). He is caught still again between the machinations of Orville Mason, the Republican candidate for a county judgeship and Alvin Belknap, the Democratic candidate. Mason and Belknap are the "psychic" as well as political opposites of each other: Mason not only comes from a poor background much like Clyde's, but he has been sexually timid (and is outraged by Clyde's use of Roberta) because he suffered a disfiguring injury as a child. Belknap, on the other hand, comes from wealth (his father had been a judge and a U.S. senator), and he had enough sexual experience to become involved in a paternity case (which his father's wealth had enabled him to escape) much like Clyde's.

Clyde is caught, in other words, between the world of his impoverished father and the world of the rich uncle, between his sense of duty to his family (and to Roberta whose situation ironically parallels his sister's) and his desire for a better life outside the family, between his early religious training and a secular world of material values, between his experience in the city and the small town mentality that eventually judges him, between the different temperaments of the prosecuting and defense attorneys, and between the opposing political parties who see the value of his case.

Caught between such conflicting impulses and conflicting forces, Clyde's will is negated. We see him torn, held, suspended in time. He is torn when he receives at one and the same time Roberta's pathetic letters pleading with him to marry her and Sondra's carefree letters inviting him to Twelfth Lake. He is torn when he accidentally finds himself with his rich friends in front of Roberta Alden's house in Blitz and "hesitates" (he did not know "whether to go on or not") to knock at the door and ask road directions. He is torn in the boat on Big Bittern as he contemplates murdering Roberta, "a balanced combat [going on] between fear (a chemic revulsion against death or murderous brutality that would bring death) and a harried and restless and yet self-repressed desire to do—to do—to do—yet . . . a static between a powerful compulsion to do and yet not to do" (492). He is torn when he is about to be arrested, an inner self telling him to run away while another argues that Sondra is too valuable a prize to sacrifice: "run, run, do not linger! yet lingering, and thinking *Sondra*, this wonderful life!" (552). He is torn between telling Mason the truth or a fictitious story—not once but twice—when he is arrested (571) and again when his lawyers are planning his defense (607).

While Clyde's will is cancelled out, negated by antithetical forces, the relationship between opposing characters is a dynamic and not a static one. Dreiser actually suggests that these relationships generate their own chemical energy, and that the character with the most dynamic personality can physically control and dominate another. One of the reasons that Dreiser uses descriptive passages with technical terminology and jargon is to suggest that the force one character exercises over another comes from a continuum that is greater than both of them. In Lycurgus, when Clyde is lured by Rita Dickerman, "There was something heavy and languorous about her body, a kind of ray or electron that intrigued and lured him in spite of himself" (205). Clyde is drawn to Roberta in the same way, helpless to ignore her "because of so strong a chemic or temperamental

pull that was definitely asserting itself" (254). When he then
meets Sondra, the force of her presence is greater than any
women he has yet met. Just as Clyde is drawn from one physical
realm to a more heightened one, he is drawn from one woman
by another more compelling: "How different [Sondra was]
to Rita and Zella . . . her effect on him was electric—thrilling
—arousing in him a curiously stinging sense of what it was to
want and not to have" (219–20). Dreiser literally believes that
there is an "electric" effect (cf. 429), an actual charge and dis-
charge of energy between Sondra and Clyde—one that negated
the power that anyone else had over Clyde—ideas probably
derived from the mechanist, Jacques Loeb. Sondra was a "newer
luminary—he could scarcely see Roberta any longer, so strong
were the actinic rays of this other" (315). During the trial,
Jephson's physical and emotional strength supports Clyde,
keeps him going when he is about to weaken. Jephson continually "fixes" Clyde "with his eye" (716–17, cf. also 704 and
714). When his mother arrives, Clyde finds even another
source of energy and strength outside himself (see 752–53).
He does not completely break down under his ordeal in the
death-house because stronger men and women comfort him—
first Miller Nicholson, the Buffalo lawyer who has been sentenced to die ("His presence and companionship during the
exercise hour . . . could help him endure thus") and then
once again his mother ("her strength seemed to be going all
to him, until she felt she must leave or fall") (770, 810).

Just as a city or a beautiful house or even a luxurious room
can create a mood in Clyde, so a stronger personality can exert
a force over Clyde. The energy here compellingly links the
inner man to a larger force—a force in nature itself. Once Clyde,
for example, fixes upon murdering Roberta, he cannot rid himself of the idea: it takes physical shape. The idea comes to
him after he reads in *The Times-Union* about a girl who
mysteriously drowned in a Massachusetts lake. He cannot get
the item out of his mind, the import of it continuously "thrust-
ing itself forward, psycho-genetically, born of his own turbulent, eager and disappointed seeking" (463).

Dreiser suggests that the idea really stems from a larger
source by linking it with the story of the fisherman and the

genie from the *Arabian Nights,* a book whose influence dominates *An American Tragedy,* and even parallels its plot. When
the poor fisherman pried the top off the strange box he had
brought up in his net from the bottom of the sea, he finds himself suddenly in the power of the huge genie which had been
trapped in the box. The genie would have killed him if he had
not been able to trick it back into the box, clamp back the lid,
and throw it into the sea. Cylde's reading about the mysterious
drowning releases the forces which now control his thoughts—
like "the efrit emerging as smoke from the mystic jar in the net
of the fisherman," a force that comes "from the depths of some
lower or higher world never before guessed or plumbed by him"
(463).

Unlike the fisherman, Clyde is unable to get "the genie"
back in the box. When he calls Roberta, for example, and asks
her—with murder in mind—to meet him at Fonda, "it seemed
as though the Giant Efrit that had previously materialized in
the silent halls of his brain, was once more here at his elbow."
The key idea comes in the next clause: he "was being talked
through—not actually talking himself" (471). Forces "talk
through" Clyde, speak to an other and secret self, a kind of
"darker or primordial and unregenerate" self that he never
knew existed (464).

As Clyde contemplates murdering Roberta, Dreiser juxta-
poses his thoughts against scenes which Clyde sees from the
train window ("Those five birds winging toward that patch of
trees over there": these birds eventually become the wier-wier
bird in Big Bittern) as if nature itself were a part of his thought
or his thinking a part of nature (*see 473–79*). Clyde's "darker
or primordial, and unregenerate" self finds its "equivalent," a
physical parallel, in the setting at Grass Lake and later at Big
Bittern: The "green slime" at Big Bittern that lies beneath piles
of rotten wood (457) corresponds to that "darker self" that
speaks to Clyde from his depths (*cf. 461 and 472*). Grass Lake
with its water "black or dark like tar" and its dark pines which
stood like "watchful giants . . . ogres almost" (480) corresponds to Clyde's dark and brooding thoughts, controlled by a
giant or ogre: once he is on Big Bittern with Roberta, the "dark
water seemed to grip Clyde . . . to change his mood." He

seemed to be in the grip of some "mighty hand" which had cast the lake there as he might a "black pearl" (*489*). Dreiser believed that inner and outer reality could not be separated and that no motives were purely subjective.

As Clyde reacts to his environment, and as he reacts to the presence of other characters, so he reacts to the presence of nature itself, a scene creating a mood in him which reinforces murderous thoughts. Clyde is in the hands of an overwhelming psychic force whose power—like an Aladdin genie—cannot be denied once it has been called into play. In "Notes on Life," Dreiser refers to this genie phenomenon as an "invisible, immaterial agent of a Universal Mind." The symbol of this universal spirit is the wier-wier bird, whose eerie cries haunt Clyde before, during, and after his plan to murder Roberta. This bird—or one like him—follows Clyde through the novel. Before the automobile accident in Kansas City, "a flock of crows rose and winged direct toward a distant wood" (*124–25*). When he first sees the wier-wier bird, it was flying "into some darker recess within the woods" (*459*). When he comes the second time to Big Bittern, Clyde sees a flock of birds from the train flying once again toward a distant woods (*476*). The woods is Big Bittern itself, and the birds bent upon getting there suggest the inevitability of Clyde's fate.

As Clyde's fate is inextricably connected with Sondra, so is the bird itself. Sondra writes Clyde that when she was riding her horse one morning "a bird flew right up under Dickey's heels" (*433*). At Twelfth Lake, Sondra was "poised bird-like" in flight (*455*), and later she comes and goes "like a bright-colored bird" (*546*). Just before Clyde is arrested, he stands paralyzed, knowing that he should and yet unable to run, "the while vesper sparrows and woodfinches sang" (*552*). While one may ponder the significance of woodfinches, and then prudently stop short of making the connection between wood (Big Bittern?) and finches (Finchley?), a critic is certainly on safe ground in seeing the wier-wier as a bird of fate (Dreiser seems to pun on the Anglo-Saxon word "wyrd"—that is, fate: "the weirdness of it [the bird]," "the weird . . . cry," "that devilish bird . . . the wier-wier"). The bird, of course, is a romantic symbol, a visitor from a transcendent realm, its song the voice of nature itself. Dreiser adds a gothic quality to the symbol, making the bird reflect a demonic element inherent in both nature and in Clyde's "darker" self, its cries anticipating Roberta's death cry and Clyde's end.

Just as the gothic element in romantic literature suggests a subterranean void—a dark, inverted force inherent in nature —so Dreiser suggests the same black force is at work with the wier-wier bird. Like the romantics, Dreiser never believed that this force dominated all nature—that nature was totally malevolent. While scenic elements can create or intensify a black mood, the same setting can be a testimony to life's beauty. In fact, while the dark waters of Big Bittern "grip" Clyde and "change his mood," he is dimly aware of "the insidious beauty of this place! Truly, it seemed to mock him—this strangeness—this dark pool, surrounded on all sides by those wonderful, soft, fir trees" (489). At Twelfth Lake, after Roberta's death, Clyde can see that behind and beneath his horror lies the "beauty" of life. As he stands under the stars, he sees "the mystic, shadowy water," listens as the pines seem to talk when they ripple in the breeze, hears the night cry of the birds and owls (which suddenly disturb him), and is over-awed by the "wonder and glory of all this" (547).

Whatever forces are at work in nature, they seem to have two selves—just as Clyde has two selves. One evening, significantly at dusk, while he is contemplating Roberta's murder, he frightens himself with his thoughts and begins to walk faster "seeking to outwalk and outthink or divert some inner self" (461).

In a world where antithetical forces seem to be at work in nature, in society, and in man, appearance often belies reality. If an inner force wars within Clyde, another force wars outside. Gilbert Griffiths, Clyde's look-alike cousin, is the projection of this other self. On the surface, the differences between Clyde and Gilbert appear to be only accidental: Gilbert's status comes from his birth, and he seems to embody all the privileges that also belong to Clyde if his father had not been disinherited. In reality, the differences between Clyde and Gilbert are essential ones: Gilbert is "dynamic and aggressive" while Clyde is "soft and vague and fumbling" (216). Just as Asa and

Samuel Griffiths differ in temperament (Dreiser probably had Mendel's laws of recessive genes in mind here), so Clyde and Gilbert are essentially different.

In Dreiser's world, there is a gulf between what we see and its meaning, between appearance and reality, between the realm of chance and accident and the realm of essence and inevitability. Accidental events seem to dominate the novel. Clyde gets his job at the Green-Daidson Hotel when he applies for a job as a soda jerk in a drug store; he is forced to move away from Kansas City because of the automobile accident; he meets his uncle by chance at the Union League in Chicago; he is made foreman of the shrinking room because it is the only job open when his uncle happens to see him doing menial work; Roberta is placed in Clyde's department after she comes to Lycurgus when a friend happens to see a workers-wanted sign; Roberta meets Clyde by chance on Crum Lake; Roberta moves into the fateful bedroom when her boardinghouse friends happen to see her out with Clyde after she had told Grace Marr that she was going home for the weekend; Clyde is the chance victim (Dreiser uses the word "accident") (*314*) of Sondra's plan to make the detested Gilbert jealous; and Roberta Alden drowns when the boat tips over after Clyde has abandoned the idea of murdering her.

Yet behind the realm of accident is the realm of causal sequence and inevitability. Given Clyde's conflicting character—his desire for money and pleasure in opposition to his ineptness and passive nature—it is only a matter of time before he will overreach himself. Dreiser's use of repetitive form—one scene anticipating and repeating the next—is in perfect harmony with the logic of Clyde's character. As Clyde shows a complete lack of will and sense of duty when he spends the fifty dollars on Hortense Brigg's coat instead of helping his pregnant sister, so his desire for Sondra Finchley will once again negate his will and sense of duty when he refuses to help—in fact, plans to murder—Roberta. Just as he will run away from those who are seriously injured in the Kansas City automobile accident, so he will swim and then run away from the drowning Roberta.

The events in Kansas City duplicate in a sense those in Lycurgus. While the situation in Kansas City and Lycurgus is very much the same, the consequences of Clyde's passivity are very different. When Clyde has to choose between helping his sister or Hortense Briggs and between remaining in or leaving Kansas City, his life and death do not depend upon his predictable choice. When he has to choose between helping or murdering Roberta and between saving or letting her drown, his life and death do depend upon his (again) predictable choice. Clyde is thus lured from a simple moral situation to a more complex one. His nature—his desire, his ignorance, his passivity—is fixed, and the conflicting forces both inside and outside him create the context that lead to his destruction.

While chance (Roberta's pregnancy, for example) seems to play an important part, the lawyer Belknap escaped from the same kind of sexual dilemma that led Clyde's undoing: the elements which shaped Clyde—his poverty, ignorance, and inexperience—once again determine his fate. Accident, to this extent, is only a catalyst which arrests and develops the essential self. Accident becomes a part of the inevitable sequence of events: fate cannot be divorced from character, character cannot be divorced from the forces which shape and determine it, and the forces which shape and determine character cannot be divorced from the accidents that often awaken the "dark, primordial, and unregenerate" second self dormant in us all. In his "Notes on Life," Dreiser wrote that there is "no chance— only a strong seeming of it. . . . Chance is another name for our ignorance of causes." [5] If Clyde Griffiths seems to be, in part, the product of gratuitous events, it is only because he himself did not fully understand the deterministic nature of his own background and we do not fully understand the darker workings of forces that transcend even environment.

Dreiser very carefully prepares us for the inevitable. One scene not only anticipates the next, but one scene repeats another. When Clyde first speaks to Roberta, for example, he is boating on Crum Lake. When he asks her to step into his canoe, he tells her, " 'It's perfectly safe . . . you won't be in any danger' " (260), a remarkable irony in a scene that anticipates Roberta in the boat at Big Bittern. In fact, the whole episode on Crum Lake anticipates and prepares for Big Bittern. When Clyde has Roberta on Big Bittern he notices that "overhead was one of those identical woolly clouds that had sailed above him at Crum Lake on that fateful day [when they met]" (*486*). While the effect may be forced, it conclusively demonstrates how Dreiser linked one scene with another that preceded it.

The progression from scene to scene becomes more complicated as Clyde moves up the social ladder. In fact, as he moves up, his relationship among the various characters becomes as fixed as his fate, and Dreiser establishes a kind of "ratio" relationship among the characters: Roberta *is* to Clyde as Clyde *is* to Sondra, just as Roberta *is* to Clyde as Clyde *was* to Hortense Briggs (*see 311*). Dreiser completes this ratio by making Hortense Briggs a lower-class Sondra Finchley (*see 320*), and he reinforces it by describing Clyde meeting Roberta in a way that parallels Sondra meeting Clyde. When Clyde sees Roberta on the banks of Crum Lake, he asks her to get into his canoe with these words: " 'Oh, please don't say no. Just get in, won't you?' " (*260*). Later, when Sondra sees Clyde in front of her house, she first (in this world of appearance and reality) mistakes him for Gilbert. When she finally asks him to get into her chauffeur-driven limousine she uses almost the same words that Clyde spoke to Roberta: " 'Won't you get in, please, and let me take you where you are going. Oh, I wish you would' " (*305*). As a series of birds flying toward a distant woods anticipates the wier-wier bird at Big Bittern, so the meeting of Roberta and Clyde anticipate the meeting of Clyde and Sondra. Clyde's fate is inextricably involved with the fate of others, and the forces which work in and through him affect others as well.

The very beginning of the novel, in fact, anticipates the end. The novel begins with these words:

> Dusk—of a summer night.
> And the tall walls of the commercial heart of an American city of perhaps 400,000 inhabitants—such walls as in time may linger as a mere fable. (*7*)

The last chapter of the novel begins:

> Dusk of a summer night.
> And the tall walls of the commercial heart of the city of San Francisco—tall and gray in the evening shade. (*811*)

The emphasis upon dusk and walls is thematically important.

The novel opens and closes at dusk; Clyde plots the murder of Roberta at dusk (*461*); Roberta drowns at dusk (*491, cf. also 494*); Clyde is arrested at dusk (*566*); and at the end of a prison day he receives the letter from Sondra which marks "the last trace of his dream . . . that moment of dusk in the west" (*789*).

Throughout the novel, the gloomy shadows of inevitability hang over Clyde, his day is over before it even begins, just as he walks throughout the novel between the walls of the city, the walls of the Lycurgus factory (high red walls which ironically "suggested energy and very material success") (*180*). Like fate, the walls of society close in on Clyde, centripetally, and it is most significant that to get from Three Mile Bay to Big Bittern one has to go "between towering walls of pines" (*457*). These walls lead straight to "the gray and restraining walls of Auburn [prison] itself" (*755, see also 807*).

At the end of the novel, Dreiser has so firmly established the theme of inevitability that almost every word has either double meaning or can be read in a double context. As Clyde, for example, approaches the electric chair:

> his voice sound[ed] so strange and weak, even to himself, so far distant as though it emanated from another being walking along side of him, and not from himself. And his feet were walking, but automatically, it seemed. . . . There it was—at last—the chair he had so often seen in his dreams—that he so dreaded— to which he was now compelled to go. He was being pushed toward that. (*810*)

A second self (the hidden self that acted at Big Bittern) accompanies Clyde to the electric chair (which has usurped the "dream," just as another kind of dream kept Clyde running from the very beginning), and Clyde "automatically" (his whole behavior has been a matter of conditioned and automatic response to stimuli) is "pushed" (he has been compelled and pushed by other forces from the very beginning) toward the fate that so long awaited him.

This passage—like most passages in *An American Tragedy* —is heavy with irony. As Clyde anticipates the dream of marrying into the upper class, his dream is being cut out from under him by a machine-like sequence of events that he never really comes to understand. There is an incongruous gulf between what Clyde expects and what actually happens to him. Whereas the reader can anticipate Clyde's fate, Clyde himself is always insensitive to what is about to happen. It is most ironic, for example, that Clyde, who will plot the murder of Roberta, becomes indignant when Esta's consort deserts her (*see 100*). It is again ironic that just before Clyde meets Roberta in his uncle's factory, "the large number of girls and women upstairs seemed very remote and of no consequence" (*233*). It is ironic that Mason and later the townspeople take an immediate dislike to Clyde because they think that he is rich. It is ironic when Clyde's desire for money gets him into trouble and his lack of money prevents him from getting out of it. It is ironic that Clyde is condemned by a society that believes in absolute justice, but he lives in a society in which money has created a double standard of justice—where Belknap, unlike Clyde, is saved by his father's money from the unpleasant consequences of a premarital affair (*see 592*), and where the doctor to whom Roberta first goes has performed abortions for the girls from wealthy families (*see 400*). It is ironic that Clyde plans to murder Roberta and is prosecuted by Mason—people with whom he shares the same background and the same drive to succeed, and people who are really very much like him. It is ironic that Clyde, first driven by the desire to live in an elegant world, and then abandoned by everyone but his mother, should be given two books in death-row—the *Arabian Nights* and *Robinson Crusoe* (*776*). It is ironic that Clyde believes in an Aladdin world of magic but lives in a world of causality—that he should think of himself as a "pagan" and be prosecuted and put to death by a strictly religious community. It is ironic that the American dream should be associated with the westward movement, for as the Griffiths family moves westward—from Grand Rapids, to Detroit, to Milwaukee, to Chicago, to Kansas City, to Denver, to San Francisco—they get poorer and poorer.

The cruelest irony of all is that Clyde is really innocent of murdering Roberta. As Dreiser carefully tells us, Clyde does not have the strength of will to murder her, and he strikes Roberta unintentionally with the camera (*see 492*). Clyde makes this perfectly clear to Reverend McMillan; but because Clyde was angry at the time of Roberta's death, and because he was glad that Roberta drowned, Reverend McMillan tells Clyde that he is guilty of murder in his "heart" (795). Although Clyde is legally innocent, McMillan believes that he is guilty before God and, as a result, fails to give the governor the facts that could save Clyde's life (*see 804*).[6] Thus, Clyde, who struggles all his life to out-distance the slums and to move beyond his fanatically religious parents, is condemned by both society and the church for a crime he never legally committed. Certainly this kind of irony, in part, is responsible for the emotional impact—and the effect of *An American Tragedy* stems from more than just a rough accumulation of detail and incident.

An American Tragedy is a major work of art—a supreme narrative accomplishment. In no other novel was Dreiser more fully in command of idea and method, theme and literary technique. In no other novel did he ever again so effectively reveal the innocent dreamer caught in a web of antithetical forces—the victim of the imbalance within himself, his society, and nature itself.

11

Russian Pilgrimage
and American Causes

On September 27, 1926, Dreiser dined in Paris with the anarchists Emma Goldman and Alexander Berkman. Emma had been born in Kovno, Russia on June 27, 1869 and came to America with an older sister in 1885, spending the rest of her unhappy childhood in Rochester, New York. On Friday, November 11, 1887, four men (Albert Parsons, August Spies, Adolph Fischer, and George Engel) were hanged for their alleged complicity in the Haymarket Bombing (three other suspects were eventually pardoned by Governor Altgeld). This was the most important day in Emma Goldman's life. From this point on, she was in spirit and later in fact an anarchist. When she left Rochester in November of 1897, she went to New York where she became involved with the movement, and where she became the lover of (among other men) Berkman.

When Carnegie's board chairman locked out the workers

at the Homestead, Pennsylvania plant of the Carnegie Steel Plant, three guards and ten workers were killed on July 6, 1892 in a clash between the workers and the Pinkerton agents. Intent on vindicating the laborers, Berkman went to Pittsburgh and shot and seriously wounded Frick, for which he was sentenced to twenty-one years in prison. Emma was sent to Blackwell's Island the next year—the year of the 1893 Panic—for inciting the unemployed to riot in a Union Square mass meeting. Eight years later, she came close to losing her life when officials tried to link her with Leon Czolgosz, who assassinated President McKinley. Always in imminent danger of being deported for pro-labor and (later) anti-war speeches, she also refused to give up such other radical causes as the emancipation of women, free love, birth control, and the defense of Thomas J. Mooney who had been found guilty of bombing the San Francisco Preparedness Day parade. When Emma and Berkman (who was by then released from prison) attacked the conscription laws as well as America's war policy in general, they were arrested in 1917, sentenced to two years in federal prison, and then deported to Russia. What they found in Russia was perhaps the greatest disillusionment of their lives. Upset with the general conditions of the workers, outraged by the persecution of fellow anarchists, they both felt that Russia had merely replaced the heartless czars with an equally heartless bureaucracy. When they left Russia, they were literally without a country, unwanted in both Europe and America.

After her dinner with Dreiser, Emma wrote (September 20, 1926) that her friends had turned against her and that she was lonely. "Imagine my joy to find you so eager and so intensely interested in my struggle." The next month (October 22, 1926), she wrote Dreiser from Montreal, asking him to help her find a publisher who would advance her two years money to write her autobiography. Over two years later (January 7, 1929), Dreiser wrote that he wanted to include her in his *Gallery of Women*. She was horrified to find that he believed she murdered Frick. She admitted that she knew about the plot; but "it was Berkman and not I" who did the shooting—and Frick did not die but recovered from his bullet wounds. She suggested that he read Hippolyte Havel in *Anarchism and Other*

Essays—also Frank Harris' and William Marion Reedy's portraits of her. She concluded: "I hope that you are not as mixed up about other facts in my life as you seem to be about this [the shooting]."

Dreiser's life had some strange parallels with Emma's. He had arrived in Pittsburgh the year after the Homestead strike, was vitally interested in the cause of labor, and spent days walking the streets trying to reconstruct the events of the year before. On December 27, 1913, Emma invited Dreiser to a New Year's party ("bring along Miss Hayman," read the invitation) sponsored by the Mother Earth Publishing Association, Emma's and Berkman's press. Dreiser in time would also become interested in the "new" woman, would advocate free love and birth control, would oppose American intervention in the First World War, would visit the new Russia—from which (like Emma) he would return somewhat skeptical, and would (in the thirties) come to the defense of Tom Mooney.

After he dined with Emma in 1926, he realized that her life reflected the crucial issues of the times, and he used her story —or at least the spirit of it—in the portrait of Ernita in *A Gallery of Women*. At the end of "Ernita," the girl turns to Dreiser (that is, the narrator) and says, " 'In my youth and zealotry I had imagined that Communism could and would change the very nature of man—make him better, kinder, a real brother to his fellows. Now I am not sure that Communism can do that. But at any rate it can improve the social organization of man some and for that I am still willing to work.' " [1] While Dreiser never was optimistic about communism changing the very nature of man, he did believe that it could "improve the social organization of man," and these words better describe his own political attitudes than they do Emma Goldman's.

When Dreiser met Emma Goldman in Paris in September of 1926, he was at the very top of his career. *An American Tragedy*, which had been published in December of 1925, had sold almost thirty thousand copies and made eighteen thousand dollars in royalties within the first six months after publication. Dreiser had big money for the first time in his life. In March of 1926, he sold the rights of *An American Tragedy* to the movies for eighty thousand dollars (in January of 1931, he would receive an additional fifty-five thousand dollars for the "talky" rights).

Like most of Dreiser's business transactions, these were made under great emotional stress and with much unpleasantness, including a scene at the Ritz Hotel in which Dreiser threw a cup of hot coffee in Horace Liveright's face when Liveright demanded twenty thousand dollars from the movie rights. While most of the commentators put the blame on Dreiser for this misunderstanding, the correspondence reveals that Liveright had gone back on his word. On March 8, 1926, Liveright wrote Dreiser about the possibility of Patrick Kearney adapting *An American Tragedy* for the stage. As producer of the play, Liveright wanted fifty percent of the motion picture rights, but would settle for less, because "it's extremely doubtful that *An American Tragedy* can ever be done on the screen. Tremendous pressure would have to be brought on Hays to let him pass it." Liveright also doubted that a movie company could handle the theme with integrity, which later proved to be true. On March 11, 1926, Liveright wrote Dreiser again, asking for one-third of the movie rights in case the play ran ten weeks in New York to an average business of $12,500 or better. He later, however, deleted this clause when Dreiser objected to it and when, if the contract were held up, he would be unable to get Glenn Hunter to play Clyde and Jane Walker to play Roberta (as it turned out, Morgan Farley and Katherine Wilson finally played these parts). In future talks, Liveright settled for ten per cent of the movie rights because, as he had stated in his March 8 letter, he did not expect the movies to buy the story. When Jesse Lasky and Walter Wanger offered Dreiser eighty thousand dollars, Liveright insisted that Dreiser had promised to give him everything over sixty thousand dollars. Dreiser was outraged, threw the coffee in Liveright's face, and accused Liveright (who was on Lasky's payroll) of working with Lasky to bring down Dreiser's price. Liveright denied this (in a letter dated March 26, 1926) and, unaware of a marvelous contradiction in terms, said that "After all, in spite of my absolute loyalty to the Famous Players, I played the cards for you."

Dreiser would have broken with Liveright, if the publisher

had not offered him (June 2, 1926) a handsome contract. Dreiser was to get twenty per cent of the retail price of his books, to receive a drawing account against royalties of five hundred dollars a month, to become a director of Boni and Liveright and oversee the publishing of his own books, Boni and Liveright to spend ten thousand dollars in advertising *An American Tragedy* between June and December, 1926 and to place an ad each week of 1927 in the *New York Times* book supplement, Boni and Liveright to buy the publishing rights of *A Traveller at Forty*, and Boni and Liveright to publish a limited edition of Dreiser's collected works in the fall of 1927. While all these terms (the edition of Dreiser's collected works, for example) were not kept, Dreiser was satisfied for the moment.

In December of 1926, Dreiser moved into a sumptuous duplex apartment at 200 West 57th Street. Despite his new security and wealth, Dreiser turned at this point in his life to attacking American materialism. He was particularly hard on Hollywood, where he claimed the producers and directors held the young actresses in sexual captivity,[2] while the movies themselves titillated the American public with vapid plots free of any social or moral problems: "The average American-made films give everything that money can buy—high-salaried puppets, costly sets, elaborate costumes—and yet—almost, not entirely—they have failed to arrive at anything worth while." [3]

Dreiser was equally severe on Miami, where he went for a vacation immediately after the publication of *An American Tragedy*. He scorned the real-estate boom (although he invested two thousand dollars in a lot that later washed out to sea), the get-rich quick schemes, the gaudy buildings, and the cheap and tawdry people: "Money, money, money! And yet with all those weary, dreary crumb-pickers in those wretched down-and-out houses near the business heart. Oh I loathe it all. *All.*" [4] Even Paris incarnated the new-materialism: "A form of hard commercialism has intruded itself everywhere." [5] Dreiser best expressed his exasperation with commercialism in "American Restlessness." The American people, he maintained, move from place to place because they continually aspire and desire a better life. Their restlessness reflected a spirit of mind that had been at work from Renaissance times—from the very breakup of a stratified, aristocratic society. This spirit has "never stopped," he asserted, "has not even to this day completely lost its momentum anywhere in the world. But in America . . . the pace appears to have been accelerated." [6]

Dreiser hoped at this time that Russia might offer an alternative to "American restlessness." The Revolution seemed to promise much, and a number of radicals—Max Eastman, Robert Minor, Scott Nearing, Michael Gold, and Joseph Freeman—had made the pilgrimage to Russia in search of a new millennium, although (like Emma Goldman and Alexander Berkman) Eastman was bitterly disappointed with what he found. As the editor of the *Masses* and the *Liberator*, Eastman had given himself to the cause with radical zeal. When the *Masses* fought against conscription during the First World War, Eastman, Floyd Dell, Art Young, and the other editors found themselves on trial—facing a possible ten-year prison sentence. The first trial ended with a hung jury, William Hillquit, the successful socialist lawyer, pleading their case. When Hillquit could not be at the second trial, Eastman handled the defense himself—and brilliantly and eloquently persuaded eight jurors to bring in a not guilty verdict, after which the government dropped the case.

Unlike Eastman's, Dreiser's trip to Russia stemmed more out of curiosity than commitment. Perhaps because Dreiser expected less than Eastman, and perhaps also because he lacked Eastman's political sophistication, he was more impressed with what he found in Russia—more impressed than even he realized at the time. While *Dreiser Looks at Russia* is not a completely favorable description of Russia after the Revolution, Dreiser was enthusiastic about the worker's living and working conditions, the new education, and the emancipation of women (which included liberalized divorce laws and attitudes toward sex). He was equally pleased that Russia lacked a flock of lawyers, "quack or robber" doctors, realtors ("his documents, booms, and grafts"), and advertisers. These blessings, however, did not eliminate all evils, and Dreiser complained repeatedly about Russian dirt and unsanitary conditions (his fastidiousness is almost amusing), about the Rus-

sian's leisurely temperament, and about governmental propaganda and spying.

Dreiser was far from consenting to Russian communism.
He still believed in what he called "equity," and he wanted a
"balance" between the men who directed the state and the
workers who ran it. After all of Dreiser's protests about the
despicable conditions of American labor, one is startled to hear
him say that in Russia "a little too much was being done for
labor and too little for the brains necessary to direct it; that
labor was being given an undue share of the fruits of the land."
He concluded, "I cannot even conceive of a classless society
any more than I can conceive of life without variations and
distinctions." [7]

Dreiser seemed to be debating himself throughout this
book. When he interviewed Alexander Janen, a factory director, he disagreed with Janen's attack on capitalism. "I went
on to inquire," said Dreiser in a passage that overwhelms the
reader familiar with his earlier political writing, "where America would be without its capitalists, money geniuses, investors,
and what not else." Dreiser then "traced the rise and services"
of Vanderbilt (railroads), Jay Cooke (financing the Civil
War), John D. Rockefeller (oil), Pullman (sleeping car),
Carnegie (steel), Armour (meat), Ford (automobile), Hearst-
Crocker-Stanford (Union Pacific): "I explained," he continued,
"what they had done for a land that then needed to be developed and developed quickly by genius functioning individually and for gain." Dreiser insisted that while the rugged
individualist and the masses needed each other, they also
needed to function "in balance," so that one would not completely dominate the other. Arguing from a concept of nature,
he concluded, "nature was by no means entirely collective or
entirely individualistic." [8]

Despite this flag-waving, Dreiser found—and this is significant to his intellectual development—that the Russians were
far less restless than Americans. Even Europeans and American
citizens living in Russia seemed more content. Dreiser quoted
Madame Litvinov, the English wife of the Foreign Minister,
who said that when she was living outside Russia she was
restless because she was always competing with others for

contacts, clothes, and social position. Since these goals did not exist in Russia (where clothes are generally poor and where social advance is impossible), Russia offered a sense of peace, almost like that which comes with the oriental sense of non-attachment. Dreiser believed that in Russia the individual had sublimated his personal desires and was more concerned with the fate of the state itself, so that "one's future and one's subsistence is bound up with that of the entire nation," and that this brings "a sense of security, which for some at least replaces that restless, painful seeking." [9] This is the germ of an important idea in Dreiser's thinking, his later interest in the Quakers stemming from this belief that they had found a worldly peace by renouncing material goals in the name of a higher, non-material presence. Dreiser's transition from communistic to Quaker thought was far less difficult than most of his critics have suggested. In fact, Dreiser wrote Warner Clark (July 9, 1934): "As I see it, I find very little difference between what the Friends are seeking to do here and what the Communists are seeking to do in Russia. Both are laying aside the profit motive in order to help mankind to a better level and a happier life." Dreiser reiterated this view in a letter (December 1, 1938) to Rufus Jones, the Quaker president of Haverford College.

The *Liberator*, which succeeded the *Masses* in 1918, became *The Workers' Monthly* in 1924 and had given way in 1926 to *New Masses*, edited by the doctrinaire Mike Gold. Gold had spent the First World War in Mexico avoiding "imperialist" conscription, and in politics was far more radical than the editors of the old *Masses*. Gold quickly recognized the value of Dreiser's sympathy for Communist Russia, and in a letter written on *New Masses* stationery (March 22, 1928), he complimented Dreiser on his Russian articles in *The World*. Where Gold left off, others picked up. Encouraged by Dreiser's newfound politics, radical groups began to call upon him. The first such call came from the John Reed Club, which had an office at 10 East Fourteenth Street and a membership of eighty-two—made up of writers, artists, educators, and scientists (Floyd Dell, John Dos Passos, Clifton Fadiman, Kenneth Fearing, Joseph Freeman, Michael Gold, Horace Gregory, Robert Herrick, Alfred Kreymborg, Joseph W. Krutch, Scott Nearing, and Edmund Wilson, among others). Dreiser joined the club in March of 1930 to question as well as to protest "the purely religious motives behind the 'holy crusade' of Pope Pius XI, the Archbishop of Canterbury, Bishop Manning, Rabbi Wise, and other ecclesiastes" who were discrediting the Soviet Union by a call for mass prayers (scheduled for March 16 and 19) against communism. Dreiser said the plan smacked of vested interests, that capitalists were trying "to bring about a holy war against Russia." The corporation and the banks "are becoming all; the individual nothing." [10]

Once sure of his radical interests, the John Reed Club called upon Dreiser for repeated favors. On June 27, 1930, for example, Carl Van Doren, Edmund Wilson, Waldo Frank, Burton Rascoe, and John Dos Passos asked him to help raise money for the International Labor Defense. Four months later, the club sent Dreiser a telegram in which they maintained that "The Communist Party is the only organized group who show [sic] any great resistance to capitalism in America," and in which they asked him to join a writer's group that was supporting the Communist Party ticket (William Z. Foster and James W. Ford) in the 1932 election. This Dreiser did, sending to the New York *Times* (July 5, 1932) his statement attacking the other parties and supporting the communist ticket: "The political programs of Republicans, Democrats, and Socialists, no matter how skillfully camouflaged, reflect only minor differences."

From 1930 on, Dreiser thought more in abstract than in personal terms. He had moved further and further away from the kind of experience that would give him the perspective and point of view of a Hurstwood. He still sympathized with the poor, but from afar. When Dorothy Van Doren requested (on October 30, 1930) an article on New York's unemployed for the *Nation*, a "pictorial" story like that of Hurstwood in *Sister Carrie*, she was very disappointed with what Dreiser sent her: "Instead of a picture of how the men in New York City who are out of work think and look and feel, you have told us how many there are."

While Dreiser's politics were not controlled by the American Communist Party, he was being deeply influenced by it. He did almost no literary work during the thirties, giving his time and energy to the study of science and to political causes. The three political concerns that absorbed much of his time were the three *causes célèbres* of the Communist Party in America during the thirties: (1) the Scottsboro case, (2) the Harlan mine strike, and (3) the Thomas J. Mooney case.

On April 6, 1931, nine Negro boys—two of them fourteen years old, all of them minors—were sentenced to be electrocuted on July 10 for allegedly raping two white girls who had been riding a freight train in Scottsboro (Jackson County) Alabama. The boys had boarded the slow freight out of Chattanooga at different spots along its route. One boy (Olen Montgomery) was nearly blind and wanted to consult a Memphis eye doctor; two brothers (Roy and Andy Wright) were running away from home along with two friends (Heywood Patterson and Eugene Williams). The remaining four boys (Clarence Norrie, Ozie Powell, Charles Weems, and Willie Roberson) were going their separate ways. When a fight broke out on the train between the Negroes and seven white boys, the white boys jumped off and complained to railroad guards, who telephoned ahead and stopped the train. Two girls—Victoria Price and Ruby Bates—travelling in male attire, had been with the whites. When the train was stopped, they were taken into custody, at which time they claimed that the Negroes had raped them. When sperm was found in their vaginas, the Negro boys were charged with rape and taken on March 25th to Scottsboro (the county seat) where an armed mob tried unsuccessfully to lynch them.

Less than two weeks later, they were brought to trial. Two court-appointed attorneys failed to talk to their parents, to subpoena eye-witnesses, or even to cross-examine state's witnesses. The death verdict for eight of the nine boys (Roy Wright was remanded to juvenile court) came within a few hours, while ten thousand men from all over the county (the population of Scottsboro was fifteen hundred) hooted outside the court house, where a brass band played "There'll Be A Hot Time in the Old Town Tonight."

If the defense lawyers had bothered to investigate, they

would have discovered that Victoria Price and Ruby Bates were prostitutes. They had been travelling with Jack Tiller and Lester Carter (both of whom had just been released from the chain gang), had had sexual relations with these men the night before, and had been abandoned when the men jumped off the train after the fight with the Negro boys.

The case received no attention in the North until the death sentence was announced. At this time, the International Labor Defense (the group that the John Reed Club had asked Dreiser to join) took an interest, and the National Committee for the Defense of Political Prisoners, with Dreiser as Chairman, came to the aid of the boys. In an open letter to Governor Miller of Alabama, released May 18, 1931, Dreiser, Lincoln Steffens, Franz Boas, Malcolm Cowley, Edward Dahlberg, Burton Rascoe, and many other writers signed a statement which read in part:

> no state in this union has a right to speak of justice as long as the most friendless Negro child accused of a crime receives less than the best defense that would be given its wealthiest white citizen.

They called the trial a "legal crime" and pledged their efforts to bring about justice.

Dreiser used his personal influence in his attempt to free the boys, and he also wrote many letters to influential people and groups, such as the Association of Southern Women for the Prevention of Lynching (July 13, 1931). Although he resigned as chairman of the NCDPP on January 28, 1932, Dreiser remained an active member of the group. On March 22, 1934, for example, he wrote "They Shall Not Die," an eloquent defense of the Scottsboro boys.

Without the help of Dreiser and his group, the Scottsboro boys would have died in the electric chair. Even with their help, the boys were found guilty at another trial (even though Ruby Bates had become a surprise defense witness and claimed that the rape story had been invented by Victoria Price). When this verdict was once again appealed, a third trial ended with the same death sentence. When this was appealed—this time to the Supreme Court—a fourth trial was set for January

20, 1936. Almost five years after the boys had begun their fateful trip, they were still in Death Row. At this trial, however, Haywood Patterson, Andy Wright, Charles Weems, and Clarence Norris were convicted—but Roy Wright, Olen Montgomery, Eugene Williams, and Willie Roberson were freed. It turned out that the Scottsboro Defense Committee had "agreed" to the state's proposal to free four of the boys immediately and the others within the next year. When the state failed to keep its promise, the Defense Committee published in 1938 the terms of the verdict—but by this time the world had lost interest. Andy Wright, the last of the boys to be released, did not get out of jail until June 9, 1950—almost twenty years from the time that he was arrested.

Despite the justice of its cause, the National Committee for the Defense of Political Prisoners was a tool of the American Communist Party—and the Party was as much interested in the publicity as in the fate of the nine boys. Within his own correspondence files, for example, Dreiser had a letter from Earl Browder, complaining about the NAACP, whose efforts were competing with the NCDPP. The motives of the Communist Party in the Harlan miner's strike were equally ambiguous.

When the National Mine Workers of America (AFL) and the National Miner's Union (a communist group) were fighting to control the Pittsburgh miners, William Z. Foster and Joseph Pass asked Dreiser t6 help the communist cause. Dreiser went to Pittsburgh (June 24, 1931) and released a statement through the United Press (June 26, 1931) attacking the AFL as being a tool of the corporations. William L. Green, president of the AFL, denied Dreiser's charges and then wrote him a three thousand word open-letter insisting that the AFL had always had the miner's interest at heart, that the communists were more interested in world revolution than the miners, and that Dreiser had been duped by the Party. Dreiser sent off a hurried note to William Foster and Earl Browder before he answered Green on July 17, 1931. Browder gave Dreiser a point by point rebuttal of Green's letter. "There is not a single issue . . . that Green meets squarely," Browder replied. He maintained that Green accepted the basic principles of capitalism, that he refused to see that the policies of the AFL and the National Civic Federation "are worked out by the same people jointly . . . which includes leading capitalists," and that Green never denied that the union leaders desire "to become capitalists and leave the working class." According to Browder, the AFL functioned to bring bigger profits: "In every industry where the capitalists consider that they can get along without the AFofL, there the AFofL does not exist." Browder rebuked Dreiser for thinking that injunctions could be used against the employers: remember, he said, that "the government which issues the injunction stands above the classes" and is a "class instrument of the capitalists."

When the strike moved into the Harlan, Kentucky coal fields, the fight once again raged between the communist union and the AFL—and Dreiser was once again a voice for the Party. In a New York *Times* interview (September 28, 1931), he noted that a dozen men had been killed in the Harlan fields since May, that the miners' homes had been destroyed, that the soup kitchens had been dynamited, that mine guards had been deputized (Dreiser underlined this fact), that children were starving (again underlined), and that some operators made profits of twenty-five per cent on their company stores. During these months, he continued his correspondence with Earl Browder and the Communist Party of the United States. Browder, in fact, returned two chapters of *Tragic America* (letter dated October 20, 1931) "with a few remarks in pencil" and "suggestions for points to be made in the preface."

In October of 1931, Dreiser invited eighteen distinguished citizens (including Senators Norris, La Follette, Shipstead, and Couzens; also Felix Frankfurter, Charles Taft, Daniel Willard, Henry W. Anderson, Roy Howard, and William Allen White) to investigate the Harlan coal fields with him. When to a man they refused, Dreiser invited his more radical friends: John Dos Passos, Josephine Herbst, Lester Cohen, Samuel Ornitz, Bruce Crawford, Melvin P. Levy, and Mr. and Mrs. Charles Rumford Walker. Browder advised (October 29, 1931) that Dreiser not invite Arthur Garfield Hays because Hays had been active in the Scottsboro case for the NAACP and would "indirectly link you up also with his friends of the NAACP in the publicity . . . [and thus] weaken the effect of your own participation," a letter that once again revealed the ulterior motives behind the communist's involvement.

When Dreiser arrived in Harlan, he set up his committee as an investigating board. His plan was to publicize his findings and gain sympathy for the miners. All did not work, however, as planned. Herndon Evans, the publisher of *The Pineville Sun*, the local paper, was obviously on the side of the owners. During one of Dreiser's inquiries, Evans interrupted him and the investigator found himself being investigated:

"What is your annual income?" Evans asked Dreiser.

"Approximately $35,000," Dreiser replied.

"Do you give any of it to charity?"

"No."

"That's all," said Evans

While Dreiser explained that he distrusted the big charities, and that if one averaged his income over his life period it would be "very moderate," every newspaper, except the New York *Times*, described Evans as humiliating Dreiser. "Dreiser Bested" ran the headlines of the Lewis, Idaho *Tribune* (November 7, 1931).

If this was a humiliation, it was slight compared to what followed. As imprudent as ever, Dreiser had taken a woman with him to Kentucky. When she disappeared into his hotel room one night, a detective in the hire of the mine owners put a string of toothpicks outside the door. When the toothpicks were still standing in the early hours of the morning, his deductions became the next day's headlines. The Los Angeles *Examiner* gave the woman's name as Marie Pergain and described her as a "vivacious young blonde, whose status with the investigators was never divulged" (November 9, 1931). When Dreiser returned to New York the next day, he held a news conference and maintained that he was impotent ("You may lock me in the most luxurious boudoir with the most attractive woman in the world, and be convinced that we are discussing nothing more than books of art or some aesthetic problem of one kind or another"), an excuse that did not convince the Bell County Grand Jury, which on No-

vember 9 indicated Dreiser and Marie on charges of adultery—
and Dreiser on November 16 on charges of criminal syndicalism. Although the charges were later dropped, Judge Jones
demanded that the Governor of New York return Dreiser to
Kentucky. Dreiser replied with his own attack on the mine
owners and on Judge Jones.

Dreiser had previously taken verbal shots at Judge Jones,
charging in a news release (November 12, 1931) that miners
had been arrested for owning a copy of *The Daily Worker*,
that no miner had ever been called for jury duty, that the
miners had been deprived of fire arms, that Jones sent the
penniless miners two hundred miles away for trial, thus virtually depriving them of a hearing before sentencing, that Jones
favored the United Mine Workers Union (AFL) over the
National Mine Workers, and that Jones's wife had a financial
interest in the Harlan Coal Field Mine. Dreiser followed this
with another release (December 6, 1931), charging that Sheriff
Blair had deputized the mine guards that had raided the
strikers' homes, that the rich mine-owners ruled by terror and
strike breaking (that they actually shot protesting workers,
intimidated women and children, dynamited soup kitchens,
and harassed relief workers), and that the Red Cross did not
help the starving miners unless they promised to leave the
communist union. Dreiser carried his battle into the next year
when, on February 26, 1932, he blamed the Associated Press
for a biased account of the Harlan strike ("The Associated
Press stressed two facts: First that a miner, had as a former
mine contractor, once earned five hundred dollars in a single
month. Second that Mr. Dreiser's own income in the last year
or two had been rather large"), getting the assistant general
manager, Jackson S. Elliott, to admit that Herndon Evans of
The Pineville Sun "has been . . . on the other side of the
controversy."

This publicity, however, did not enhance Dreiser's public
image. Sherwood Anderson, addressing a group of college
boys, was shocked to find that his audience believed Dreiser
had gone to Harlan for the publicity. Anderson responded
(December 6, 1931): "Ye gods. Even the young [refuse] to
believe that any man can do anything for clean reasons. Taking

for granted that . . . artists . . . are also business men . . . or grubbing movie stars." He maintained that if Dreiser could be extradited and found guilty of criminal syndicalism, then what the country needed was "more criminal syndicalists."

Earl Browder also appreciated Dreiser's Harlan work. He wrote (November 24, 1931), congratulated Dreiser, and told him that while he (Browder) was out of town Dreiser could consult William Foster or William Weinstone when he needed to know the Party's position.

Despite his intimate relationship with the Communist Party, Dreiser denied at this time that he was a communist. When asked his political affiliation, he replied that he was an "Equitist," by which he meant that he desired a "fair break for all" (New York *Herald Tribune,* November 22, 1931). There seems to be no reason to doubt Dreiser's own description of his political position. Never once during these months of strife did he ever say that he wanted to abolish capitalism. What he wanted was a more even balance between the poor and the wealthy.

Dreiser's correspondence at this time with two men named Mooney well illustrates how he moved emotionally back and forth between the upper and the lower classes. One Mooney was James D., Vice-President of General Motors in charge of foreign sales. The other Mooney was Thomas J., prisoner number 31921 at San Quentin, who was serving a life sentence for supposedly killing ten persons in the bombing of the 1916 Preparedness Parade in San Francisco. While the Vice-President of General Motors invited Dreiser to his mansion at Oyster Bay, prisoner number 31921 pleaded with Dreiser, often in letters smuggled through the prisoners' underground, to help get him out of the prison in which he had already spent fifteen years. In a letter dated July 8, 1935, the General-Motor's-Mooney recalled the day that Dreiser visited him at Oyster Bay, at which time the radical novelist and the business executive were becalmed in a sailboat and spent a leisurely afternoon floating around Oyster Bay, discussing philosophy and economic theory while their legs dangled in the water (truly a modern tale of a tub). On May 29, 1930, while on a car trip through the Southwest and California, Dreiser visited the San Quentin-Mooney, after which he said at a press conference that "If Mooney is not freed, he should, by rights, be taken out of prison by force." He regretted the way "government is moving toward an oligarchy. The government is run in Wall Street," he continued, "not in Washington." With his impressions of Russian bureaucracy fresh in mind, he concluded: "The difference between the four Wall Street banking houses that run this country and the Soviet central control committee is the difference between Tweedle-Dee and Tweedle-Dum." [11]

Thomas J. Mooney's story goes back to July 22, 1916. On that day a bomb exploded killing ten and injuring forty at the San Francisco War Preparedness Parade. Mooney was indicted for murder, along with his wife Rena, Warren K. Billings, Israel Weinberg, and Edward D. Nolan. Mooney was a member of the Moulder's Union, Local 164, and hated by the local street car company for his attempt to organize the motormen and conductors. Billings was the former president of the Boot and Shoe Workers' Union. Nolan was chief of the pickets in the local machinist strike. And Weinberg was on the executive board of the Jitney Bus Operators' Union (which was in competition with the local street car company).

The anti-labor force in San Francisco, particularly the United Railroads of San Francisco and the Pacific Gas and Electric Company, were out "to get" Mooney, and they hired the Pinkerton Detective Agency's Martin Swanson to do it. In July of 1916, he tried to bribe both Warren Billings and Israel Weinberg, offering them each five thousand dollars to testify that Mooney had participated in a bombing incident at San Bruno, California. When Billings and Weinberg rejected Swanson's offer, they also went on his black list. After Mooney was indicted, Martin Swanson actually became District Attorney Charles Fickert's special deputy. Fickert had dismissed indictments against the heads of the Pacific Gas and Electric Company and the United Railroads when these officials became implicated in a San Francisco graft scandal.

On February 24, 1917, Mooney was convicted, primarily on the testimony of two witnesses: a jobless dope addict named John McDonald and a cattle dealer named Frank C.

Oxman. McDonald testified that he saw Billings arrive at Stewart and Market Streets at 2:00 P.M. There Billings supposedly dropped a suitcase and walked to a saloon from which emerged Mooney. This story, however, was indeed suspect: his description of the men did not fit either Mooney or Billings. Moreover, a chance photograph taken at 2:01 P.M. (as a clock in the background proved) placed Rena and Tom Mooney on the roof of the Eilers Building, more than a mile from the explosion. Five year's later, McDonald admitted that Swanson, Fickert, and others had made him perjure himself.

Oxman, the other witness, testified that he saw Mooney arrive in Weinberg's jitney bus, Mooney carrying the supposedly bomb-filled suitcase. (The suitcase held a steel pipe loaded with dynamite, around which had been stuffed bullets, ball-bearings, and jagged pieces of iron. Some believe a timing device caused the explosion, but others deduced that the suitcase was dropped from a building.) Oxman's testimony was equally suspect: the only vehicles that travelled down Market Street previous to the explosion were the official photographer's car and an ambulance. Moreover, Oxman said that a friend could corroborate his story. When the friend (named Rigall) was investigated, he produced letters Oxman had written him, offering "two hundred dollars in the clear" to testify as "a expurt witness. You will only haf to anser three & four questions and I will post you on them." Oxman was brought to trial for perjury—and acquitted. The Supreme Court refused to grant Mooney a retrial, maintaining that Oxman's letter (admitting perjury) was not a part of the trial evidence.

In retrospect, it is clear that Billings and Mooney were the victims of a well-organized plan to wipe out labor agitators in the San Francisco area. Mooney was condemned to die by hanging, while Billings was sentenced to life in prison. When the cases of Mrs. Mooney and Weinberg came up, the evidence by that time was so obviously perjured that they were both acquitted and the charges against Nolan were dropped. When the outraged voice of labor was finally heard, President Wilson asked for clemency; and on November 28, 1918, Governor W. D. Stephens of California commuted Mooney's sentence to life in prison.

After this, Mooney suffered one frustration after another. All of the governors of California were uninterested in his plight. While parole was often within Mooney's grasp, he repeatedly refused this possibility because it suggested initial guilt. On November 15, 1928, Dreiser wrote Governor C. C. Young, who was sympathetic to Mooney, but Young rejected Dreiser's plea for a full pardon. Young was followed by Governor James Rolph, who had been Mayor of San Francisco at the time of the bombing. Rolph, obviously prejudiced, held a public hearing on the case, appointing as his chief advisers Judge Matt Sullivan and Lewis Byington. Judge Sullivan was a friend of District Attorney Fickert and a corporation lawyer. Lewis Byington was also a corporation lawyer and a relative of the chief lawyer of the Pacific Gas and Electric Company. No one was surprised when this group found Mooney guilty: their ninety-page report spent ten pages on the case and eighty pages attacking Mooney as "unpatriotic," as "radical," and as "anarchistic."

On November 6, 1932, Dreiser spoke along with Lincoln Steffens before eleven thousand people in San Francisco's civic auditorium. The crowd warmly applauded Dreiser and booed the mention of Governor Rolph. The principal speaker was one Paul M. Callicotte who maintained (his story was later discredited) that he had planted the fateful suitcase. After the meeting, the crowd paraded through the city singing the "Internationale" and waving red flags.[12]

When the liberal Culbert A. Olson became Governor of California, Mooney was finally released from San Quentin. Convicted on February 24, 1917, released on January 7, 1939, Mooney spent twenty-two years in prison for a crime that he never committed. Warren Billings was not released at this time because he had a record of prior convictions. Billings, the forgotten man in the case, grew each year more and more bitter —finally breaking with Mooney and accepting (against Mooney's advice) parole instead of pardon.

The Harlan strike, the Scottsboro trial, and the Mooney case were *causes célèbres* for the Communist Party; and while Dreiser participated actively in each cause, it is unlikely that

he would have become involved (as he had not become involved with Sacco and Vanzetti when they were executed in
1927) if his attention had not been directed by the Communist
Party.

The Communist Party could so move Dreiser because he
had given his heart to Russia after the 1927 journey. The
journey was a pivotal point in his life, turning his attention
toward politics in the same way that his summer at Woods
Hole turned his attention toward science. Without this political
interest Dreiser would not have written a book like *Tragic
America*.

Loaded with statistics, *Tragic America* was a broadside
attack on American corporations, the church, and even the
big charities. Relying heavily on Myer's *History of American
Fortunes*, Dreiser went at tedious length through the history of
American big business, showing the way the trusts created
inequities between capital and labor's share of the profits, how
they controlled the American press, how they bribed and influenced national and state legislatures, and how they were
responsible for miscellaneous other evils. Dreiser saw the corporation as the serpent in the garden of the new world: it had
betrayed the promise of the frontier by greedily acquiring
immense amounts of land (Dreiser began with Congress giving
the Ohio Land Company 100,000 acres in 1792 and ended
with Congress giving the railroads 155,504,944 acres between
1850 and 1872)—a point William Faulkner would make with
far more literary skill in "The Bear."

As in *Dreiser Looks at Russia*, Dreiser's main concern was
with the lack of "equity" between capital and labor. Once
again arguing from a concept of nature, he maintained that
"Nature's way is a balance." A look at history, he went on,
shows us "the same balance between the ruling power and
the masses as can be found between the sun in nature and the
planets." The primary law of government, he insisted, is that
"the executives of a nation can, by the law of nature, take no
more power to themselves than the people will that they take."
Dreiser concluded: "Personally I am for a reconstruction of
our economic life in order to restore that balance." [13]

As one might expect, *Tragic America* was not well received by the general public. In a New York *Times* review (January 24, 1932), Simon Strunsky pointed out that Dreiser claimed that the "Methodist-Episcopals" had 893,881 missionaries, most of them in China. Yet the actual number of all American missionaries, representing forty denominations, was slightly over 8,000. Strunsky tabulated a score of other factual mistakes, and then concluded: "why should Mr. Dreiser have plunged into the jungle of concrete information where 891,000 Methodist missionaries in China are just as possible as 891 missionaries would be, and $2,000,000 a day railroad revenue is just the same as $2,000,000,000, and the American people's readiness for communism is demonstrated by Mr. Dreiser's 'rather fancying' that they are?"

Even though Dreiser attacked both the big corporations and the big unions ("they are led by the Greens and the Walls whose business it appears to be to reconcile them [the workers] to the rule and almost charity of Big Business"), *Tragic America* was not even well received by the communist critics. In his *New Masses* review of *Tragic America*, Bennett Stevens rejected Dreiser's thesis that big business had betrayed the possibility of an "ideal" Republic, modelled on the concepts of the "framers of the Constitution." When the "true" revolution came, the Constitution would also have to be swept aside, Stevens declared. He objected even more strenuously to Dreiser's belief that the federal government could oversee strikes, insisting that the government was a tool of the corporations. While he was pleased with Dreiser's attack on the non-communist unions, he was displeased that Dreiser did not explain how the "left-wing unions" could better help the workers.[14]

As Stevens' review well suggests, Dreiser was far from a doctrinaire communist. Like most of his other attitudes, his politics rested more on an emotional than an intellectual base. Yet the Communist Party—with its proletarian and secular emphases—obviously had emotional appeal. When Dreiser suggested this to Sherwood Anderson, Anderson wrote (December 21, 1931) that he was dubious about the virtues of communism: "It may be the answer and then again it may only be a new sort of puritanism."

12

Toward Communism

The Dreiser-Mencken correspondence had broken off in March of 1926, after Mencken had unfavorably reviewed *An American Tragedy* in that month's *American Mercury*. He had described Dreiser's novel as "a vast sloppy, chaotic thing of 385,000 words—at least 250,000 of them unnecessary." Mencken's attack on Dreiser had been in part personal. He wrote Helen Richardson (January 30, 1946) that Dreiser had angered him when he visited Baltimore on December 12, 1925, the day before Mencken's mother died. Over twenty lears later, Mencken remembered that Dreiser had called upon him while Helen waited in a freezing car. He especially resented Dreiser's "aloof indifference to my mother's illness. It was a long while afterward before I felt close to him again."

The split between Dreiser and Mencken, however, had a deeper basis than mutually hurt feelings. The two friends were moving ideologically further and further away from each other. By the mid-twenties, Mencken was politically old-hat (one recalls what Jake Barnes and Bill Gorton say about Mencken in *The Sun Also Rises*); and by the thirties, Mencken and Dreiser were politically at odds. With the Hoovervilles and farm foreclosures, the time moved out from under Mencken. He had appealed to the intelligentsia when he had attacked the stupid conventions and the outrageous hypocrisies of the middle class, and the religious fanaticism and rigidity of mind of the lower class, especially the Fundamentalists. With the depression, the lower classes became a kind of economic hero: novelists attacked the dry rot of the very rich (for example, Fitzgerald's *Tender Is the Night*), or they sentimentally elevated the common man, particularly the displaced worker, to a position he did not deserve in a world that suddenly became black and white (as in Steinbeck's *The Grapes of Wrath*). A new kind of romanticism had won out—the common man endowed with a new dignity, the sentimentalized victim of a system which had cruelly exploited him. Mencken was a social —and not political—critic; and when the "booboisie" was more to be pitied than hated, his caricatures were no longer funny. Unlike Dreiser, he never moved from his distrust of the social and religious structure to a distrust of the political and economic system.

Dreiser's distrust was moving him toward communism. He was drawn toward communism in the early thirities because he felt that the Republican and Democratic parties had "sadly merged" their views. Dreiser first believed that the NRA was an attempt to bring about prosperity "not for the masses, but for the classes" [1] Although Dreiser warmed slightly to Roosevelt, his feelings once again cooled when Roosevelt seemed intent on getting America into the Second World War. Dreiser also hated the do-gooders like New York Police Commissioner Mulrooney, who asked him (March 7, 1932) to support the Big Brother movement because "crime is the result of wrong leadership." While Dreiser never answered Mulrooney's letter, he circled the word "crime" and wrote in the margin of the letter that "[crime] is more the result of economic inequality & gross social *injustice* [Dreiser's emphasis] Drop the big brother nonsense and work for something worth while." Since Dreiser saw nothing "worth while" to work for within the American party system, it is not surprising that in "America and Her Communists" (October 31, 1931), he called for a third party based on "Marx's attack on the limits of capitalism." [2]

Although there was a "cool" period in between the two dates, Dreiser's zeal for the Communist Party was as great in the early thirties as it was when he actually joined the Party in August of 1945. He refused, for example, Max Eastman's request (April, 1933) that he condemn Russia for the way it handled Trotsky. In 1925, Eastman had published *Since Lenin Died*, which revealed the means by which the "triumvirate" had slandered and then demoted Trotsky in their final take-over.[3] Eastman had eventually retreated to his four-room farm house in Croton-on-the-Hudson after he had been expelled from the Party and had been attacked—often viciously—by his former friends. Even Trotsky himself had repudiated Eastman's charges, and it would remain for history to vindicate Eastman's assessment of Stalin. Unlike Eastman, what reservations Dreiser had about Stalin were subsumed by his enthusiasm for the new state.

> I am so much interested in the present difficulties in Russia [he replied to Eastman] and in Russia's general fate, that I am not prepared, without very serious consideration, to throw a monkey-wrench such as this [the support of Trostsky] could prove to be, into their machinery.

Only three months before, Dreiser had refused, at the request of the John Reed Club's Executive Board, to support Charles Yale Harrison. Harrison, who wrote Dreiser on January 20, 1933, had just resigned from the *New Masses* when Trotsky's daughter committed suicide. As late as February 6, 1937, Dreiser was still getting letters (this one from the American Communists for the Defense of Leon Trotsky) and still refusing to support Trotsky.

Because Dreiser could never reconcile his political ideals with the reality of American politics, he leaped beyond America and bestowed his romantic expectations, his vivid sense of possibility, upon Communist Russia. "More and more, as I observe the world," he wrote in July of 1933, "I am satisfied that the Russian revolution is the one and only thing that has opened the door to a more equitable, more creative and more human social order." [4] As Dreiser became disillusioned with American politics, he also became disillusioned with American communism—but, significantly, not Russian communism, which was far enough removed to survive in Dreiser's dreams.

Dreiser saw that American communism had a hard row to hoe because "at the present time America does not possess that class-consciousness so necessary for it." [5] When Dallas McKown wrote him that he was trying to establish an organization like the National Committee for the Defense of Political Prisoners, but free of the American Communist Party, Dreiser replied (June 9, 1932) that such a group might be useful because the American masses could not understand or be moved by the Communist's "highly involved intellectual and idealistic terms." Dreiser felt that if the Communist Party were to succeed in America, it had to become indigenous and grasp problems peculiar to America, problems that could not be dictated from abroad. When he wrote Max Eastman at this time (June 14, 1933), he said that he had great difficulty accepting the American Communist Party, particularly their infighting and their squabbling over power.

> What I cannot understand [about American Communism] is why there are so many groups [78 in all] and why they waste so much time critically belaboring each other and ridiculing each other for their interpretations of Marx, when the world situation and particularly the American situation requires a united front against a very obvious problem.

Eight months later (February 6, 1934), in another letter to Eastman, Dreiser specified the radical "factions." He complained of the feuds between men like A. J. Muste (Chairman of the American Workers' Party) and Alfred Bingham (executive secretary of the Farmers-Political Federation). Muste gave radical priority to the worker, Bingham to the farmer. Dreiser felt that this squabbling was needless, since they were both working for the good of "the general mass" and "both agree that the white collar class must be included."

Dreiser was far more interested in securing benefits for the masses than in supporting American communism with its doctrines that were often more relevant to conditions in Russia than those in America. The struggle within the Party only supported Dreiser's belief that all men—communist or capitalist—were naturally selfish. He wrote James D. Mooney (December 16, 1931) that Marx and communism frighten the masses, and he wrote to Bruce Crawford (January 15, 1935) that "I despair of communist efforts in this country. There are too many groups, too much quarreling, and the mass sentiment of America seems to be more anti than pro." Crawford, the communist editor of *Crawford's Weekly*, had accompanied Dreiser to Harlan. In an earlier letter (September 22, 1932), Dreiser had told him that "I have put the oars in the boat and am floating." He added: "I now see things I did not see anywhere as clearly when we were both in Kentucky."

The inequality between the classes—a concern that Dreiser had voiced thirty-five years earlier in his *Ev'ry Month* essays —was now an obsession. In almost all his articles—and even his personal letters—he would touch upon this subject, as if talking about it helped. "I feel that the immense gulf between wealth and poverty in America and throughout the world should be narrowed," he wrote (January 20, 1933) to Ralph Fabri, who had painted Helen Richardson's portrait for him. "I feel the government should . . . effect the welfare of all the people—not that of a given class." He began to feel that the machine—more than the Communist Party—was the source of new hope. On September 22, 1932, he wrote both Bruce Crawford and Chales E. Yost that America needs "the technician as a part of a newer kind of state." While he did not elaborate, Dreiser had in mind Howard Scott's economic scheme called Technocracy, which was just beginning to get public attention.

Scott and his associates began with the fact that employment reached its highest peak in America in 1918, while production reached its highest peak in 1929—at a time when the employment rate was declining. The reason for this inverse ratio between employment and production was obvious: the machine reduced the need for labor and yet produced more goods than could be turned out by hand. The source of economic evil, Scott insisted, was not with the machine but with the system. While the energy in a ton of coal remained fixed, the price of the coal continually changed. Under the price system, the goods were made not to use but to sell—and sell for a profit. The number of goods sold determined the profit, which is why each producer wanted to increase his market (at home and abroad) and to cut the cost of production. The use of machinery achieved both these ends: the machine mass-produced goods with less need of labor.

In order to buy machinery, however, the owner had to secure credit; but before one paid for the most heavy machinery, it was obsolete; and the industrialist had to borrow once again by issuing more bonds and mortgages—and paying interest on these debts. In order to pay the debt, he then had to sell more goods. When the debt increased faster than the sale of his goods, the system broke down—and this, said Scott, is what happened in the Depression of 1929. Even when a wealthy family (like Ford) had more money than it could personally spend, it could only reinvest this money—always with the expectation of getting profit or interest from the investment. This forced the debtors to borrow more in the hope of raising production sales. Not only was the worker left out of this cycle, he was its victim.

Since Edward Bellamy anticipated in *Looking Backward* (1888) many of Scott's ideas, Technocracy was not really new. While Scott had been at work on his theory since 1919, Technocracy would have had little appeal between 1933 and 1937 if the foundations of American capitalism had not been rocked by the Depression. Scott wanted to do away with all debt instruments (bonds, stocks, debentures) based on money values. While vague about who should control the machines, he believed that an engineer could calculate the amount of goods the machine could produce in a fixed period of time; these goods could then be divided by the number of the population and distributed on a pro rata basis (through "energy certificates," the total number not to exceed the amount of goods produced).

This was the plan for which Dreiser had been looking: Scott not only curbed the bankers and speculators, but he gave the masses an equal share of the fruits of invention and industrial genius. Dreiser wrote as early as 1932: I see now "the enormous significance of the machine in any equitable society, and the need of the technician as a part of a newer kind of state." [6] Since Dreiser had always thought of the universe as a machine, he could give imaginative consent to a machine society, and he saw Technocracy as the new hope.

Yet he also saw that Technocracy needed a political sponsor, and he hoped that Upton Sinclair would warm to the idea. Sinclair was running for governor of California in 1934 on the EPIC (End Poverty in California) ticket; and in a sympathetic portrait of Sinclair, written before but published in *Esquire* after Sinclair had lost the election, Dreiser parenthetically endorsed Scott's theory, thereby linking Sinclair and Scott, whether they wanted to be linked or not (Sinclair saw a connection with fascism). He called for an Engineer Dictator to take control of industry. Capitalism, he maintained (rephrasing Scott's idea that capitalists believed goods were made to be sold and not used), restricted and limited production, kept goods scarce and prices high. The Engineer Dictator would have control over raw material, machinery, and labor; and he "could flood and bury and smother the people of America with an avalanche of goods and services such as no Utopian dream ever conceived of." [7] A year later, Dreiser wrote Sinclair (November 25, 1935), thanked him for sending the *National EPIC Magazine*, and encouraged Sinclair to endorse Technocracy, "because I cannot see how your programs of production for use can be divorced from the technical programs of Howard Scott. . . . The two movements should be harmonized" (Dreiser was even more emphatic about merging the EPIC movement and Technocracy in another letter to Sinclair written on December 27, 1935).

From 1933 to 1935, Dreiser also wrote a series of essays in support of Scott's ideas, although in some cases he went beyond what Scott expected from Technocracy. In "Challenge to the Creative Man" (November, 1933), for example, he insisted for the first time that capitalism be abolished and that the workers control production.[8] He felt that there were other motives—fame, recognition, intellectual curiosity—that could inspire the individual as much as money, and he praised the Soviet Union for uniting practical and creative energy.[9]

His attack on the corporation had suddenly become an argument *for* individualism. In "Why Capitalists Praise Democracy" (July, 1934), he pointed out that the trusts defend capitalism in the name of individual incentive and yet work to destroy such incentives. Until the trusts "abandon monopoly," he concluded, "let us have an end of this hypocritical hoopla concerning the rights of the individual, the values of democracy, and the need for preserving them at whatever cost." [10]

Dreiser had expressed this idea more softly in an earlier essay, "Individualism and the Jungle" (January 2, 1932), in which he said that society is not a jungle, that the masses should be protected from ruthless exploitation by a favored few, and that history had been working to suppress rugged individualism (an idea that presupposed teleology and thus contradicted his mechanistic beliefs). What America needed was "a limited form of individualism which will guarantee to all, in so far as possible, the right, if there is such a right, to life, liberty, and the pursuit of happiness; also an equitable share in the economic results of [group labor]." [11] Dreiser repeated this argument in "Harlan Miners Speak" (1932) and stated it once again in his review of the play *They Shall Not Die* (March 24, 1934).

These were significant changes in Dreiser's thinking: individualism was still a good—but it must have limits. The theory of rugged individualism, he wrote in "What Is Democracy?" (December, 1940), "ignored . . . the consideration of 'what happens if everybody bolts for the exits in a theatre fire.'" What worked for one era would not necessarily work for another—and Dreiser suggested that the age of rugged individualism was nearing its end.[12] He now felt—and this is perhaps the most significant change in his thinking—that planned action could do what he previously thought that only blind force could achieve:

> For there can and will be change . . . [which will come with] thought—and after thought, action toward ushering in the new day—not merely stubborn and angry and blind use of force on both sides.[13]

Behind these changes in Dreiser's thinking was his belief that the machine could bring the new millennium. The machine will permit "the support of more people on earth," he wrote Sherwood Anderson (January 2, 1936). Several years later, when Anderson visited him in Los Angeles, they discussed the function of the machine in the new society. Anderson was less enthusiastic than Dreiser: "the machine for all it brings in the way of benefits," he wrote Dreiser after he returned home (November 23, 1939), "brings at least an almost equal hurt." And while Dreiser's enthusiasm for Technocracy did not wane until the late thirties, he never convinced Upton Sinclair that Scott's ideas were sound, nor could he persuade Scott himself to align Technocracy with a political group or movement.

Although Dreiser was giving more attention to Technocracy than to the American Communist Party during the mid-thirties, we know from his correspondence with the National Council for the Defense of Political Prisoners that he was still active in communist causes. On February 7, 1935, he went to the Chinese consulate to protest the political harassment of Agnes Smedley, a political critic, who feared for her life in Shanghai, China. On April 18, 1935, he wrote Warden Holohan of San Quentin about James McNamara (the anarchist who had blown up the Los Angeles *Times* building in 1910), complaining that McNamara's cell was recently raided and left-wing books were taken, including Dreiser's *Tragic America*. In one instance, Dreiser leaped before he looked. On April 5, 1932, Patrick Kearney (who had adapted *An American Tragedy* for the stage) wired him that he had been fired from Universal Studios because he was a member of the John Reed Club. Dreiser attacked Universal in a news release only to learn from Forrest Bailey of the American Civil Liberties Union (April 19, 1932) that Kearney had been fired for drunkenness—not because he was a member of the John Reed Club—and that Kearney was already back on the payroll. Bailey told Dreiser that Kearney had also wired Joseph Stalin, whom we trust was less disturbed about the matter than Dreiser. While Dreiser's impetuousness here is understandable, it is also characteristic of his political mentality: he acted impulsively, was easily angered by the big corporations, and would support the underdog even though he did not always have the facts.

By the mid-thirties, Dreiser had so many political irons in the fire that none was really hot. He was still willing to lend his name to communist causes, especially if the request came from Moscow itself. He was also trying to convince both Howard Scott and Upton Sinclair that Technocracy should merge with the EPIC movement. In the meantime, he had changed his mind about Roosevelt, whom he supported instead of the Communist Party in the 1936 election. In a New York *Times* statement, he praised the President because he had saved the nation in a time of crisis by establishing a kind of socialism (although he later qualified the word "socialism").[14]

Dreiser might have continued to vacillate among a number of political positions, if war had not broken out in Spain. On February 8, 1937, he responded to a plea from Roger Chase of the American Friends of Spanish Democracy to help send ambulances to the Spanish front. On July 13, 1938, he sailed for Paris to attend the *Rassemblement Universal pour la Paix*, sponsored by the League of American Writers. After speaking at the meeting, Dreiser journeyed to Spain itself, arriving in Barcelona from Paris on July 30, 1938, where he spent the next three days visiting the Ebro River battlefield. In the New York *Times*, he vividly recorded his impressions of the simple people who were tired of war but determined and resigned to the Loyalist cause. On September 15, 1938, Dreiser was the guest of honor at a dinner for three hundred, with Malcolm Cowley as chairman, sponsored by the America League of Writers. In his speech, which was also carried over WQXR, Dreiser drew heavy applause when he said that the United States "cannot take the position of an innocent and harmless people" and still carry on trade, banking, and other relations with countries which "openly threaten to bring about the war we so much dread."[15]

The war in Spain swung Dreiser once more toward the communist cause. When Alfred M. Bingham told him (August 16, 1939) that *Common Sense* planned to run a symposium based on the growing fear that our present civilization would be destroyed ("The question might be asked, whether the present fear for Western Civilization indicates a genuine parallel to the collapse of Roman civilization"), Dreiser responded with "The Dawn Is in the East," a whole-hearted endorsement of communist Russia. Since life itself is nothing but flux, every civilization must expect change, Dreiser maintained. Civilization will not pass. It will proceed in a new form—and Russian communism will be the next dawn, will mark an advance and not a decline in western history. Significantly, before Dreiser released this article, he asked Ruth Kennell, who had been his translator throughout his Russian trip, if he should support the Soviet cause. Still faithful to the USSR, Miss Kennell (in a letter dated September 20, 1939) eagerly endorsed Russia.

If Dreiser needed Miss Kennell's advice, it was probably only to confirm his own feelings about the course of international events. As early as 1932, he saw war approaching and blamed it on the capitalists' desire to protect their interests both at home and abroad. He pointed out at this time that America was caught between Russian and Chinese communism and lordly Japanese ambitions. He maintained that America hoped that Japan would invade Manchuria and put a stop to communism, after which the western world could suppress Japan. He also insisted that both American and European capitalists wanted war because it would help the economy.[16]

As Dreiser blamed the First World War on England and her colonial empire, he believed that England was once again manipulating events to bring about a Second World War. England had supposedly used Germany as a cat's paw to defeat Communist Russia, but Hitler had finally turned against England, his real enemy. "England, which represents the capitalistic system, wishes to destroy the non-profit systems."[17] As justice would not come to America until there was an "equity" between the workers and the owners, so also it would not come to the world "until fair play between capital and labour in the various nationalities has been established."[18] The USSR, he said, could best bring equity between nations because it was

no longer an experiment but a proved success affecting the health, education, social welfare and hourly development of nearly 200,000,000 people, who no longer face enforced ignorance and hunger and social degradation but the marvelous privilege of working one for all and all for one.[19]

Once again more interested in national and world affairs than either science or literature, Dreiser welcomed the opportunity to write another political book. While his main concern in *America Is Worth Saving* was with showing why America should not go to war for England, he was also concerned with showing that both English and American capitalism had suppressed the masses and prevented economic equity. He began his book with a catalogue of changes from the invention of the electric light bulb to the discovery of uranium 235—and then maintained that the only thing that had not changed was the poverty of the masses and the comfort of the classes. "Forty-one per cent of all our [American] familes live on an average of $758 a year," he maintained. Eight million families face starvation while another eleven million are fighting the cruelest poverty.[20]

He believed that government actually worked to keep the imbalance between the rich and the poor. Perhaps with Howard Scott's thesis in mind, he pointed to the way the government stored surplus gasoline, destroyed surplus meats, ploughed under surplus cotton and potatoes, and poured oil on mountains of surplus oranges. "Our system of distribution is geared to an economy of scarcity," he concluded (20).

Dreiser once again maintained that the machine could offer the masses a way out of their predicament, and here he is clearly reflecting the lingering influence of Howard Scott's Technocracy. We have to accept the burdens and the benefits of the machine: "we have no choice but to go forward to the inevitable social implication of our technology" (24).

He wanted the capitalist system changed—and changed immediately. The corporation was the source of almost all economic evils: it created monopolies, polluted government, censored the press and the radio, and suppressed labor. As long as our economic system exploited the masses, America would continue to be selfish (183). If our economic system fairly distributed the country's wealth, the individual would be more altruistic and less dissatisfied.

Dreiser's journey toward communism was also a journey toward brotherhood and selflessness, qualities he admired in the Quakers. Cowperwood and Solon Barnes represented extreme points of view. Both died, interestingly enough, disappointed with what life had brought them: they were victims of American extremes, of an economic system that was out of balance, of an ideal that was impossible to realize and a reality that would never be ideal.

Dreiser felt that the evils of capitalism in America were the economic evils of the world. He insisted that the capitalistic countries, particularly England and France, had tried to destroy democracy (and here he really meant socialism or communism) wherever they found it: in Finland, in Spain (1936–38), in Germany (by destroying the Weimar Republic and actually assisting Hitler who finally turned on them) and in Russia (where "for the first time in history the intervention doesn't come off") (*33*). He insisted once again that England plotted with Hitler to conquer Russia and that Hitler had "double-crossed" England before England could double-cross him (*46*). His main evidence was a long list of German capitalists who supported Hitler and then another list of English capitalists who supported the Germans:

> Those [the German capitalists] were the men behind Hitler. But who was behind them? Beyond a doubt, their brother-monopolists in the "democracies." . . . We know that Vickers of England has business connections with the German arm trust. . . . The enormous increase in the profits of Hitler's monopolistic-backers in Germany since 1933 was really given them by the City of London under the standstill agreement of Germany's foreign debt. Schroder's Bank was known in London as the "bridge" between Hitler and Lombard Street. (*194*)

American capitalism was supposedly behind English capitalism, and Dreiser even implicated his old friend, James D. Mooney, the General Motor's executive in charge of foreign sales and investments who had received Hitler's "order of the German Eagle" for service to the state of Germany (*202*).

While no one could deny that capitalistic money was invested throughout Europe prior to the Second World War, to base a capitalistic plot upon a series of common investments overloaded the evidence; *America Is Worth Saving* was hardly a definitive study of the causes leading to the war. Dreiser's book does, however, reveal his growing despair with capitalism —both American and international capitalism—and shows him on the doorstep of Russian communism. Russia, he said, is the only country in the world that has substantially helped the masses (*137*). In contrast, 742 American corporations control half the cash assets of the country, half of the capital assets, two-fifths of the other assets, and nearly two-thirds of non-tax-exempt investments. The fate of the masses was inextricably connected with the fate of the corporation: "Our jobs depend on them." This is what the corporations wanted, because now they can "take complete control of the government, as they did in Germany, Italy and Spain, so that the shackles on the people may be legally fastened" (*226–27*). Dreiser concluded *America Is Worth Saving* with an address to the people: he pleaded that they rise in mass and use their collective power to keep America out of the war and to delimit the power of the corporations. "Only the mass can get America out of the mess" (*292*).

Dreiser had great trouble getting *America Is Worth Saving* published. The book was originally contracted by Oskar Piest of the Veritas Press, who knew of Dreiser's antiwar sentiments. When Piest saw Dreiser's draft of the book (then titled *America Keep Out!*), he was very displeased. He wrote Dreiser (October 2, 1940) that he particularly disliked its communist leanings, told him that Russia was as much a terroristic state as Germany or Spain, and asked him to delete Chapter 14 (in which Dreiser claimed that English and American finance had cooperated with Hitler to destroy democracy) and to omit his discussion of American finance. Three weeks later Piest's doubts about publishing the books had increased, and he was trying to break his contract with Dreiser. In a letter dated October 24, 1940, he said that the federal government would think he was part of the Nazi propaganda machine if he published Dreiser's book. Since Piest was an alien, he feared that this would ruin his chance to become an American citizen. This was the the fourth time in Dreiser's life (his experiences with *Sister Carrie, The Titan,* and *The "Genius"* were the other three) that a publisher had tried to break his contract with Dreiser.

William Lengel, Dreiser's good friend and agent, had anticipated Piest's decision not to publish Dreiser's manuscript. He wrote Dreiser (September 19, 1940) that the "Book was designed to show the futility of America getting into war and to show that our interests lie in our developing our national identity." He said that Dreiser had wandered "afield" when he insisted that "our salvation rests in Communism rather than in the development of democracy within the frame-work of the Constitution." He later asked (August 16, 1940), "Is it really necessary for you to be so hard on the English so as to injure your own publishing record in Great Britain?"

Despite Lengel's objections to Dreiser's book, he arranged (November 4, 1940) to have Modern Age Books take over Piest's contract, if Dreiser would repay out of his eventual royalties the $5,000 advance Piest had given him. When Dreiser declined, Piest, anxious to get out from under Dreiser, was willing to take a loss on the advance; and he told Lengel that he would settle for $1,775 (that is, for the return of his last advance to Dreiser, minus Lengel's commission and an attorney's fee).

While these deliberations were going on, Modern Age Books also had second thoughts. Lengel wrote Dreiser (December 5, 1940) that his new publisher was afraid of a libel suit. The next day, David Zablodowsky of Modern Age Books wrote Dreiser directly that "Two printers have, in succession, refused to print the book," because they felt that it was libelous and un-American. Modern Age Books then gave the manuscript to its own lawyers, who were also wary. Their particular concern (as a letter dated December 17, 1940 reveals) was with Dreiser's attack on the Red Cross, which he had inserted in the galleys. When Dreiser refused to delete this material, Lengel wrote him (December 30, 1940), "Why not sell or give that part [on the Red Cross] . . . to Ellmore of *Friday*. Then you would at least have the satisfaction of seeing it published."

When they finally settled this issue, Zablodowsky insisted that Dreiser break completely with Piest so that he would not be considered Piest's tool, since Piest was an alien. When

Dreiser, however, refused to repay Piest, except out of his royalties, Zablodowsky wearily gave in. Like most of Dreiser's business dealings, the publication of *America Is Worth Saving* was awkward and unpleasant. As usual, the man most hurt was a friend, this time Lengel, whom Dreiser accused of betraying him. A man of great patience, Lengel replied (January 3, 1941) that "at all times my efforts have been directed solely in *your* behalf—a fact which seems not to have impressed you." Even the title of the book was a source of difficulty: Zablodowsky wanted to call it *Is Peace Worth Saving?*, Dreiser *America Wake Up and Live*, before they compromised on *Is America Worth Saving?*, which they changed to *America Is Worth Saving* because it sounded less un-American.

If Dreiser had had a crystal ball, he could have saved himself the difficulties of publishing *America Is Worth Saving*. In June of 1941, three months after his book was published, Hitler broke his nonaggression pact with Russia, and Dreiser suddenly found that he was for American intervention. While he hated to see England aided, he did not want to see Russia destroyed. He quickly put aside all theories about international capitalistic plots and wrote: "We are calling for all aid to both the Soviet and British people in order to defeat Hitlerism." [21] If in the next few years Dreiser lapsed into relative political silence, the reasons are perhaps understandable.

Politically, the last four years of Dreiser's life involved waiting and watching. His sympathies were with Russia, and he followed with great interest the fighting on the western front. His old friends, like George Douglas and Sherwood Anderson, were dying each year, and his own health (he had a serious kidney problem) was not the best. He did get satisfaction from an occasional talk with such liberal visitors as John Howard Lawson. He was also writing Mencken again, having picked up on November 26, 1934 a correspondence that had stopped on March 5, 1926. Although the first six years of this renewed correspondence was chilly, it had thawed by the forties. Mencken congratulated (October 2, 1939) Dreiser for "The Dawn Is in the East," especially his attack on England. Yet Dreiser's pro-Russian attitude disturbed him. He wrote later

(November 27, 1940): "Have you turned Communist? I certainly hope you haven't."

Dreiser had not turned communist, but he probably would have if Earl Browder, who was suspect of Dreiser's independent and unpredictable views, had not repeatedly refused his request to join the party.[22] Between 1940 and 1945, Dreiser wrote a dozen essays ("The Soviet-Finnish Treaty and World Peace," "What Is Democracy?", "The USSR Today," "Churchill and Democracy," "The Russian Advance," and many more) in support of Russia in general and Russian communism in specific. As Mencken followed this drift, he wrote Dreiser (April 1, 1943): "I simply can't follow you in your belief in Comrade Stalin. To me he seems to be only a politico like the rest, and if anything worse than most."

Dreiser's new enthusiasm for the Communist Party stemmed from many factors. He had never recovered from his Russian journey of 1927 and was deeply moved by the courage of the Russian people as they fought insurmountable odds and routed the Germans from their country. He had become less convinced that economic change would come from within America: Technocracy was a pipe-dream, and the Communist Party in America was still racked with dissension (Dreiser told Mencken that he communicated directly with Russia). Moreover, Dreiser's thinking had become more international, and he began (as we have seen) to desire not only equity between classes but equity between nations. Paradoxically, he thought that dialectical materialism would eliminate acquisitive instincts and create a Quaker-like sense of fraternity. At the same time, he believed that communism would suppress religion and create a secular attitude toward both sex and divorce. Also, his novels were more read in Russia than in the United States and, at Dreiser's request, Stalin had deposited a $34,600 royalty check in Dreiser's Los Angeles account. And finally, in July of 1945, William Z. Foster, Dreiser's old friend, became head of the American Communist Party, succeeding Earl Browder who had never wanted Dreiser as an official member of the Party. While some critics maintain that Dreiser's joining the Party was an impulsive act of an old man, Dreiser had been moving emotionally and intellectually toward this decision for many years. In July of 1945, he requested membership in the Party, and on August 7, 1945 Foster officially welcomed him into the American Communist Party of the United States. Foster's letter expressed hope for a new world—one free of fascism and true to the promises of the Moscow, Cairo, Teheran, Yalta, San Francisco, and Potsdam Conferences.

On February 4, 1946, Mencken wrote Helen that he could never have followed Dreiser this far.

13

The Larger "I"

Theodore Dreiser never overcame the effect that early poverty had on his life. From childhood through to adulthood, he desired to escape, to break away from its restrictions. His revolt against the family was first a revolt against the father who had impoverished the family; and his revolt against the family merely anticipated his later revolt against institutions—first the Church and then the government which favored men of wealth and position over the poor and the oppressed. Dreiser's life was motivated more by hate than by love. Although he championed their cause, he did not really love the poor. His sympathy for the poor—even the criminal—was a reverse kind of sympathy, more a hatred for the rich and the well established.

Even after the publication of *An American Tragedy*, when he had a great deal of money, Dreiser suffered from what Helen called his "poverty complex," never really thought of himself as wealthy, and believed that Horace Liveright and others were trying to cheat him out of his new and hard-earned security—a security to which he would never be accustomed. Most of this intensity stemmed from his desire to rise above institutions and conventions, to live the heightened life, free from restrictions.

Herbert Spencer's ideas had a natural appeal. Struggling to overcome the limits of his own family, working just to survive in the city, he could readily believe that life was a battle between conflicting forces. All his energy up to this point had been directed at overcoming and surmounting the obstacles that seemed continually to be in his way. Like the characters in his novels—Carrie, Jennie, Cowperwood, Eugene Witla, and Clyde Griffiths—he wanted to free himself of his past, move beyond the limits of his birth, the limits of his environment, and finally the limits of moral and social conventions. Although Cowperwood is a businessman and Witla an artist, they are more similar than dissimilar: both are self-made men who are a law unto themselves and, as a result, both are in continued conflict with a society which tries to restrain them. Dreiser's characters want to soar, to fly above ordinary men, to be free of all restrictions. They are modern-day Icaruses, flying beyond the prison of family and culture, rising on the wings of their imagination, even though their illusioned view of self will be scorched by the reality of the sun.

More than any other novelist in the twentieth century, Dreiser described the "new" Horatio Alger hero, without morals or principles, pulled by desire. Dreiser depicted a cruel and selfish world, a world in which men use and are used by others, a world in which true love is impossible. While there are moments of tenderness between his characters—Hurstwood and Carrie, Jennie and Lester Kane, Cowperwood and Aileen, Witla and Suzanne, Clyde and Roberta—these moments are betrayed. True to Horatio Alger, Dreiser equated women and money. In fact, in *The Financier* and *The Titan,* when the woman has lost her looks, her market value decreases, and she is replaced (literally "bought off" as in the case of Aileen Butler) by a younger, more attractive model. In every one of Dreiser's novels, women are bought and purchased: Drouet buys Carrie with an expensive meal and money for clothes as

Hurstwood buys her with the promise (a false one, to be sure) of his money. Senator Brander wins Jennie with gifts of money as does Lester Kane, who is Jennie's main source of security. Frank Cowperwood marries Lillian Semple for her money, and in turn wins Aileen with his own money and vitality, and later Berenice whom he finances and supports practically from childhood. Hortense Briggs sees Clyde as an easy source of money for a new coat; Roberta sees him as an avenue to the Griffiths family; and Sondra sees him (at least at first) as a means to make the snobbish Gilbert jealous, just as Clyde sees her as a means to social status.

In a very real way, money is power, the source of all values, in Dreiser's fiction. Take away a character's desire for money and nothing happens in the novel: Carrie would not live with Drouet; Hurstwood would not steal from the safe; Jennie would not become Kane's mistress; Cowperwood would not marry Mrs. Semple or play the market; and Clyde would not murder Roberta. One can find two kinds of characters in Dreiser's novels—the "haves" and the "have-nots." The haves, he believed, created their own values, clawed their way to get and keep their money. The have-nots either lacked the fierceness to succeed in the struggle or, like Dreiser's father, had given up the fight because they thought it un-Christly.

Dreiser had no sympathy for Christian meekness, felt it was a self-destructive illusion. He also had no sympathy for the genteel sense of manners, feeling that it only disguised the true nature of reality. He dismissed both the Christian and genteel values because he felt that they rested upon dubious premises. He was particularly skeptical that there was some kind of relationship between the good life and material success. In *Sister Carrie*, he suggested that there was no relation between failure, success, and moral law; he pursued the theme even deeper in *Jennie Gerhardt* when he showed a sincere woman, truly in love, punished unjustly when she violated the moral law; and Dreiser used the theme again in the Cowperwood trilogy and in *The "Genius"* when he showed Cowperwood and Witla, self-enclosed, laws unto themselves, contemptuous of both genteel and mass values. Witla and Cowperwood, however, are blind in thinking that they can, like modern-day Icaruses, fly beyond conventions—just as blind, in fact, as the moralists are when they "close the eye and turn away the head as if there were something unclean in nature itself." [1]

Dreiser came more and more to believe that if there were any final truths, they could be discovered in the workings of nature itself. In 1915, he had tried to get a stack permit at the New York Public Library in order to read books on natural and physical science, and in *Hey Rub-A-Dub-Dub* he attempted to work out his own theory of man and the universe. After he published *An American Tragedy*, he had the financial means—for the first time in his life—to pursue his scientific concerns, and from 1927 until he died in 1945 he was obsessed with highly abstract and scientific questions about the nature of man and reality. This obsession led him to write thousands of pages of notes that he hoped to turn into a book, a final credo. Dreiser never finished this project, but his "Notes on Life" are on file at the University of Pennsylvania, and they reveal his attempt—perhaps pathetic, perhaps sublime—to give order and meaning to his own life and to his universe, a final attempt to explain the meaning of his years of struggle.

In "Notes on Life," Dreiser hoped to prove—to himself and the world—that the universe was a machine and that man was a part—at best a tool—in its workings. If there were a plan behind the machine's operation—and Dreiser came more and more to believe that such was the case—the plan was not evident to man and probably never would be. The machine was in motion, the universe in flux, and this is about all that one could say for certain. The atoms that made up the individual were in flux in his body; the individual was in flux in the big cities; and the planets were in flux in their galaxies. All matter was energized—that is, electrified. Out of the boundless ether of space-time came matter-energy, and out of that came life as we know it. Matter was continually wearing itself out and disappearing into the ether, at which point it was being renewed at its source. This original energy accounted for all life. Thus all life had a common source, and the universe was a boiling sea of electrons and protons. This fact was basic to all human existence, led to cosmic correspondences, and created a tension in man he could never overcome: lightning reflected the turbulence of cosmic existence, caused "children to cry, grown-ups to have the blues, stock markets to collapse, the sea to churn." [2] Until the universe itself was at peace, Dreiser maintained, there would be no peace within men.

The only truth in life was the truth of change. The individual lived and died, seasons changed, and civilizations prospered and decayed. This did not mean, however, that matter was created anew. As a materialist, Dreiser believed that the universe—that all matter—had limits and was fixed in quantity, growing toward a moment of fulfillment, at which time it would run down, and the whole process would be repeated. Out of such flux and change came contrast, and Dreiser repeatedly stressed the significance of contrast. He believed in the "equation inevitable": that one force engendered its opposite, and that knowledge depended upon seeing life in terms of opposites—good through evil, beauty through ugliness, mercy through cruelty, sorrow through joy, love through hate, youth through age, wealth through poverty, and strength through weakness.

There was no absolute good or evil. In fact, good and evil were inextricable and could not be separated; one was a part of the other, a part of the same process. Life fed on life; man like the animals had to kill in order to eat; and what was good for man in this case was evil for the animals: it all depended upon a point of view—a relative and limited point of view. Man thus had no fixed point of reference. His mind was merely another kind of machine, a highly structured nerve mechanism that registered impressions and responded to stimuli.

For Dreiser, all life moved in a circle, was in continuous motion, but going nowhere. The universe had a limited amount of matter which was forever changing, diminishing, and replenishing itself. Man was born to die—a fact that kept life mysterious and led to man's sense of awe and wonder in the face of the unknown. Change and contrast, the old and the new, the flux of matter, the meaningless repetition of life—these beliefs are the foundation of Dreiser's view of man and the universe.

Dreiser tried in a systematic way to develop these ideas in "Notes on Life." Fortunately, we have the means of talking about this treatise as Dreiser perhaps intended. In a letter dated

January 26, 1935, he gave to George Douglas, whom he hoped would work on this project with him, an outline of what he was attempting to do. The first part of his book would have been titled "The Essential Tragedy of Life." Here Dreiser had in mind ideas that he had taken from Herbert Spencer over forty years earlier: the belief in a dualistic existence, the pull and tug between contradictory and contrasting forces, the relationship between the "continuously tragic [and] cosmic elements which can never be escaped." Man could not escape tragedy and comedy because (as we have already seen) all life was in motion and men were caught between extreme states of being. All knowledge stemmed from experience with self-perpetuating dualities—from the ironic awareness that the individual affirmed his existence in the face of a larger order that negated it.

After discussing "the essential tragedy of life," Dreiser planned to discuss "The Myth of Reality," an idea that he had worked out in part in the essay "You, the Phantom." [3] In this section of his book, Dreiser would have treated man's pathetic limitations. If there were final answers to the mysteries of life, man did not have the means to find them. While the individual liked to feel otherwise, he was not necessary to the workings of the universe. Man was mere matter with the illusion of being more. He was born to press "pathetically against his wretched limitations, wishing always to know more and more, and as constantly being denied." [4] In "You, the Phantom," Dreiser maintained that the individual was nothing "but a mechanism for the mind and the intention of some exterior and larger mental process which has constructed me and these minor entities [that is, atoms] which help to make me what I am." Until almost 1935, Dreiser believed that the "exterior force" was blindly mechanistic. As he grew older, he came more and more to believe that there might be a Creative Intelligence at work behind the flux and change of life, even though he was still far from consenting to a God or even to teleology. If there were a final purpose inherent in the universe, man was not a part of that purpose. If there were a Creative Intelligence, it had its own happiness—and not man's—in mind and was realizing itself at man's expense, man being a mere adjunct to a larger

process of creation. "I am," said Dreiser, "not wholly and individually living—but being lived by something else that has
constructed me and is using me, along with all other forms and
creatures and elements and forces, for [unknown] purposes of
its own." [5]

"The Myth of Reality," the belief that man lives independent
of exterior forces, was only one of a series of modern "myths"
that Dreiser was intent on dispelling. The other "myths" can
be summarized briefly.

THE MYTH OF INDIVIDUALITY: By this phrase Dreiser meant to
suggest that because man was a part of a larger process of life,
he had no individual existence. He was a manufactured object,
made by the billions. Man "is not living, but is being lived by
something which needs not only him but millions like him in
order to express itself." [6] Forms are thus "atoms built into
things." While individual men are as different as individual
atoms, in groups their individualism is canceled out, and neither their individuality nor their group nature is within control
of their own will." [7]

THE MYTH OF THE CREATIVE POWER OF MAN: Man did not invent or record anything that was not first in nature. The swordfish had a sword before man, the sabre tooth tiger a sabre, the
mosquito a stiletto, the elephant a spear. Birds could make
windows before man. The milkweed and the dandelion had,
long before men, parachutes which carried their seeds through
the air. Nature, older and more intelligent than man, was the
source and set the limits of man's creative genius. This was true
of the painter and the novelist as well as the inventor: the man
who partakes of the creative power of nature itself merely "reflects" rather than "creates" the reality of his art.

THE MYTH OF POSSESSIONS: Man can never fully satisfy his
desire. Nature is larger than the individual; its resources will
never be exhausted; and man was born to want. "We are never
further from our wishes," Dreiser wrote, "than when we imagine we possess what we have desired." [8] This idea is central
to both *Sister Carrie* and *An American Tragedy,* both Carrie
and Clyde revealing man as an overreacher. Our last view of

Carrie is in her chair, rocking away, like the flux of life itself, never to be satisfied, always yearning for more than she can ever acquire.

THE MYTH OF FREE WILL: Since man is a machine, a medium through which a larger force works, he lacks free will. "Our ego belongs to the universe or creative energy," Dreiser once wrote, "and has only such response as nature provides." [9] Man was in reality bound to a mysterious universe in which some principle outside of him held the totality together, and his will only appeared free. Included among Dreiser's notes was a quote from Schopenhauer, which exactly summarizes Dreiser's own views of free will: "Spinoza says that if a stone has been projected through the air had consciousness, it would believe it was moving of its own free will. I add only to this that the stone would be right." [10]

THE MYTH OF INDIVIDUAL THINKING: Some greater intelligence was working behind the electro-chemical phenomena of life, an intelligence that man at best intuited. All individual thinking was limited, and no individual could grasp the full meaning of nature. As a result, the universe was both infinite and unknowable, and knowledge was only a form of ignorance: the more that men knew the more they realized how much they did not know.

THE MYTH THAT IGNORANCE IS EVIL: Men seek complete self-fulfillment and understanding but are "deceived by emotions [and] desires . . . like the naive player of any game." We cannot abolish ignorance "without abolishing knowledge." Thus, while each man is a part of the same machine and acted upon by the same stimuli, his ignorance of his common nature and common plight cuts him off from other men. And yet ignorance is not evil because it gives life its mystery. "Nature is a secret" —and this is the source of man's awe, the origin of the sublime. [11] In one of his "Notes on Life" folders, Dreiser discussed the way the mystery and awe of life affect man's nature, how "the mountains and plains . . . change men—transmute them from one thing to another." He was particularly interested in the Himalayas which "seem to speak to men in deep tones . . .

[and yet] so loftily ignore men as something puny and unimportant," creating a humble race of men with their "brooding Buddahs and Brahamans," their "Mahatmas and motionless Pundits and yearning Gandhis!" [12] Man is finite; nature is not. Man's memory is limited because the "old must be forgotten" so what "has evolved will appear new." [13] Man dies before he can remember enough to see the pattern of repetition clearly. If it were not for man's ignorance, for his sense of the awe and mystery of life, art would be impossible. The artist's vision is only partial, but he sees more than average men and has the ability to organize his insights into the work of art. As a result, "art is like . . . a power house," a dynamo that has drawn its energy from nature. The work of art thus reflects both man's awareness and his ignorance of the beauty and meaning that surrounds him.

THE MEANING OF "MORALITY AND IMMORALITY": There is no such thing as absolute good and evil. Each order of being in the universe tries to realize itself, and what may be "good" for its own sense of being and fulfillment may be "evil" for those other species with which it comes in contact—as the frog eats the butterfly, the pig the frog, and man the pig. Man is innocent because "mysterious forces express themselves through man," and one cannot say whether these forces are working for good or evil because "nature not man is the inventor of life, and if there is evil, nature is guilty." [14] Man, in other words, is moral—nature is not. Man creates his own sense of morality, a morality that sometimes becomes—as with both Christian and genteel values—a fiction of the mind, completely removed from the principles inherent in nature. When man turns the other cheek, he is turning from nature. When he lives by a gentlemanly code, he is being blind to the brutality that surrounds him. The unscrupulous titan embodied Dreiser's ethical man. When Dreiser came to hate the titan, came to believe that reformers could help change the competitive world in which the industrialist so selfishly functioned, he was, of course, contradicting the main principles of his mechanistic beliefs. The capitalism that Dreiser came so much to hate was really consistent with his belief in self-interest. Moreover, as a mechanist,

Dreiser should have accepted what nature had wrought, should have accepted society as he found it. In trying to change man's social condition, he contradicted both his belief in a Creative Intelligence and his belief that man was powerless to act against forces beyond his control—contradictions he either did not see or did not allow to bother him.

THE NECESSITY FOR LIMITATION: Man is limited by the mechanism of his body (his appetites and passions), and his environment (immediate and solar). The matter that makes up the universe is fixed and limited, although it does take different forms. Nature has a principle of balance within it, even though matter does not remain constant, and life is a perpetual struggle. The bacteria that carry disease through the human body are not trying to kill but to live. "Life flows into new forms, and these forms wage war or arrange an armistice." Because matter is limited, it repeats itself. Time does not march, only matter; time is matter in motion. When we detect change, we become aware of time, and time has no existence apart from changing objects. For Dreiser, time was extended in space—and at one with matter and energy in space: "time is nothing but the measure of the duration of something, and the only something it can measure is matter or energy—or matter-energy—two phases of the same thing." [15]

THE MYTH OF THE PERFECT SOCIAL ORDER: Just as Dreiser believed that matter was limited, he believed that the Utopian state was impossible. The perfect state was impossible because life was built upon a system of contrasts; and while contrasts suggest the possibility of alternation, they also "suggest a machine that cannot or does not change but goes on repeating itself hopelessly." [16] Thus "society never advances; it recedes at once on one side as it advances on the other. Its progress is only apparent, like the working of a treadmill." [17] While society undergoes continual changes—becomes civilized, Christianized, rich, and scientific—"for everything that is given something is taken." Dreiser maintained that while there is "a contrast between the well-clad . . . American . . . and the naked New Zealander," one had only to "compare the health of the two to see that his aboriginal strength the white man has lost." [18]

THE MYTH OF DEATH: In his essay, "The Essential Tragedy of Life," Dreiser insisted upon the insignificance of man. The total design, he said, may have purpose, but an individual man has no more purpose than the "atoms of his internal mechanism [have] success, fame, or great life." The individual existence is thus inconsequential to the larger order. Death is the process by which matter renews itself. Death is the key to life, the means by which man is kept ignorant of cosmic secrets. "Without death," Dreiser wrote, "no life." [19] In this context, life is a delusion, a myth, a mirage. Man aspires to realize himself, to achieve worldly possessions, to make himself eternal, when in reality a force larger than man—a force which perpetuates the flux of life—negates all aspiration and cancels the human will.

Dreiser planned to round off "Notes on Life" by considering how the creative energy expressed itself here on earth. This section surely would have been repetitive (he planned to treat the already discussed subjects of desire, beauty, mercy, secrecy, and justice) as would his conclusion (which would once again treat his theory of "the equation inevitable"). The whole book, in fact, would certainly have been inchoate, scientifically naive, and hopelessly confused, simply because Dreiser was not on sure ground when he came to such complex scientific and philosophical questions. What he was doing in this work was projecting his own sense of self, his idea of life as combat, into the universe. It is most interesting that Dreiser's final image of the universe was that of a "greedy self," fulfilling its being at others' expense. Ironically, in this view, he found a kind of release from his own sense of conflict. Since the universe was an all-absorbing ego—a larger "I"—it embodied all life in its desire for fulfillment, and the individual might just as well not struggle against it.

Dreiser's final cosmic views do not, however, resolve the contradictions within his thought: he admired the rugged individualist and yet believed in the supremacy of the masses, saw men as the hopeless dupes of their illusions and yet was sorry that man's dreams bounced off the rocks of indifferent mountains, believed that organized groups (like the Communist Party) could bring about political change and yet maintained that man was powerless to alter his condition because he was a mere tool of a cosmic machine. At the end of his life, Dreiser submitted himself to the larger, natural process, one that was using him and the Communist Party for reasons that they neither knew nor understood. Even in his last days, when his own views were mellowing, Dreiser still needed to feel that fate was outside of him, that the story of Hurstwood and Clyde—the story of his helpless father—was really the story of all men. Dreiser did not really eliminate his sense of self: he merely extended it. He did not abandon his overwhelming ego: he transfigured and projected it into nature. In one sense, Dreiser let nature absorb him. In another sense, he absorbed nature. Dreiser's consent to a Creative Intelligence was an act of faith, just as his joining the Communist Party (with all his doubts about communism) was an act of faith, the same kind of faith that he had so bitterly hated in his father. In *An American Tragedy*, Clyde returned to his mother and her religion at the end of the novel. Dreiser saw a cruel irony in this return to the religion of Clyde's father. And yet, even if we did not have *The Bulwark* to prove it, we could still see that in his last years Dreiser was also coming back to the family, back to the old home and the father, back to many of the ideas he had spent his whole life trying to reject.

Despite the contradictions within his philosophy, Dreiser externalized his sense of conflict in his fiction; depicted the pull of desire and the struggle for money and power; revealed the fear of treachery and the betrayal of trust and love; described the play of chance and accident; and portrayed the destructive nature of time, the illusion of strength, and the reality of man's limitations. No other twentieth-century novelist has so clearly described man's fragile and precarious nature—precarious in the face of his own greed and self-righteousness, and in the face of a capricious universe. Dreiser depicted a mechanized cosmos which operated beyond man's understanding and without his comforts in mind. Dreiser's novels were a personal expression of his individual temperament.

More than any other novelist in the twentieth century, Dreiser has been criticized for his view of reality, been judged more on the quality of his ideas than on his ability to use them in his fiction.[20] As inchoate as his ideas may appear, they are not inchoate in the fiction. Moreover, Dreiser considered himself a realist because only the view of life he expressed in his fiction seemed "real" to him. Like any supreme egoist, he was puzzled by those who could not share his own beliefs, his own sense of experience. To these critics he gave the only answer that he could give:

> On thinking back over the books I have written, I can only say . . . this has been my vision of life—life with its romance and cruelty, its pity and terror, its joys and anxiety, its peace and conflict. You may not like my vision . . . but it is the only one that I have seen and felt, therefore, it is the only one I can give you.[21]

14

"The Bulwark"
and "The Stoic"

In the fall of 1912, Dreiser met Anna Tatum at the Plaza Hotel in New York. Miss Tatum, young and pretty with light blond hair, had recently graduated from Wellesley College. From a very conservative Pennsylvania Quaker family, she was looking for a larger life and had arranged to meet Dreiser with hopes of becoming a part of the New York literary and art world.

She had first written Dreiser from Fallsington, Pennsylvania on November 7, 1911, just after she had read *Jennie Gerhardt*. The letter was sent to Dreiser's apartment address (3609 Broadway) and forwarded to him in London, where he was staying under the solicitous eye of Grant Richards. While Miss Tatum said that she wept over *Jennie Gerhardt* and that she particularly liked his characterization of Lester Kane, she (surely to Dreiser's amusement) added: "I doubt whether you have ever really known a Jennie Gerhardt such as you have created." [1] Miss Tatum then went on to disagree that love is more important than pride (which for some reason she believed Dreiser had maintained in *Jennie Gerhardt*). "I cannot," she said, "believe that love and pride are enemies. It was Lester Kane's tragedy not that he had them both, but that he had too little of both." She felt there was no character in *Jennie Gerhardt* who embodied "pride in its noble sense."

Dreiser was never one to spurn the interest of a pretty, literate young girl, who also seemed to be personally attracted to him. When he wrote her defending *Jennie Gerhardt,* Miss Tatum replied on December 20, 1911 that she was moved by the novel but that ultimately it went against her temperament. She also took this occasion to warn Dreiser about becoming too "flowery" and writing in an "exalted, pseudo-lyric strain," becoming the first of Dreiser's critics to see the danger of this tendency, anticipating Lionel Trilling's remarks by almost forty years.[2]

In time, Anna told Dreiser the story of her father—a man of firm religious belief who was physically broken when his children rejected the old religion and turned toward a more compelling secular world. The story obviously touched a chord in Dreiser's own experience: Mr. Tatum repeated the history of Dreiser's own father, and Anna duplicated his own temperament and his desire for freedom. While Dreiser decided at this time to make a novel out of this situation, *The Bulwark*, like so many of his other novels, would have a long period of gestation. In fact, it would not be published until 1946—thirty-four years after Anna Tatum told her story to Dreiser and when Dreiser himself was dead.

Dreiser first postponed *The Bulwark* because of his work on *The Financier, The Titan,* and *The "Genius."* He had turned his attention to it after *The "Genius,"* and Liveright was still expecting the manuscript as late as August, 1920. Late in 1919 or early in 1920, however, Dreiser abandoned this story for *An American Tragedy.* By this time, he had long broken with Anna Tatum, and for the same reasons that the Greenwich Village artist Willard Kane (Dreiser obviously modelled Kane on himself, keeping the name of the character that Anna so admired in *Jennie Gerhardt*) breaks with Etta Barnes: Anna was getting too serious and making too many emotional de-

mands. Dreiser, who was never bashful about making demands
on his women, wanted the affairs to be on his own terms, and
he could be ruthless when the women became possessive.
Most of Dreiser's women were as much in love with Dreiser
the novelist as Dreiser the man. On March 16, 1914, Anna
wrote Dreiser, who was not answering her letters, "Oh Dodoe,
how much I love you," and then "and how much I love even
more the artistic ideal." Miss Tatum also mentioned in this
letter that "Father has been ill again—and I think is destined
to die soon." Such was the case, and like Etta Barnes, Anna
Tatum was taking care of her father when he did die.

Anna did not write Dreiser again for almost twenty years.
On October 10, 1932, she wrote asking for work (in 1934 Dreiser
let her write a scenario of *Sister Carrie*) and mentions, "I
read some time ago that you were thinking of doing *The Bulwark*. Now that my mother is dead I don't mind." Dreiser was
so busy with his political and scientific interests in 1932, however, that he did no work on *The Bulwark*. He picked up the
story again in 1942. On April 2nd of that year he wrote
Mencken: "Believe it or not, I am working on *The Bulwark*."
Putnam, now his publisher, expected a manuscript in June. In
July of 1942, however, he wrote Lengel, "The book is not
ready yet and will not be for some time. Not that I am not
working on it or getting along with it but it is a very intimate
and touchy problem in connection with religious family life—
and, like the American Tragedy, I find it difficult." [4] Dreiser
was not exaggerating his problem. He did write about a fifty
page introduction to *The Bulwark* in 1943, but in September of
1944, he had all but abandoned the novel when Marguerite
Tjader Harris volunteered to come West and help him. For
over a year they worked faithfully, usually from nine in the
morning until four in the afternoon, in Mrs. Harris' little cot-
tage on Cadet Court in the Hollywood Hills.

In 1942, Louise Campbell had sent Dreiser his earlier
drafts of *The Bulwark*—so they had Dreiser's fifty-page introduction; an early typescript treating the wedding of Solon
and Benecia, the birth of the children, and the developing
gulf between the generations; and a third typescript treating
Solon's first years in banking, the changes that took place in

American finance after the Civil War, and the developing gulf between the old banker and the new capitalist. Two other typescripts—one treating Solon's early years, and another the Barnes household—were not of much use.

As in the past, Dreiser had clipped stories from the newspapers which might be of use in *The Bulwark*. He had, for example, the reports of exposed bank frauds and money schemes—the kind of transaction that so bothers Solon Barnes in the novel. He also had a clipping about a Ralph Hewitt Steurer, who stole fifteen hundred dollars for a girl friend from the Farmers' Loan and Trust Company—an incident which Solon reads about in moral shock and with great indignation.[5] He had another clipping from the New York *World*, March 1, 1903, about an employee who robbed the Hotel Beresford—an incident that has remote parallels to the way Walter Briscoe robbed the Traders and Builders Bank (96-97). Most important, Dreiser had clippings (not among his papers at U. of P.) about Lorlys Elton Rogers whose story becomes Stewart's in the novel.

When Dreiser first thought of making *The Bulwark* into a novel, he had intended to show how helpless the religious man is in a changing and turbulent world. The emphasis was to be on Stewart who, like Dreiser himself, felt temperamentally cut off from the father. Since Dreiser abandoned *The Bulwark* to begin *An American Tragedy* and since he used much of the earlier manuscript in the 1946 version of his story, it is not surprising—even though thirty years elapsed between gestation and birth—that there are many similarities between *The Bulwark* and his earlier novels.

The old mechanistic motives, for example, while less obvious in *The Bulwark*, are in many ways just as compelling here as in *An American Tragedy* and earlier novels. Solon is held by the "chemically radiated charm of" Benecia (37). An attractive girl can "move" Stewart "with a kind of energy that was electric" (195). When Solon first enters the impressive Traders and Builders Bank, he is as "overawed" and as "confused by the magnificence of it all" (75) as Clyde Griffiths was when he entered the Green-Davidson Hotel. Dorothea responds in exactly the same way, "the lavish splendor" of her cousin Rhoda's house suddenly opening "a magic world . . . to her" (*152–53*). Again like Clyde, Stewart is moved by the color and motion of life, particularly by the flux of the city (*cf. 117 and 196*). As Clyde's desires grow upon what he sees, so Stewart's first sexual experience with Ada Maurer intensified his desire for more sex. As Dreiser put it, this experience "aroused in his mind the endless possibilities of further conquests" (*215*). This is the same device Dreiser had used in all his previous novels, appetite expanding in proportion to what it feeds upon.

In all of Dreiser's novels, from *Sister Carrie* to *The Stoic*, he showed a world breaking up, and the people in it—particularly the young—becoming more restless. Dreiser's whole narrative point of view depends upon a world in transition, in flux, dominated by change. As he did in most of his novels, Dreiser set *The Bulwark* against a panorama of time. Not only do Solon's and Benecia's parents die in the course of this novel, but their deaths are juxtaposed against the birth of the children (Hannah Barnes, for example, dies four months before Isobel is born, Isobel's birth the next narrative incident after the death). Their deaths are also juxtaposed against the return of new life (the day Aunt Hester died, for example, Isobel comments on the beauty of Spring) (*see 90 and 140*). Life goes on in the face of death, and no man can be a bulwark against time and the changes that it brings. As the story of the Barnes family is told, one character—the faithful servant Joseph—is present from beginning to end. Growing more decrepit in each chapter, he stands as a kind of physical testimony to both the constancy of temperament and the mutability of man, time cancelling such fidelity (cancelling an "older and better order of things," as Solon sees it) (*242*), as a physical force works beyond man's power to stop it. Dreiser is guilty of romantic nostalgia here, a trait from which his ambitious and yearning younger characters seldom suffered. Yet if Solon learns anything in *The Bulwark*, it is that time will not stand still, that he cannot stop or turn back the clock, and he comes to accept what time brings him. This stoic attitude provides the link between Solon Barnes and the Frank Algernon Cowperwood of Dreiser's next novel.

The theme of time and of change is an essential one in *The Bulwark*. The change in the Quaker's way of life gave Dreiser a vehicle to treat the more general change taking place in America and even Europe. In all of Dreiser's novels—sometimes clearly, sometimes vaguely—one can make out the fixed world of the past. This is as true in the autobiographies and the travelogues, where we can see the breakdown of the old aristocracy (*cf. Traveller at Forty*) and of the old values (*cf. Hoosier Holiday*), as it is in the novels where such change has led to a new mobility and a struggle for wealth and success in a turbulent and frenetic world. The loss of a stratified society has led to a time of desire (as the title *Trilogy of Desire* suggests) and a time of frustration (as the plight of Carrie, Clyde, Eugene, and even Cowperwood also suggests). All of these characters have one trait in common—restlessness. And this is the trait which Solon Barnes, the bulwark of the past, so dislikes in the world about him (he is shocked, for example, by the instability of the cashier in a Trenton bank—certainly another Hurstwood—who is dissatisfied enough with his plight to abscond with a large sum of money, leaving his wife and child behind) (*cf. 139*). Solon equally dislikes this spirit of restlessness in his youngest children (*cf. 147*). In fact, as they become more restless, he becomes more authoritarian: as Etta and Stewart "thirst for a freer and still freer form of life" Solon "grew more and more conservative and wary as to the conduct of the family in general" (*218*). In *The Bulwark*, as in Dreiser's earlier novels, one force generates in equal proportion its opposite.

Again, as in Dreiser's earlier novels, there is the "chance" moment of exposure. Stewart is seen at the Orpheum Theater by a friend of his father's (*137*), and Etta is seen with Willard Kane by a friend of Orville's, just as Hurstwood was seen with Carrie, Cowperwood with Aileen, Witla with Suzanne, and Roberta with Clyde. While these characters try to act in secret, they are always seen when they think they are most hidden. Instead of being a chance event, these discoveries reveal man's vulnerability, show the discrepancy between what he thinks is happening and what is really happening, and suggest a larger realm of being at work outside of the individual.

Because there is a realm of being outside the power of man's will, the individual is often the victim of seeming accidents. As in the earlier novels, *The Bulwark* shows how evil can come about accidentally. As a child, Solon unwittingly killed a catbird, an event that clearly reveals what man in his ignorance can do—and what can be done to him (*cf. 21–23*). This scene, of course, anticipates the death of Psyche Tanzer which is seemingly a matter of chance. As the safe shuts on Hurstwood, as the boat overturns on Clyde, Bruge has no intention of killing Psyche. In *The Rake*, the early version of *An American Tragedy*, Dreiser intended to show how an ambitious young man committed murder by mixing bromo-seltzer with hydrocyanic acid and potassium. He had expected the mixture to produce a slow death with the symptoms of diphtheria. Instead the chemicals combined to produce a stronger and more deadly poison, brought on immediate death, and revealed the intention of murder. When Victor Bruge mixes his aphrodisiac (really a depressant) with Psyche's coffee, he is ignorant that she has a heart condition. In all of these events an element beyond man's understanding is at work, and in all of these events the accident brings about inevitable consequences because the same fixed causes are consistently and persistently in operation, revealing a common condition. The fate of Walter Briscoe, for example, who steals fifteen hundred dollars from the Traders and Builders Bank so he can entertain his high-living girl friend, anticipates the fate of Stewart, who steals money from his family to entertain Ada Maurer. As in Stewart's case, "his father was so severe with him, his home life so narrow, that he could not resist the temptation to embark on a freer happier existence" (*97*).

In this context, Stewart Barnes becomes another Cldye Griffiths: they are both from strongly religious homes, have sensual natures, love the glittering city, need more money than they have (Stewart's wealthy father gives him very little), and are completely bewildered by the old values and want to break the chains. Dreiser, in fact, establishes the same kind of relationship between the restless, rebellious, and less pretentious Stewart and his smug, self-satisfied, conservative older brother Orville that he did between Clyde and his cousin Gilbert. Yet where Dreiser had in *An American Tragedy* put the emphasis upon youth, in *The Bulwark* he put it upon age. Dreiser had always depicted the father from the point of view of the son. Now he was depicting the son from the point of view of the father. The points of view in each novel, despite this divergence, overlap in their focus upon a violently turbulent and changing America, a secular world of new wealth, new machines, and new morality. When Solon is the "bulwark" of the past, Clyde wants to tear down such walls (the metaphor dominates *An American Tragedy*) in his headlong rush into the future. Dreiser sees them both caught in the same destructive force—each the other's antithesis in this world where one has seemingly engendered his opposite.

Even though they represent different points of view, Dreiser could sympathize with both Solon and Clyde. While he had little respect for Solon's dogmatic mind and his fear of new experience (Solon is as much a book-burner as John S. Sumner), Dreiser admired Solon's selflessness and his belief that men, the stewards of God, should help man in general and not over-zealously pursue money. At a time when Dreiser was about to join the Communist Party, he saw Solon Barnes not only as an oppressive expression of the old authority but—strangely enough—as a time-worn advocate of the communistic idea of shared wealth. Like his father before him, Solon believed " 'that God intends all forms of trade and wealth for the benefit of all men' " (45). Like Dreiser, Solon believed in an economic "balance and equity," the laborer getting a fair share of the profits (*see* 220). Again like Dreiser, he is repelled by the new capitalist, men like the hungry and unscrupulous Wilkerson, who "wanted too much for himself" (220). Wilkerson and his kind have a lot in common with Frank Algernon Cowperwood: they all manipulate men and money in postwar Philadelphia—that boundless and lucrative world of high finance. To be sure, Cowperwood with his taste in painting is more cultured and refined than that rapacious Wilkerson. Yet Cowperwood is motivated first by personal interest and money and then by a sense of the beautiful. Solon Barnes, on the other hand, is motivated first by a sense of responsibility for his depositors and by the simple beauty in life and then by money. As Solon and Clyde stand in inverse relation to each other, so also do Solon and Cowperwood. Far from being inconsistent with Dreiser's joining the Communist Party, *The Bulwark* depicts two kinds of money-makers: the dying breed of Solon Barnes who feel responsible to the people, and the new crop of profiteers who feel responsible only to themselves.

Not only can *The Bulwark* be reconciled with Dreiser's joining the Communist Party, it can be reconciled with his earlier fiction and with its own seemingly conflicting ideas. The problem comes in Dreiser's suggestion that men should be selfless and not selfish. He was once again unable to extricate himself from his philosophical dilemma. While he had always suggested that the artist was keenly aware of life's beauty, he had also suggested that life feeds on life, that men live in violent combat like the lobster and the squid, and that an intense pursuit of wealth was consistent with the nature of man. At the end of *The Bulwark,* Solon observes a green fly eating a beautiful flower. Like Dreiser, he ponders why life must feed on life and decides that behind the veil, which man cannot lift, is a Creative Force which is using all life for some purpose. While man is still fragile and life tragically effervescent (we are here "for a brief summer only"), the pain and the suffering, the struggle and the combat perhaps have a hidden meaning—or so Solon suggests.

Dreiser (as we have seen in Chapter 4) had maintained in essays written before *Sister Carrie* that there was a transcendent realm of order and beauty and also a worldly realm of combat and flux. His artist (like Eugene Witla) intuited the beauty inherent in all life at the same time as his tycoon (like Frank Algernon Cowperwood) outwitted his enemies in a savage struggle for wealth. The motives came together in a character like Clyde Griffiths who can see—as he ponders murdering Roberta Alden for Sondra Finchley's money—a perverse kind of beauty in Big Bittern. When Dreiser endows his transcendental force with intelligence, he obviously softens his naturalism and adds another set of motives to his fictional world: man can be as much compelled to act in the name of beauty as in the name of money—as much motivated by his love of life as by his love of possession.

The old conflict between a love of beauty and a love of money—a basic and persistent conflict in Dreiser's thinking—is an integral part of *The Bulwark*. On the one hand, Rufus Barnes, Solon's father, can look at Thornbrough and see the beauty of the house as an end in itself ("the house affected him esthetically . . . it involved beauty") (17) and not as a symbol of what money can buy. As Dreiser tells us, "Rufus [could succumb] to a genuine poetic reaction to nature" (28). On the other hand, Rufus is caught between his desire to keep the house "simple" and his need to repair it for sale. The love of simple beauty is in conflict with a shrewd business sense. As Dreiser put it, "Just the same this grateful, religious mood of Rufus' ran side by side with the practical" (29). Solon also is disturbed by "where lay the dividing line between ambition and irreligious greed, between the desire for power and a due regard for Quaker precepts" (94).

Dreiser used the two Barnes brothers, Orville and Stewart, to show the difference between one who is motivated by a conservative desire for money and social prominence and another who is motivated by a rebellious desire for new experience and immediate pleasure. He also used the three Barnes sisters—Isobel, Dorothea, and Etta—to portray different types of behavior and values in the modern world. In fact, in these three girls we have the prototypal Dreiserian women who run through his early as well as late fiction.

Isobel is the chained, prosaic, conventional woman. A victim of her plain looks, she lacks the entré to a larger and gayer world, and she retreats into herself, pursuing an academic life and never totally accepting (*see 126*) or totally rejecting the values of her staid father. Except for her education and social standing, she has much in common with a Roberta Alden who is also caught in kind of a no-man's land between the family and a world of romance which she has only glimpsed. Behind this type of character stands Sara White and her authoritarian father, whom Dreiser depicted in "A True Patriarch" in *Twelve Men*.

In contrast to Isobel, Dorothea is the frivolous and ambitious egoist. Once her cousin Rhoda introduces her to high society, she has no trouble—with her good looks and youthful vitality—of making her own way. Like a female Clyde Griffiths, she also is caught between her drab family and a heightened world which proves to be a greater force. Like Clyde, she is shrewd, calculating, and selfish. Unlike Clyde, she has the proper social credentials and a native intelligence: she gets what both she and Clyde wanted when she marries into a wealthy and socially prominent Philadelphia family. "Temperamentally antagonistic to all the restrictions that had been imposed on her at home," she is strongly related to such other self-seeking and yearning characters as Carrie Meeber, Aileen Butler, and Hortense Briggs as well as to the smug and self-satisfied Sondra Finchley.

In contrast to both Isobel and Dorothea, Etta is the artistically inclined, freedom-seeking new woman. Dreiser, of course, knew many of this type, saw them every day in the Village, and even discussed them at length in a *Gallery of Women*. Dreiser obviously used Anna Tatum as the model for Etta, Anna who wrote Dreiser, "Oh Dodoe, how I love you and how I love even more the artistic ideal." Like Anna, Etta wants "a world quite apart" (*108*), the world of the artist, and she not only rejects the simple, religious ways of her father but she also rejects the world of social pretense and money. She feels that "there is a wisdom that is related to beauty only" (*107*). As Rhoda Wallin opens the door to a new life for Dorothea, Volida La Porte—the name itself is an obvious play upon the French *velléité*: desire, and *la porte*: the door—does the same for Etta. Volida gives her the new French novel—Balzac's *La Cousine Bette*, Flaubert's *Madame Bovary*, and Daudet's *Sappho*—all books about the new woman. Volida is herself the new woman: she has no desire to marry (in appearance she is masculine looking), wants instead to make her way in the professions, particularly one in which she can change the disparity "between the rich and poor around them" (*167*). While the relationship between Volida and Etta seems homosexual, Dreiser never develops these implications. He stresses instead how Volida inculcates in Etta the spirit of selfless dedication and the desire for a bohemian freedom. To use Dreiser's own language, Volida opens the "door" and lets Etta seek an "essential self":

It was a door to a different world she was seeking, a complete escape from the atmosphere of repression and religion that was weighing upon her so heavily. Volida represented to her the right to think and do what she felt to be essential to herself, as well as the affection and understanding for which her whole nature cried out. (*162–63*)

Not only is Etta in pursuit of an "essential self," she is also in pursuit of "some special essence of life" which only the artist could reveal (*167*). Dreiser's new woman is really a romantic visionary: a rebel, interested only in those things she can respond to in mood and emotion (*244*), she is in pursuit of an idealized self which she vaguely feels can be realized through the artistic life.

Through Etta and Solon Barnes, Dreiser was giving consent to Shelley while rejecting Babbitt, giving consent to John Burroughs and Henry David Thoreau while modifying—but not dismissing—Herbert Spencer. The ideas here were latent in Dreiser's early writing, and *The Bulwark* is not a radical departure in Dreiser's thinking. He merely shifted the magnifying glass, showing the man of big business aware of a higher principle than money, showing Spencer's realm of antithetical forces being absorbed—contradictions and all—within Thoreau's oversoul—that is, on a transcendent level of beauty and order. Dreiser created a larger self within the universe—a self that was also greedy and seeking, but a self within which the individual could be absorbed. Even though the will of the larger self might be inimical to man in general, it offered a release from individual desire and self-seeking. It also offered the means to reconcile life's contradictions. Opposites now only appear to be in conflict, just as two men climbing different sides of the mountain will eventually find themselves together on the top.

When Dreiser saw the pursuit of beauty as an alternative to the pursuit of wealth, he was, of course, extolling the selfless artist and condemning the rapacious businessman—a fact which might have been a source of amusement to Dreiser's publishers, especially Horace Liveright, with whom Dreiser's business dealings were hardly other-worldly. Dreiser could be more contemptuous of Babbitt in his seventies, surrounded by material comfort, than he could in his thirties, trying to make a go of it as a free-lance writer and novelist. Perhaps the real difference between Sister Carrie's restless desire and Solon Barnes's final peace was the difference between Dreiser's own early thirst for experience and fame and his final sense of tired commitment. *The Bulwark* may better reveal Dreiser's state of physical decline than a resolution to his philosophy. As oriental philosophers teach, once one is able to shut out the material world—the physical realm that so compelled and fascinated Dreiser's characters, even the Stewarts of his final writing— one is better able to give himself to contemplation and to concentrate on the inherent beauty and the mystical "way."

Solon becomes more resigned to life as he is softened by unhappy experience and mellowed by the years. When Etta returns to him, she notices that "the stern light that shone in his eyes" was gone (*250*). Solon is no longer the rigid, authoritarian, unforgiving father who dominates his children. Once he is able to break down his own ego, he is able to perceive the Creative Spirit—able even to communicate his goodwill to the puff adder which crawled (Dreiser was telling a personal story) over the toe of his shoe when it perceived that he meant no harm. As Solon tells Etta,

> "Daughter, until recently I have not thought as I think now. . . . God has taught me humility—and, in His loving charity, awakened me to many things that I had not seen before. One is the need of love toward all created things." (*254*)

If Solon Barnes started out as Dreiser's father, he ended up (except for perhaps the consent to a Christian God) as Dreiser himself—or at least as the seventy-five-year-old Dreiser liked to think of himself. In a sense, through Solon Barnes, Dreiser was coming home.

While there is a more relaxed attitude, Dreiser did not suddenly move from philosophical mechanism to a kind of transcendentalism. As we have seen, the two ideologies warred within him from the turn of the century on. A Spencerian mechanist and a romantic idealist, Dreiser sometimes saw a creative intelligence absorbing the seemingly unreconcilable, combative forces in both society and nature. Life fed on life—

but perhaps with a (selfish?) purpose if one could view the combat from a higher plane.

Solon finds a moment of peace by giving consent to such a possibility. His consent, however, cannot and does not change the physical world in which he lives: in the physical world the struggle is fierce and man is fragile; pleasures lure on Solon's children; and material rewards and comforts encourage the unscrupulous man of big business, whom Solon rejects. Solon, in fact, is very much a part of the dialectic, his religion an inverse expression of the secular—a reaction of the old to the new. *The Bulwark* still reveals a world of force and counterforce. While some of the motives here are the same motives we find in *Sister Carrie*, Dreiser emphasized, not added, another dimension—a transcendent realm of being. This emphasis softened the play of mechanistic forces and allowed the artist romantic dignity.

The added dimension is present once again in Dreiser's next and last novel—*The Stoic*. Both Solon Barnes and Frank Algernon Cowperwood have Pennsylvania Quaker backgrounds. While Solon struggles to preserve his religion, Cowperwood never sees any relationship between Quaker teachings and the business world of post-bellum Philadelphia and Chicago. Solon Barnes and Frank Cowperwood have very different temperaments, respond differently to the values of a materialistic society, and become different kinds of men—one, in fact, becomes the inversion of the other.

Cowperwood does not really change in character in *The Stoic*—nor does his world differ radically from that of *The Financier* and *The Titan*. We are told (on the very first page), for example, that Cowperwood was a man of "determined and almost savage individualism" (*1*) and that (three pages later) he followed " 'the line of self-interest, because . . . there is no other guide' " (*4*). We are also told that life consists of forces at work, using men like tools, so that events happened because they "sprang out of conditions which life itself, operating through him [Cowperwood] and others, had created and shaped" (*47*). As in Dreiser's other novels, the two elements described—Cowperwood's selfishness and the combative forces of life—are related, and the world of force justifies his ruthlessness. In a sentence which reveals the logic of Dreiser's philosophy as clearly as he would ever express it, he tells us: "The man [Cowperwood] was ruthless, but in a way which the jumbled interests of life required" (123). Cowperwood finds little to admire in religion, believes that "the strong [use a] . . . belief in a god to further the conquest of the weak," (137) maintains that "men killed to live" (137), and that this is a basic truth of life.

Like all of Dreiser's ambitious characters—Carrie, Eugene, Clyde, the youthful Cowperwood himself—Cowperwood has little interest in the past (*see 137*) and concentrates on realizing what the future holds. This frame of mind is a constant source of narrative irony in *The Stoic* because throughout the novel we hear the tick of the clock. The *ubi sunt* theme dominates this novel: "Time! Time! Time!" we are told, "Always the erosive process at work" (*41, cf. also 108*). At one point, Cowperwood ponders why he is working so hard, scheming once again, trying now to push through a London underground transit system, when he has more money than he can ever use. Dreiser's question here was a very personal one, for he also was working hard—struggling through both *The Bulwark* and *The Stoic*—when he also did not need the money. In "Notes on Life," Dreiser had maintained that life is a game and that we play it because there is nothing else that we can do. Cowperwood comes to the same conclusion in *The Stoic*. As De Sota Sippens, one of his assistants, tells him: life is " 'some sort of game that I'm here to play . . . I guess that's the answer: to be doing something all the time. There's a game on, and whether we like it or not, we have to play our parts' " (*113–14*).

This metaphor significantly undercuts a belief in teleology, and final purpose. In "Notes on Life," Dreiser replaced the idea of evolution with involution. All matter and all energy, he maintained, is fixed and constant; while matter expresses itself through different and various forms, it can neither increase nor decrease. Hence life repeats itself and all motion is circular. This is the "truth" that Berenice Fleming learns in *The Stoic*. She goes to India, studies oriental philosophy, and learns that all life is like the throw of the dice. " 'Suppose the dice falls in this ratio: 5-6-3-4,' " the guru tells her. " 'We take the dice up and throw them again, and again. There must come a time when the same number will fall again, the same combination will come'" (296). The atoms of the universe, he continues, are like thrown dice; and while an infinite number of "throws" may pass, eventually the same atoms, like the same sequence of thrown dice, will combine into groups, with "group intelligence," these bodies serving "'as vehicles for higher forms of consciousness'" (296).

Behind the veil of chance (an accidental event is usually in the center of Dreiser's novels) is thus a realm of inevitability (in all of the novels the "accidents"—that is, the roll of the dice—set up an inevitable sequence of events and bring fixed laws and forces into play). Behind the realm of matter is a higher consciousness (which Clyde seems to intuit at Big Bittern and which creates an ironic distance between the way a character sees and is seen). Behind the linear sequence of events is the circular and repetitive motion of life (which explains the repetitive structure, the incremental progression, and the circular design—particularly in *An American Tragedy*—of Dreiser's fiction). And beyond the will of each character is the possibility of self-fulfillment ("'all the possibilities of life are in the germ,'" the guru tells Berenice) which lures men toward a final destiny and which keeps them chasing an ideal self down the circular corridors of time. Eugene Witla and Frank Algernon Cowperwood are single-minded in their rush to realize an essential self, while Clyde Griffiths overestimates his possibilities, and Solon Barnes is unable (at least at first) to reconcile the Witla and the Cowperwood that battle within him.

The contradictions that exist in Solon Barnes exist first in Dreiser the man. He identified with and gave imaginative consent to the accomplishments of a Charles Yerkes and yet believed that such a man was an antithesis to the artist who pursued the highest ideals. He glamorized the heightened life of the rich and yet felt this life existed at the expense of the poor—in fact, perpetuated their condition.

These contradictions remained more or less latent in his early work. As Dreiser, however, became more interested in social causes—in establishing an "equity" (to use his word) between the rich and the poor—he had to find the means of reconciling his mechanistic philosophy (which justified the ruthless and energetic tycoon) with his romantic idealism (which justified altruism and the values of art).

In *The Bulwark*, Dreiser tried to resolve these contradictions through the character of Solon Barnes. In *The Stoic*, he tried once again—this time in his portrait of Berenice Fleming. He does this by insisting that one has to be washed of desire before social commitment is possible. When Berenice Fleming accepts and is "absorbed in Brahman," she loses her sense of desire. When she is once a part of the larger "I," she is better able to see the discrepancies between rich and poor and thus better able to help the afflicted.

If Berenice Fleming moves beyond Frank Cowperwood, then we have come full circle: Cowperwood embodied the spirit of desire, is completely selfish, and his life is consistent with a world of force and counterforce; Berenice is "absorbed in Brahman," is washed free of "self" and desire, and is able to dedicate her life to others. On a spiritual plane, the physical extremes are resolved, and the world of combat gives way to love.

While *The Stoic* offers a syncretistic resolution to thematic extremes, the novel still functions in terms of those extremes— Frank Cowperwood embodying the principles of materialism, Berenice Fleming of spiritualism—and *The Stoic*, if perhaps Dreiser's worst novel, is his most ambitious attempt to find in romantic idealism the means to negate Cowperwood's savage motives.

One can find countless literary parallels to *The Stoic*, all of them within the tradition of romantic literature. Hart Crane's *The Bridge*, for example, tries to reconcile the terrestrial with the supraterrestrial, man with the higher forces of nature. While Crane is not concerned with the conflict between selfish and altruistic motives, he is concerned with the gulf between man and the machine world. At the beginning of the poem, we have the "iron-dealt cleavage"—modern man as a "bedlamite" cut off from himself and nature, living in an unreal world, a manufactured realm of the "cinemas" with their flickering and fragmented images, a world where the sun has become an acetylene torch and "elevators drop us from our day" or we "scuttle" from the subway (perhaps built by Yerkes-Cowperwood). Like Dreiser's later characters, the poet seeks a higher and larger "I," a synthesizing plane of reality. Like Columbus in the "Ave Maria" section of *The Bridge*, he is searching for India, where Berenice discovers final "truth." Like Berenice, he finds himself being absorbed into a higher, transforming substance, participating in a kind of primitive dance-of-death-and-new-life which links his will with "The old gods of the rain [who] lie wrapped in pools," domed by iron mountains. This act becomes "the bridge" between the material and the spiritual. When the poet at the end of the poem comes up from the underground, he finds himself once again in the city, the iron Brooklyn Bridge now a kind of sea flower ("whitest Flower,/ O Answer of all,—Anemone—"), the machine and nature metamorphically at one.

Like Crane, Dreiser in *The Stoic* tried to reconcile dualities, affirmed that the contradictions of life are more apparent than real, and insisted that the individual has to free himself of greed before he can combat it in others. Ironically, the Creative Intelligence, to whom Berenice gives consent, is really an extension of the greedy self. Dreiser escaped from his overpowering ego by projecting it into the universe. The way back—the peace beyond understanding—becomes a fiction of the mind, a means of surrendering will and desire to the higher reality which is all absorbing. As Berenice Fleming put it, when this happens she could "brush completely out of her consideration the whole Western materialistic viewpoint which made money and luxury its only god" (286). At odds with the physical world, Dreiser created a transcendental world wherein an idealized self could find fulfillment. Torn between material and esthetic values, Dreiser extended this conflict into the universe itself and surrendered himself to the forces that work for their own self-fulfillment. Although these forces are as greedy as their inventor, when Dreiser's characters become absorbed within this larger "I," they find peace and a release from material desire. This was the best Dreiser could do in his attempt to escape from the romantic dilemma; and he was playing games with himself when, in *The Stoic*, he buried Frank Algernon Cowperwood— in more ways than one.

15

The Crossroads of the Novel

Dreiser's novels must be read against the genteel tradition. James Russell Lowell (1819–91) was only eight years dead when Dreiser began to write *Sister Carrie*. This was the Lowell who attacked Thoreau, scorned Walt Whitman, and praised William Dean Howells, Edmund Clarence Stedman, Thomas Bailey Aldrich, and Richard Watson Gilder. This was the Lowell who had no sympathy for the Haymarket Square anarchists (he described them as "ruffians well hanged"). This was the man who believed that no author should write what he did not want his daughter to read, thus reducing the content of literature to the experience of the inexperienced.

William Dean Howells embodied the values of a Lowell, which is why Lowell praised him. Dreiser had little sympathy for either Lowell or Howells. In his essay "The Great American Novel," Dreiser linked Howells with Henry James and said that he was "too socially indifferent and worse, uninformed, save for *Their Wedding Journey*." [1] *Their Wedding Journey* (1871) is Howells' first novel, although it is really not a novel at all but a travelogue account of Howells' honeymoon which took him and his new wife from Boston to New York, up the Hudson River, to Niagara Falls, and down the St. Lawrence to Quebec. As a travelogue, *Their Wedding Journey* is similar to *A Hoosier Holiday*, which might explain Dreiser's fondness for it. Like Dreiser's travelogues, Howells gives us vivid impressions of the cities he visits (New York, especially Broadway, Rochester, and Buffalo), mixing these impressions with social commentary.

While Dreiser and Howells were never fond of each other (Howells disliked *Sister Carrie*), they had much in common. Like Dreiser, Howells was the ambitious son of unprosperous parents (his father was a printer) who lived in a small Midwestern town (Ferry, Ohio), yearned for the larger life which only the city could supply, and he was a journalist before he became a magazine editor. Here the parallel stops. When Howells wrote a campaign biography of Lincoln, he was appointed in 1861 to the American consul in Venice. When he returned to the States in 1865, he joined the staff of *The Nation* and then in 1866 became assistant editor of the *Atlantic Monthly* and was later the editor, from 1871 (the year Dreiser was born) to 1881. In 1888, he went to New York where he contributed to *Harper's Magazine* before taking over as editor of the *Cosmopolitan.*

Although Howells disliked *Sister Carrie,* one of his own novels, *A Modern Instance* (1881), is similar to Dreiser's first work. Like Carrie, Bartley Hubbard is an ambitious and amoral product of a small town (Equity, Maine). Although he soon reveals a tainted and corrupt nature, he still manages to marry Marcia, the wealthy daughter of the local squire (who disapproves of the marriage) and comes to Boston to make his fortune in journalism. Just as Dreiser described Carrie struggling to find work in Chicago, Howells described the Hubbards' bewildering attempt to find lodgings they can afford. Like Carrie, Bartley eventually succeeds, first as a free-lance writer and later as a journalist; and like Carrie (or Eugene Witla or Clyde Griffiths) Bartley is willing to subordinate moral scruples to his desire for success and money (there was a "decay of whatever was right-principled in him," Howells tells us). While Bartley is amoral, Marcia has an innate sense of goodness and virtue. While her heart pulls her toward Bartley, her conscience pulls her away from him: her rigid awareness of right and wrong adds a dimension of moral certainty that is absent in Dreiser's novels.

A Modern Instance reaches its climax when Bartley, after a violent quarrel with Marcia, absconds to Chicago with twelve hundred dollars of Ben Halleck's money. In Cleveland, he has a change of heart and decides to return to Boston. When he comes to buy his return ticket, however, he discovers that his wallet—with the twelve hundred dollars in it—has been stolen. "Now he could not return; nothing remained for him but the ruin he had chosen." [2] Bartley, of course, has not chosen at all. Or if he had chosen, it is to return to Boston, just the opposite of what fate decrees. While a Christian God seems to be at work in most of Howells' novels, the forces at work here seem malevolent, and Bartley is driven toward a predestined end by an accident (the stolen wallet) just as Hurstwood is driven toward a predestined end by another accident (the safe slamming shut). In fact, the stolen wallet in *A Modern Instance* and the slamming of the safe door in *Sister Carrie* have the same narrative purpose.

A Modern Instance, however, is very different from *Sister Carrie*, especially the ending which is told from the point of view of the suffering Marcia. This is, of course, a major difference, because when Marcia morally triumphs and Bartley morally fails, the Christian sense of right and wrong is put in clear perspective—just as it would have been if the story of Hurstwood had been told from the point of view of Mrs. Hurstwood. By telling the story from Hurstwood's own point of view, and telling it sympathetically, Dreiser turned the genteel novel upside down, created a ambivalent world, and wrote a novel that the Doubledays (brought up on Howells' kind of fiction) were reluctant to publish. While Hurstwood's death arouses our sympathy, no one really cares when Bartley is shot to death in Whited Sepulchre, Arizona. Marcia has gone back to Equity, where she is pursued by Ben Halleck, now a minister, who ponders whether he can rightfully marry her, since he secretly loved her from afar while her husband was alive. As the novel ends, this ersatz moral problem keeps the lovers separated and the Christian God in His heaven.

As Dreiser developed a social conscience mid-career, so did Howells. While *A Traveller from Altruria* (1894) and *Through the Eye of a Needle* (1907) reflect a Utopian socialism, *A Hazard of New Fortunes* (1890) attempts a more realistic portrait of social conflict. Basil March (of *Their Wedding Journey*) and his wife leave Boston to take over the editorial duties of *Every Other Week*, just as the Howellses left Boston when he took up with *Harper's* and later *Cosmopolitan*. When they arrive in New York, they meet a number of social types, who comment on each other's values: Mr. Dryfoos, the owner of the journal, is a self-made man from Pennsylvania. He is an uneducated farmer, who made his money in natural gas and has neither the taste nor the intelligence to know what to do with it. He is scorned by the upper-class because he is newly rich, and he fears the lower classes because they threaten his money and new security. Lindau is the Socialist whom Mr. Dryfoos comes most to hate. He has lost his hand in the war, and he hates the ruling class with passion. Dryfoos says of him: "He's a red-mouthed labor agitator. He's one of those foreigners . . . [who cause] strikes . . . break our Sabbath, and teach atheism. They ought to be hung." [3] Conrad Dryfoos, the owner's son, is a young liberal, who believes social change must come. He tells his father: "The burden of all the wrong in the world comes on the poor. . . . Every sort of fraud and swindling hurts them the worst. The city wastes money it's paid to clean the streets with, and the poor have to suffer, for they can't afford to pay twice, like the rich." All of these characters are marched toward a tour de force ending. Conrad is shot and Lindau clubbed to death during a streetcar strike (much like the one in *Sister Carrie*) when they coincidentally arrive at the same time at the scene of the strike. Old Dryfoos has a change of political heart when he learns that Conrad was killed trying to help Lindau. A Christian sense of fate—man in God's hands —runs through this novel. Both old Dryfoos and Lindau, men of extreme views, are punished in the end, the more humane and genteel views prospering, as if God blessed all who walked in the middle of the road.

As a political novel, *A Hazard of New Fortunes* does not come to terms with political realities, just as *The Rise of Silas Lapham* (1885) does not come to terms with the reality of postwar business life in America. Howells could not see or was unwilling to depict the corruption of his age. While Silas does treat a business partner unfairly, he is otherwise a model of Christian charity and scruples. And while Silas chooses poverty to dishonor, Rockefeller was ruining his competitors with deceitful deals and railroad rebates, Drew and Gould and Fiske were bribing legislators, and Elkins, Widener and Yerkes were deviously securing streetcar franchises. Granville Hicks has pointed out the gulf between the world of Silas Lapham and that of the gilded age: "One thing is clear and that is that neither the great rewards nor the great achievements would have been possible if they [the robber barons] had spent much time meditating on the problems that distracted Silas Lapham." [4]

If Howells was unable to see beneath the gilt of his age, Henry James was not even interested in the gilt. He disliked the business world; and because his grandfather had made enough money, he did not have to worry about what was going on downtown and could take the genteel life of leisure for granted. When he returned to America in 1904, he was greatly upset at the extent it had been commercialized. He voiced his discontent in *The American Scene,* a travelogue, and in *The Ivory Tower,* significantly, a novel that he was never able to finish. James admired the aristocratic world of Europe. In his *Hawthorne,* he listed the institutions that America lacked:

> No sovereign, no court, no personal loyalty, no aristocracy, no church, no clergy, no army, no diplomatic service, no country gentlemen, no palaces, no castles, no manors, nor old country-houses, nor parsonages, nor thatched cottages, nor ivied ruins; no cathedrals, nor abbeys, nor little Norman churches; no great Universities nor public schools—no Oxfords, nor Eton, nor Harrow. [5]

Yet the aristocratic world had been corrupted and was crumbling—and James knew it. His Christopher Newman gives up the seamy world of American business, tries to find himself among the dying French aristocracy, and becomes a victim of its machinations. And even though James would have us believe that Newman triumphs morally when he burns that letter incriminating the Bellegardes, it is an empty triumph: Valentine is dead and Claire is in the convent. Isabel Archer duplicates this plight. Caught between going back to America and Caspar Goodwood, or returning to Italy and Gilbert Osmond, she "chooses" Osmond, giving herself to a loveless marriage, sacrificing herself to keep the dying aristocracy alive, remaining faithful to her misguided decision to marry. Her choice is really not a choice, since she is damned either way she turns; and she is far more the victim of James's own cultural dilemma than she is a free spirit choosing nobly and heroically.

Isabel, in fact, is no more free than Christina Light, who, as we see in *Roderick Hudson*, is forced into marriage with Prince Casamassima. As Christina says in *The Princess Casamassima*, "My husband traces his descent from the fifth century, and he's the greatest bore in Europe. That's the kind of people I was condemned to by my marriage . . . intelligent mechanics . . . would be a pleasant change." [6] The princess becomes a radical and works to overthrow the society she sees as polluted and corrupt. She sweeps men before her with the power of her desire, including Hyacinth Robinson, the wayward son of a woman of the streets. His mother has murdered his father, a man of mysterious but noble background; and Hyacinth, who has been adopted by a gentle seamstress, has two different kinds of blood self-destructively flowing through his veins. When he gives his word that he will kill the duke, he kills himself instead, because to kill the duke would mean killing his father and repeating his mother's murder. While he is swept away in the cultural currents that swirl about him, he is as much the victim of James's imagination as he is the victim of his age. His end reveals that James's sentiments rested with the aristocracy and not the revolutionaries—with those who cultivated the refinements of life and not those who bluntly proposed to overturn the establishment, even though the establishment was hopelessly corrupt.

Thus James, like his principal characters, was caught between two worlds—one of the past and the other of the future: the lost aristocracy and the new industry. While the industrialist had means beyond his needs, he lacked the institutions that James so completely described in his book on Hawthorne. And while the aristocrat had his institutions, he lacked the means to support them. Since each culture was insufficient in and by itself, James's pilgrims are destined to remain incomplete, because the values they seek are the values which only society can give them. And what was true of his characters was true of James also. He exercised his will—that all-important faculty in his novels—but exercised it in a social vacuum, the victim of this cultural dilemma.

While James and Dreiser are usually contrasted by the critics, a comparison of their first novels, *Roderick Hudson* (1875) and *Sister Carrie*, offers a number of similarities. Both Roderick Hudson and Sister Carrie leave small towns (Northhampton, Massachusetts and in the holograph of *Sister Carrie* Green Bay, Wisconsin) for the big city (Chicago and Rome) which holds new possibilities and a heightened way of life. Both are trying to shed their parochial upbringing (Carrie the moral rigidity of the small town, Roderick the Puritan scruples of his family) in their search for a larger and freer way of life. Both are financed in this aim by others (Roderick by Rowland Mallett, Carrie by Drouet and later Hurstwood), and both betray the trust of the men who support them. Both are insufferable egoists, dominated by an insistent urge to fulfill their desire for success or experience. Both want more than just material pleasures—Carrie intuiting the spirit behind the flesh, Roderick motivated by the artist's sense of eternal beauty. And both are destined to fail—Carrie by continually yearning for more and more, Roderick by bestowing his desires upon Christina Light, who is fated to betray them. Roderick's death (in a fall from an Alpine mountain) is a melodramatic version of Carrie's rocking discontentedly in her chair. With both characters, the range of their vision went beyond the limits of their ability.

While there are these similarities between James's and Dreiser's novels, Roderick Hudson is most at home in the salon, surrounded by princes and men of wealth and leisure. He struggles on a much higher level of society than does Carrie, who would be more comfortable in Hurstwood's saloon, surrounded by traveling salesmen and aspiring actors. Roderick Hudson moves in the fixed, tradition-filled society of an old and corrupt Europe. Carrie moves in the more fluid, traditionless society of the new and turbulent America. Carrie and Roderick are separated by their differences in taste, by the genteel wall of manners, although in Bob Ames, Carrie meets and is attracted to a kind of Roderick Hudson. The artist in a Philistine world bridges for both Dreiser and James the gulf caused by class and social differences. As a result, Dreiser's characters function in a "vertical" way: Carrie moves up as she moves beyond first Drouet and then Hurstwood. James's characters, on the other hand, function in a "horizontal" way: the essence of each is revealed through a kind of counterpoint with his cultural opposite. Both the "Europeanized" Christina and Roderick, for example, want to realize themselves—Roderick as an artist, Christina as a woman—in a free and unencumbered way. This becomes impossible, however, because Rowland Mallet and Mrs. Light, who dominate them, have a fixed idea of what each should be. In the meantime, Prince Casamassima and Mary Garland (representing violently different cultural extremes) wait as lovers in the wings, the Cavaliere (who turns out to be the father of Christina) and the hysterical Mr. Hudson (again representing cultural extremes) having their unexpressed influence on the two principals.

Like Dreiser's *The "Genius," Roderick Hudson* is a study of the artist trying to find himself. In his novel, James makes it clear that neither inspiration (Roderick has to be inspired before he can work) nor perspiration (Singleton is both tireless and talentless) is enough to make an artist: he must also have a sense of life based on experience. This is an idea Dreiser would accept, although Dreiser's artist has more of a romantic's sense of intuition, sees more beyond the veil, and his art reflects the essences of life—as if life itself, the forces that move us all, were speaking through him. Thus Eugene Witla would not go to Rome to imitate the models of antiquity; he would go to the slums and catch the violent throb of men caught in life's struggle. Here—in the extreme contrast between what are the objects of art—one can discover the essential difference between a James and a Dreiser.

If Howells never saw beneath the surface of post-Civil War America, and if James took flight from this new era, Mark Twain also never came to terms with his age, although he made an attempt in *The Gilded Age*, which he wrote in collaboration with Charles Dudley Warner. Twain's world was the vanished realm of childhood (*Huckleberry Finn* and *Tom Sawyer*) or the vanished world of feudalism (*A Connecticut Yankee in King Arthur's Court* or *The Prince and the Pauper*).

Dreiser met Twain—in fact, met him three times. He met Twain once by accident on the street; he visited him once to interview him (unsuccessfully as it turned out) for *Success* magazine; and he met him a third time (in 1908, when he was editor of the *Delineator*) in a saloon on the corner of Irving Place and 14th Street in the Village, where Dreiser was introduced to him by two writers, whose names he could not remember. Twain himself had lived in the Village off and on. In 1900, he lived at West 10th Street; and in 1908, he was living at 21 Fifth Avenue. Dreiser was pleasantly surprised at the third meeting when Twain attacked the hypocrisy of Americans who maintain that marriage is a sacrament when in reality (and Dreiser was quoting Twain from memory) "after the first few years of marriage, men don't love their wives, and they are not strictly faithful." [7] Dreiser, who was about to leave his own wife at this time, was "exhilarated" by this talk, and Twain became one of his culture heroes. Yet, like Van Wyck Brooks, Dreiser felt that Twain never realized himself because he was restrained by American puritan conventions: "convention—convention, the dross of a worthless and meaningless current opinion—this was the thing that restrained him." [8]

Like Dreiser, Twain had married a small-town, conventional girl, Olivia Langdon, from Elmira, New York, fifty miles southeast of Cortland. Like Dreiser, Twain had worked as a reporter (for the *Territorial Enterprise* of Nevada, the San Francisco *Morning Call*, and the Buffalo *Express*, of which thanks to his father-in-law, he had a third interest). And like Dreiser, Twain was unsympathetic to the genteel tradition. In

1877, at an *Atlantic* dinner in honor of John Greenleaf Whittier, Twain described Emerson, Longfellow, and Holmes as "three deadbeats, visiting a California mining-camp, and imposing themselves upon the innocent miners." While Twain publicly apologized, he was never forgiven by the genteel critics, who looked down upon him anyway because of his popularity with the masses.

While Twain was once sympathetic to the Republican Party, he broke when it nominated James Blaine for president, and he eventually became sympathetic to socialism. He attacked Czarist Russia during the Russo-Japanese War, and he supported the Russian revolution. He was particularly sympathetic to Maxim Gorky, whom he planned to introduce to an American audience before Gorky discredited himself by coming to America and living with an actress who turned out not to be his wife (would Dreiser have blanched as Twain did?). While Twain rented a pew at the Asylum Hill Congregational Church in Hartford (the Church of the Holy Speculator, he called it), he seldom attended, even though his good friend, the Reverend Joseph T. Twichell, was the pastor. Twain hated men like John Wanamaker, the department store magnate, who founded the Bethany Presbyterian Sunday School, preached Christian charity, and then paid his female employees so poorly that many were forced to become prostitutes. Twain had no more respect for the pious John D. Rockefeller who ruthlessly crushed his competitors, big and small, in his monomaniacal efforts to establish the Standard Oil monopoly.

In the unpublished "Notes for a Social History of the United States from 1850 to 1900," Twain maintained that America became money-mad after 1850. He believed that the California gold-rush had brought on the desire for sudden wealth. This attitude of mind was intensified by the Civil War which encouraged the Wall Street banker and the railroad promoter, who profited from the war and who looted the country. They were unscrupulous men who wanted most to "get rich, dishonestly if we can; honestly if we must."

Twain's political shift was influenced by William Dean Howells, whose thinking underwent change when the Supreme Court upheld the decision against the Chicago anarchists who supposedly were involved in the Haymarket Square bombing on May 4, 1886. Four of these men were hanged, one committed suicide, and two had their death sentences commuted to life imprisonment. Howells wrote to his father at this time: "All is over now, except the judgment that begins at once for every unjust and evil deed, and goes on forever . . . this free Republic has killed five men for their opinions." [9]

Yet if Twain shared Howells' doubts about where America was going, he never wanted to do away with capitalism. If he attacked American business, he attacked the aristocracy as well —and both attacks stemmed from the same premise: Twain distrusted all institutions. He felt that beneath the institution was the man. Beneath the clothes and the pomp was nature itself. The theme of nakedness is important in Twain's work. The great man sees through the gilt of wealth and the pretensions of courtly and social conventions. He grasps truth in its naked reality. In fact, when Twain's characters most embody the natural self (Huck on the raft, the Connecticut Yankee in prison), they are naked. In a world where twins and mirror images give rise to surface similarities that distort reality, Twain had as much distrust of clothes as Carlyle.

An essential reality exists beneath the trappings of society. In *A Connecticut Yankee in King Arthur's Court*, the king is most king when he is a slave; and in *The Prince and the Pauper*, the prince is most a prince when he is a pauper. The true merits of character—an essential reality—come out when one is put to the test. One is what one has been bred to be, and this residual self always remains. Even when the king is being abused as a slave, he is still a king. The narrator notes: "And as [the king] stood apart there, receiving this homage in rags, I thought to myself, well, really there *is* something peculiarly grand about the faith and bearing of a king after all." [10]

Moral supremacy in Twain's novels comes from knowing what others do not know, and one learns by living—that is, through experience. Arthur learns the evil of slavery by being a slave; Prince Edward learns the misery of poverty by being a pauper. Both Twain and Dreiser believed in this essential point: that life is learned from life and that meaning cannot be divorced from experience. Until we reach Hemingway, we do not find another American writer endorsing what amounts to experiential knowledge and the finding of self—an essential self (a point that separated Dreiser's and Twain's characters from those in existential literature)—waiting to be realized through action.

Although Twain's view of man became more pessimistic in his last years, it was not until he wrote works like "The Man That Corrupted Hadleyburg" and "The Mysterious Stranger" that he abandoned a kind of Rousseau-like view of man: the belief that man had a kind of innate and primitive goodness which one could discover beneath the layers of artifice and pretense that came with being a social animal. Thus while Twain was never popular with the genteel critics, he did not fly in their face; and while *Huckleberry Finn* was banned in Concord, it was because Huck chose Hell over betrayal—and not because of Twain's view of man.

If Twain did not fly in the face of the genteel tradition, neither did Stephen Crane. While one might think that *Maggie* would have created the same kind of storm as *Sister Carrie*, it did not—in fact, it was highly praised by William Dean Howells, and there is a world of difference between Dreiser's and Crane's novel. Crane once wrote of *Maggie:* "It tries to show that environment is a tremendous thing in this world, and often shapes lives regardlessly." Dreiser would not have argued with this view of environment. Yet in *Maggie* Crane used environment statically, while in *Sister Carrie* Dreiser used it dynamically. Crane's Maggie is merely suppressed by her poverty and her drunken parents. Dreiser's Carrie is equally suppressed, but she has the illusion of escape. In fact, in one sense, she does escape when she becomes a stage star. In another sense, she is as imprisoned at the end of the novel as she was at the beginning, since she will always desire more than she has—will always be the victim of her appetite. Dreiser's view is much larger than Crane's: while Maggie cannot see beyond her tenement world, Carrie looks beyond the Chicago slums to at least cafe society. Moreover, while Carrie "sins" and prospers, Maggie is the mere victim of her moral collapse. When Maggie gives her body to Pete she is damned, and the assumptions here are melodramatically Christian. Maggie is as much the victim of her moral turpitude as she is of her environment. If Crane depicted the plight of the East-side tenement life, he also created a morally rigid world—the assumptions of which are strangely similar to those one finds in the world of the upper-Fifth Avenue salon, more conventional and proper even than one finds in the world of Edith Wharton.

If Dreiser was the first novelist to portray fully the motives of a Carrie Meeber, Edith Wharton returned to this kind of woman in her portrait of Undine Spragg. Ambitious, gauche, and totally amoral, Undine reveals her own unscrupulous nature when she tells Mr. Dagonet, to the astonishment of his dinner guests, that Mabel Lipscomb will probably get a divorce because her husband "isn't in the right set, and I think Mabel realizes she'll never get anywhere till she gets rid of him." [11]

An upper-middle-class Carrie (or even Clyde Griffiths), Undine aspires for social recognition and will destroy anyone who stands in her way. Although she is more intelligently and consciously willful than either Carrie or Clyde, her values are just as derivative as theirs; she likes and dislikes what the social register accepts or rejects, just as she liked her summer at the Persimon House until she heard the snobbish Miss Wincher deprecate it. She represents "the custom of the country"—that is, the ruthless spirit and drive of the new rich—which has moved into New York from the emerging industrial cities and corrupted the salon. Undine, with the help of Elmer Moffatt, cannot be denied. Someone like Ralph Marvell, who lives by the old courtesies, is incapable of coping with this new type, these shrewd and unscrupulous manipulators who have been spawned by a new, amoral and money-mad age.

Isolated by his taste and moral rigidity, Ralph Marvell is unhappy with the postwar society based on financial success, observes a new grossness of behavior that corresponds to the bad taste of the new architecture, and concludes that this society "was really just like the houses it lived in: a muddle of misapplied ornament over a thin steel shell of utility. The steel shell was built up in Wall Street, the social trimmings were hastily added in Fifth Avenue; and the union between them was . . . monstrous and factitious" (73).

As Carrie uses Drouet and then Hurstwood, so Undine uses

Elmer Moffatt and then Ralph in her climb to the top, the fates of Drouet and Hurstwood paralleling almost exactly those of Moffatt (who continues to ride the waves) and Marvell (who is engulfed and commits suicide). Like Carrie, Undine climbs even as she moves against the moral grain of the times, and climbs by dint of her own energy and force: "Her sole graces, her unaided personality, had worked the miracle" (387).

While an Undine takes advantage of the decline in the old order, the serpent in the garden is really Elmer Moffatt. He corrupts Ralph's genteel sense of morality and fair play. Mrs. Wharton tells us, "Since his transaction with Moffat, [Ralph] had had the sense of living under a new dispensation," and he was unsure that he could implant the old "reserves and discriminations" in Paul, his son (305–06). A man from the lowest level of poverty, a man with a mysterious past who marries Undine before she is taken from him by her socially astonished parents, a man who is ruthlessly and cunningly ambitious, Elmer Moffatt embodies the kind of character who, in one way or another, dominates contemporary American fiction. Seen by a Faulkner, he will become the despicable Flem Snopes (like Snopes, he even worked in the local power plant). Seen by a Fitzgerald, he will become a more practical Jay Gatsby, who actually regains his lost love with his dishonestly made fortune and dubious social credentials. And seen by a Theodore Dreiser, he will become a Frank Algernon Cowperwood, a man of energy and drive, who shrewdly forces his way to the top of the business world, buys up the rarest art treasures of Europe, and sets up one of the most impressive homes on upper Fifth Avenue. In *The Custom of the Country*, Edith Wharton, in a very real way, married Carrie Meeber to Frank Algernon Cowperwood. The novel ends with Undine already tiring of Elmer, Undine deciding that she wanted most of all to be a ambassador's wife, and Undine not sure that Moffatt "fit the picture" (591). At this moment, Carrie is about to triumph once again, this time over a kind of Frank Algernon Cowperwood—for even the titans cannot satisfy or stop her lust for riches and fame.

Dreiser admired Edith Wharton's novels—and one can see why. She described the aspiring and unfixed character in a turbulent world, a world in which new values were replacing the fixed values of the past. Dreiser admired even more Henry Blake Fuller's novels—and for much the same reason. *The Cliff Dwellers* (1893) is a novel, in fact, that Dreiser could not help liking—a novel that has much in common with his own fiction. The central character is one George Ogden, who has come to Chicago from Boston and works as a cashier for the Underground National Bank. The bank, owned by the ruthless titan Erastus M. Brainard, is housed in the Clifton, one of the first Chicago skyscrapers. Both Brainard and the Clifton symbolize the mad rush for money in post-Civil War America. They also symbolize a destructive force at work in America, even though progress and the products of an industrial civilization would suggest the opposite.

We can see the destructive element at work in Brainard's own family. As much a tyrant in his home as in his office, Brainard treats his family in the same domineering way that he treats his competitors. Ironically, the most vital and the most unscrupulous member of his family is his daughter-in-law, the former Cornelia McNobb, who is very much a Sister Carrie. She comes to Chicago from a small Wisconsin town, works first in a boarding house, then as a waitress in the Clifton restaurant before she moves into the Clifton offices as a secretary when she ambitiously masters shorthand and the typewriter. Like Carrie, Nealie loves the theater and the bright life. She is eagerly and shrewdly trying to crash into a respectable family; and no matter how bleak her future appears, she refuses to go back to the small town. Like Carrie, her self-confidence is justified: she traps and marries Burt Brainard, the banker's eldest son, who is given a half-million dollars as a wedding present.

While Burt and Abbie Brainard, the oldest children, tolerate their father, a younger daughter marries (unhappily as it turns out) against the father's will, and his youngest son leaves home to try his luck on the stage. When he fails at acting, Marcus becomes a tramp.

As the tenants in the Clifton embody the destructive personal and social compulsions of this era, so the destructive break-up of the Brainard family symbolizes the nature of the times. Like most of Dreiser's chracters, Ogden is the victim of these destructive forces. He is victimized by his brother-in-law, who betrays a family trust and misinvests the money that his father bequeathed to his mother. He is victimized by his own wife, who recklessly spends his meager salary in trying to compete with Cecilia Ingles, whose husband owns the Clifton. (Fuller says at the end of his novel that it is for such a woman as Cecélia Ingles "that one man builds a Clifton and that a hundred others are martyred in it.")[12] With his back to the wall, George Ogden, much like George Hurstwood, embezzles money from Brainard's bank, an act that enrages Brainard, whose pride has been hurt when Ogden did not marry his daughter. George is saved from prison when Marcus murders his father. He is saved from the mad mentality of his era when his spendthrift wife dies. And although he finally marries Abbie, he is saved from the destructive power of Brainard's money when Burt, without the help of his father, proves financially incompetent and loses the tainted millions. Although melodramatic and high-pitched, the plot of *The Cliff Dwellers* nicely relates the plight of aspiring characters with the plight of a money-centered world, the impulses of one realm accounting for the behavior of the other, so that individual and social motives are destructively at one.

And if *The Cliff Dwellers* has its parallels to *Sister Carrie, Jennie Gerhardt, The Financier,* and *The Titan,* Fuller's *With the Procession* (1895) anticipates Dreiser's *The Bulwark,* a novel he carried in his mind from 1912 to 1945. Like Solon Barnes, David Marshall is unable to cope with a changing America in which the old courtesies are giving way to social climbing, scheming, and financial ruthlessness. Within his own family, Marshall is confronted by his daughter, Jane, who wants to be "with the procession." She feels that life is passing them by in the new Chicago, that her family has lost its rightful place in the new society, and that they must adapt to a changing world. While Jane thinks of the family welfare, her sister, Rosy, thinks of her own immediate welfare and manipulates her way to the top of the social ladder.

If his daughters' ambition puzzles Marshall, so do the artistic pretenses of his youngest son, Truesdale, who has been educated abroad, paints with some ability, and tries to live like

a character in a French novel. When Truesdale gets into romantic trouble, he blames his predicament on America: "were
the books wrong, and only life true? No; it was the fault of
America itself." [13]

As Solon Barnes is unable to understand his children, so
David Marshall is unable to fathom his own children's restlessness, their desire for social recognition, and their indifference to
the old conventions and moral virtues. But where his children
puzzle him, Mr. Belden frightens him. Belden is his ambitious,
unscrupulous, and aggressive business partner, a man who is
eager to "move up" and to do it with any means possible. While
Marshall is completely unable to cope with Belden, his oldest
son is not. Roger, in fact, is one of the new breed, an aggressive
lawyer who can out-scheme the Beldens. While he dislikes what
his son is becoming ("He almost seemed to see the moral fibre
of Roger's nature coarsening—perhaps disintegrating—under
his very eyes") (301), Marshall would be easily ruined if Roger
were not handling his business affairs. Caught between conflicting choices—perplexed by his children and yet solicitous
of their desires, embarrassed by rugged individualism and yet
fearful of failure—David Marshall spins in a whirlpool of
events which prove too much for him. His death at the end
of the novel has been anticipated from the first paragraph.
After his death, Jane prepares to finance a college building in
her father's memory—in memory, that is, of a lost era.

Dreiser believed that Henry Blake Fuller was the first of
the realists. He wrote in 1932 that *With the Procession* "is one
of the first and, even at this date, one of the best examples of
American realism," [14] and he advised the young Edward Dahlberg (in a letter dated November 30, 1937) to read Fuller,
Harold Frederic, and Merton Lyon. Dreiser met Fuller on his
1913 trip to Chicago, where he was researching *The Titan*, but
personal friendship had little to do with Dreiser's praise. Fuller
had shown men caught in a world of flux and change, a realm
of ambiguity and ambivalence where moral alternatives (like
David Marshall's feelings toward his sons) were mutually exclusive and canceled themselves out. Dreiser was very much a
romantic-realist, and he placed his characters between roman-

tic dichotomies: the aspiring (except in *The Bulwark*) idealist in conflict with conventions or forces which delimit
ideals. While the romantics put the emphasis upon man's
aspiring nature, Dreiser put it upon man's determined nature.
Yet, while Dreiser's characters are determined, he shows them
struggling to get free; and the illusion of freedom gives his
novels a dimension that is usually lacking in other naturalistic
fiction. Carrie and Jennie, Cowperwood and Witla, struggle in
a rigidly moral society where, ironically, there is no relation
between success, failure, and moral law. Dreiser creates a
world in which morality restricts and represses natural desire,
a world in which external forces conflict with internal motives,
passion with convention.

For Dreiser, society was an antagonist, and he hated moral
timidity. In a letter to Edgar Lee Masters (March 7, 1940),
he raged against Hamlin Garland, whom he considered a literary conservative.

> What a meaningless person! He was so socially correct and cau-
> tious. I met him several times, dined at his home in Chicago and
> each time came away with a feeling of futility—wasted minutes
> or hours. He was careful of his words—almost fearful of what he
> might say or think. And in this great tumultuous world! Once he
> recited to me the "dreadful" social goings on of a group of peo-
> ple in Eau Claire, Wisconsin and when I said why don't you
> make a book of that he said "Oh, no. That wouldn't do for me.
> It seems to me something that should interest you." I think I
> said "yes, it would." Certainly I thought so.

Twenty-five years before Dreiser wrote these words, he
had attacked Ford Madox Ford on the same critical grounds.
Objecting first to Ford's tangled chronology ("once begun, it
[a novel] should go forward in a more or less direct line"),
Dreiser went on to say that Ford's Dowell is "that literary
packhorse or scapegoat on whom the native Englishman loads
all his concepts of Americans." What Dowell admires is really
English pretense, leisure, gentility, and moral scruples. This
attitude of mind makes difficult, if not impossible, "the production of any great work of art." The Dowells "make life safe,
stale, and impossible." They inculcate "impossible religious,

and moral codes," and encourage the mob "to take their frivolous existence seriously." [15]

Dreiser was rejecting in this review the genteel values. And when Dreiser rejected the genteel tradition, he was rejected in turn. Doubleday, Page tried to suppress *Sister Carrie*, Harpers rejected *The Titan* (after printing 8,500 sets of sheets) and Harper's and John Lane had deleted hundreds of pages of "woman stuff" from *The Financier, The Titan,* and *A Traveller at Forty.* The middle-class magazines gave him the same kind of trouble with his short stories. On September 7, 1917, *The Saturday Evening Post* paid seven hundred fifty dollars for "St. Columba and the River" (in which Dreiser contrasts a religious and mechanistic view of life), held the manuscript for six years, and then returned it (January 26, 1923) as too controversial. Even Mencken, the grand battler against the booboisie, rejected "The Court of Progress," writing (July 16, 1918), "a fat woman with diabetes—the normal magazine reader—would stop her subscription." On August 7, 1918, Douglas Z. Doty rejected "Love," writing "I still believe personally that it is one of the best things you've done." And on September 13, 1918, *Everybody* rejected the same story, saying "It is immeasurably far away from *Everybody*'s type of fiction." The trouble Dreiser had with the middle-class magazines was minor compared to his trouble with the upper-class and more genteel journals. *The Atlantic Monthly,* for example, rejected thirteen consecutive articles and stories between May 13, 1918 and October 10, 1921, doubly rejecting two stories ("Khat" and "Phantom Gold") which Dreiser unwittingly submitted twice.[16] Even as late as 1921, when Dreiser was thinking of leaving Boni and Liveright, he "tested" Dodd and Mead by sending them his story "Olive Brand" to see if they would hesitate to publish such material. Throughout his career, Dreiser was plagued by the timid morality of American publishing, a morality grounded in a native puritanism and encouraged by the genteel tradition. More than any other novelist, he fought the battle against genteel timidity. As Sherwood Anderson put it, "because of him, those who follow will never have to face the road through the wilderness of Puritan denial, the road that Dreiser faced alone."

A Note on Documentation

Much of the documentation in this book is to manuscripts, correspondence, and notes among Dreiser's papers left to the University of Pennsylvania (hereafter referred to as U. of P.). When footnoting holographs and discarded and revised manuscripts, I have referred the reader to the specific chapter of my source, since the U. of P. has very carefully separated such works by title. When footnoting correspondence, I have indicated in the text itself (1) the date of all letters that Dreiser himself wrote (on occasion cross-referencing these to the excellent edition of the letters by Robert Elias) and (2) the name of the person from whom Dreiser received the letter and the date it was written, since this is the way the U. of P. has filed the correspondence. When footnoting unpublished manuscripts (such as "Notes on Life" where there are no chapter headings) I have referred the reader to the box number at U. of P. within which the specific passage or material can be found. All quotations from the novels are taken, when possible, from first editions, although page references are to more accessible texts.

Chapter 1

1. "Dawn," manuscript version, Chapter 19, U. of P.; Dreiser's italics.

2. *Ibid.*, Chapter 2, p. 2, U. of P.

3. *Ibid.*, Chapter 4, U. of P.

4. *Ibid.*, Chapter 4, U. of P.

5. "Notes on Life" is one of the titles that Dreiser gave to the scientific treatise that he worked on from 1933 to 1945. There are several thousand pages of manuscript and notes—never published—which make up this document. The quoted material here is from Box 398, U. of P.

6. See *Harper's Weekly*, December 8, 1900, pp. 1165–66a.

7. "The River of the Nameless Dead," *Tom Watson's Magazine*, I (March, 1905), 112–13.

8. "Dawn," manuscript version, Chapter 15, p. 7, U. of P.

9. W. A. Swanberg in his biography rightly gives the figure of the stolen money at $3,500. Cf. *Dreiser* (New York 1965), pp. 19–20. In a passage Dreiser deleted from *Dawn*, however, he gave the figure of $15,000.

10. "Dawn," manuscript version, Chapter 45, pp. 414–15, U. of P. These pages are typed, but

Dreiser drew a line in the margin and wrote "out" next to the line and deleted these three manuscript pages from the book.

11. This correspondence is among the Dreiser papers, U. of P.

12. "Dawn," manuscript version, Chapter 45, pp. 415–16, U. of P.

13. *Ibid.*, Chapter 56A, U. of P. deleted from the published text, pp. 314 ff.

14. "An American Tragedy," first manuscript version, Chapter 6, U. of P.

15. *Dawn* (New York, 1931), p. 241.

Chapter 2

1. *Dawn* (New York, 1931), p. 191.

2. *Ibid.*, p. 377.

3. *Ibid.*, p. 44.

4. *Ibid.*, p. 78.

5. *Ibid.*, p. 294

6. *Ibid.*, p. 298.

7. *Ibid.*, p. 156.

8. Theodore Dreiser, *A Book About Myself* (New York, 1922), p. 1.

9. These columns, written mostly in 1893, are among the Dreiser papers at U. of P.

10. *A Book About Myself*, p. 231.

11. See particularly Dreiser's description of the joys and agonies of fishing, July 14, 1893.

12. *A Book About Myself*, p. 284.

13. "Odd Scraps of Melody," Pittsburgh *Dispatch*, July 7, 1894.

14. "Snap Shots of Pleasure," Pittsburgh *Dispatch*, August 18, 1894.

15. "General Booth Says Farewell," Pittsburgh *Dispatch*, November 11, 1894.

16. "Soldiers of Morganza," Pittsburgh *Dispatch*, July 5, 1894.

17. "Our Fleeting Shekels," Pittsburgh *Dispatch*, August 26, 1894.

18. "And It was Mighty Blue," Pittsburgh *Dispatch*, May 15, 1894.

19. "Hospital Violet Days," Pittsburgh *Dispatch*, May 12, 1894.

20. W. A. Swanberg, *Dreiser* (New York, 1965), pp. 65–67.

21. Arthur Henry, *Lodgings in Town* (New York, 1905), pp. 80–85. I am indebted here to John Espey, who called my attention to Henry's book, which (as far as I know) has never previously been brought into focus with Dreiser's biography.

22. In "The Early Adventures of *Sister Carrie*," printed in *The Colophon*, part 5 (March, 1931), Dreiser, for example, said "Doubleday Page decided not to put it [*Sister Carrie*] in circulation. . . . I believe [Thomas McKee's] advice was followed to the letter, because no copies were ever sold." Dreiser had told the same story to Freemont Older in November of 1923: see the *Letters of Theodore Dreiser*, ed. Robert H. Elias (Philadelphia, 1959), pp. 417–21. W. A. Swanberg finally set the record straight: see *Dreiser*, pp. 90–93. Although Swanberg was also using the Doubleday, Page correspondence as his source, his figures of the books sold and the royalties paid differ slightly from mine.

23. Arnold Hauser, *The Social History of Art* (New York, 1958), pp. 181–85.

24. *A Book About Myself*, p. 87.

25. *Ibid.*, p. 99.

26. *Ibid.*, p. 260.

27. *Ibid.*, p. 337.

28. *Dawn.*, p. 156.

29. *Ibid.*, p. 299.

30. *Ibid.*, p. 466.

31. *Ibid.*, p. 63

32. *Ibid.*, p. 167.

33. *Ibid.*, p. 167. See also p. 500.

34. *Ibid.*, p. 423.

35. *Ibid.*, p. 500.

36. *Ibid.*, p. 542. Cf. also, p. 547 and *A Book About Myself*, p. 106

37. *Dawn*, p. 542.

Chapter 3

1. Theodore Dreiser, *Hey Rub-A-Dub-Dub* (New York, 1920), p. 125.

2. *A Book About Myself* (New York, 1922), p. 19.

3. Max Lerner, *America As A Civilization* (New York, 1957), p. 417.

4. See *Hey Rub-A-Dub-Dub*, p. 84. See also Theodore Dreiser, *Dreiser Looks At Russia* (New York, 1928), pp. 153–54.

5. *A Book About Myself*, pp. 369–70.

6. *Ev'ry Month*, May 1, 1897, p. 2, column 1.

7. *Ibid.*, December 1, 1896, pp. 6–7.

8. *Ibid.*, March 1, 1897, p. 3.

9. *A Book About Myself*, pp. 392–93.

10. The Orison Swett Marden books which contain Dreiser's articles are the following: *How They Succeeded, Life Stories of Successful Men Told by Themselves* (Boston, 1901), which contains Dreiser's interviews with Marshall Field, Philip D. Armour, Lillian Nordica, William Dean Howells, Andrew Carnegie, and John Burroughs; *Talks with Great Workers* (New York, 1901), which contains interviews with Chauncey M. Depew, Paul Weyland Bartless, Alfred Stieglitz, Anthony Hope, and Frank W. Gunsaulus; and *Little Visits with Great Americans—or Success Ideals and How to Attain Them* (New York, 1905), which contains interviews with Thomas Edison and Joseph H. Choate, as well as the reprinting of previous interviews with Field, Carnegie, Depew, Howells, Burroughs, Gunsaulus, Armour, and Nordica.

11. *Little Visits with Great Men*, pp. 203–04.

12. *Ibid.*, p. 201.

13. *Ibid.*, p. 202.

14. *Ibid.*, p. 410.

15. Theodore Dreiser, *The Color of A Great City* (New York, 1923), p. 125.

16. *Ev'ry Month*, May 1, 1897, p. 21.

17. Lloyd Morris, *Postscript to Yesterday* (New York, 1947), p. 304.

18. Charles Edward Russell, *Lawless Wealth* (New York, 1908), pp. 46–47.

19. *Ibid.*, pp. 57–58.

Chapter 4

1. *A Book About Myself* (New York, 1922), p. 457.

2. Herbert Spencer, *First Principles* (London, 1893), p. 35.

3. *Ibid.*, p. 108.

4. *Ibid.*, p. 110.

5. *Ibid.*, p. 158.

6. *Ibid.*, p. 179.

7. *Ibid.*, p. 192c.

8. *Ibid.*, p. 215.

9. Theodore Dreiser, "The Realization of an Ideal," *The Color of A Great City* (New York, 1923), p. 108.

10. Theodore Dreiser, "Man and Romance," *Reedy's Mirror*, Aug. 28, 1919, p. 585. This article, which McDonald does not include in his bibliography, can be found among the Dreiser papers at U. of P.

11. *A Book About Myself*, p. 458.

12. Theodore Dreiser, "Hunting for Swordfish," *Sunday Magazine*

for July 24, 1904, pp. 11–12, U. of P.

13. Theodore Dreiser, "Our Red Slayer," *The Color of A Great City,* p. 135.

14. See *A Book About Myself,* pp. 457–58.

15. *Ev'ry Month,* March 1, 1897, p. 2.

16. *Ibid.,* p. 3.

17. Theodore Dreiser, "The Beauty of Life," *The Color of A Great City,* p. 170.

18. Theodore Dreiser, "The Car Yard," *The Color of A Great City,* pp. 72–73.

19. Theodore Dreiser, "The Flight of Pigeons," *The Color of A Great City,* p. 74.

20. Theodore Dreiser, "The Waterfront," *The Color of A Great City,* p. 10.

21. *Ev'ry Month,* December 1. 1896, pp. 5–6.

22. Theodore Dreiser, "Greenwich Village," partly handwritten, party typed manuscript, U. of P.

23. Theodore Dreiser, "Whence the Song," *Harper's Weekly,* December 8, 1900, pp. 1165–66A; reprinted in *The Color of A Great City,* p. 154.

24. *Ev'ry Month,* December 1, 1896, p. 4.

Chapter 5

1. Theodore Dreiser, *Sister Carrie* (New York, 1900). All quotations and references are from or to the Holt, Rinehart, and Winston edition, pages indicated in parentheses after the quote.

2. The differences between this section of the novel (pp. 424–27) and the article are that Dreiser added in the novel the last paragraph of p. 421, the last paragraph and a half on p. 424 and the first paragraph and a half on p. 425, the last twelve lines on p. 425 and

the first three lines of p. 426, the top paragraphs of p. 427, and part of the last paragraph on p. 427.

3. Theodore Dreiser, "Whence the Song," *Harper's Weekly,* December 8, 1900, pp. 1165–66a.

4. Theodore Dreiser, "The River of the Nameless Dead," *Tom Watson's Magazine,* I (March, 1905), 112–13.

5. F. Scott Fitzgerald, *The Great Gatsby* (New York, 1925), quote is from the 1953 edition, p. 69.

6. See also Dreiser's review of *The Man from Boston,* a play in which John L. Sullivan acted, St. Louis *Globe Democrat,* February 27, 1893, p. 10.

7. Dreiser's letters to John Howard Lawson were published in *Masses and Mainstream,* VIII (December, 1955), pp. 20–22.

Chapter 6

1. Theodore Dreiser, *Jennie Gerhardt* (New York, 1911), p. 208. All quotations and references are from or to the Dell edition (1963), pages indicated in parentheses after the quote.

2. Nathaniel Hawthorne, *The Scarlet Letter* (New York, 1958), p. 75.

Chapter 7

1. Theodore Dreiser, *The Financier* (New York, 1912 and 1927); *The Titan* (New York, 1914); *The Stoic* (New York, 1947). All quotes are from the following editions, pages indicated in parentheses after the quote: *The Financier* (Dell edition, 1961), p. 312; *The Titan* (Dell edition, 1959); *The Stoic* (Doubleday edition, 1947).

2. Among the books about the stock market, Dreiser read the following:

Charles A. Conant, *Defense of the Stock Exchange* (Boston, 1903).

Francis L. Eames, *History of the New York Exchange* (New York, 1894).

Arthur Crump, *The Work of Wall Street*, ed. S. A. Nelson (New York, 1907).

Arthur Crump, *The ABC of Wall Street*, ed. S. A. Nelson (New York, 1909).

Arthur Crump, *The ABC of Stock Speculation*, ed. S. A. Nelson (New York, 1902).

Arthur Crump, *The Theory of Stock Speculation*, ed. S. A. Nelson (New York, 1901).

John R. Dos Passos, *Treatise on the Law of Stock Brokers and Stock Exchanges* (New York, 1882).

Henry Clews, *Twenty Eight Years of Wall Street* (New York, 1888).

3. Charles Edward Russell, "Where Did you Get It, Gentlemen?" *Everybody's Magazine*, XVIII (1907–08).

4. Edward Lefèvre, "What Availeth It," *Everybody's Magazine*, XXV (1911).

5. See Waldo R. Brown, *Altgeld in Illinois* (New York, 1924), pp. 235–41.

6. *A Book About Myself* (New York, 1922), p. 108.

7. *The Evening World*, June 14, 1913, p. 3.

8. Theodore Dreiser, "You the Phantom," *Esquire*, II (November, 1934), 25.

9. Theodore Dreiser, "Notes on Life," Box 190, U. of P.

Chapter 8

1. Theodore Dreiser, *The "Genius"* (New York, 1915), p. 312. All quotes are from the World edition (1963), pages indicated in parentheses after the quote.

2. Percy Bysshe Shelley, "A Defense of Poetry," *Criticism: The Major Texts*, ed. Walter Jackson Bate (New York, 1952), pp. 429, 430, and 432.

3. *Ibid.*, p. 432.

4. *Dawn* (New York, 1931), p. 332.

5. *Ibid.*, pp. 367–68, italics mine.

6. *A Book About Myself* (New York, 1922), p. 260.

7. *Ibid.*, italics mine.

8. *The Letters of F. Scott Fitzgerald*, ed. Andrew Turnbull (New York, 1963), p. 462.

Chapter 9

1. Theodore Dreiser, *A Hoosier Holiday* (New York and London, 1916), p. 173.

2. John Reed to Upton Sinclair, November 6, 1918: cited by Daniel Aaron, *Writers on the Left* (New York, 1961), reprinted as an Avon Library book, p. 84.

3. For a discussion of Dell's attack on Mencken, see Aaron, p. 126.

4. Theodore Dreiser, "More Democracy or Less? An Inquiry," *The Call Magazine*, Nov. 30, 1919, pp. 6–7.

5. *Ibid.*

6. "Americans Are Still Interested in Ten Commandments—For the Other Fellow, Says Dreiser," *The Call Magazine*, March 13, 1921, U. of P., p. 7.

7. *Hey Rub-A-Dub-Dub* (New York, 1920), p. 79.

8. After he was separated from Jug, Dreiser found it convenient not to marry again by insisting that Jug would not give him a divorce, which was in part true. He did not marry Helen Richardson until Jug died in 1942, although it appears clear that he could have married her earlier if he had really wanted.

264 *Notes*

Dreiser prized his freedom, particularly after he just left Jug, and he made this clear to such friends as Anna Tatum (whom he met in 1912, and who becomes the model for Etta in *The Bulwark*) and to Kirah Markham (whom he took away from Floyd Dell, and who lived with him in New York from 1914 to 1916).

9. Theodore Dreiser, "Fulfillment," *Chains* (New York, 1927), p. 314.

10. *Ibid.*, p. 320.

11. Ernestine De Jongh is modelled upon Florence Deshon, a Hollywood actress, who carried on a two-way romance with Charlie Chaplin and Max Eastman. For over a year, she lived with Chaplin in Hollywood. When she was seriously ill for over a month, she returned in August of 1922 to Croton, New York, where Eastman had a small farmhouse. Eastman took her to his own doctor, who discovered that she had been three months pregnant and that the fetus was dead. If the doctor had not operated immediately, Florence would have died. Eastman discusses these matters in *Love and Revolution* (New York, 1964).

12. Emanuela is modelled on Ann Watkins, a literary agent and free-lance writer that Dreiser knew in New York. Emanuela's escape from Scheib is based upon an experience Ann Watkins had with Fritz Krog, one of Dreiser's assistant editors on the *Bohemian*. See W. A. Swanberg *Dreiser* (New York, 1965), p. 170.

13. Olive Brand is modelled on Edith De Long Smith, the wife of Edward H. Smith, one of Dreiser's most faithful friends.

14. Esther Norm is modelled on Mary Pyne. She was married to Harry Kemp, the "Byron of the Village," and was a close friend of

Hutchins Hapgood, whom Dreiser depicted in this story (to use Hapgood's own words) as a "Svengali figure, romantically evil." See Hutchins Hapgood, "A Victorian in the Modern World* (New York, 1939), p. 430. Hapgood would get his revenge when, to Dreiser's everlasting discredit, he challenged Dreiser to discuss publicly Dreiser's feelings about the Jews. See Hutchins Hapgood, "Is Dreiser Anti-Semitic," *The Nation*, April 17, 1935. See also "Dreiser Denies He Is Anti-Semitic," *New Masses*, XV (April 30, 1935).

15. Theodore Dreiser, "Lucia," *A Gallery of Women* (New York, 1929), republished by Fawcett as a Premier Book, pp. 133–34.

16. *Ibid.*, p. 149.

17. Theodore Dreiser, "Regina C——," *A Gallery of Women*, pp. 255–56.

18. See the *Letters of Theodore Dreiser*, ed. Robert H. Elias (Philadelphia, 1959), pp. 375–83.

Chapter 10

1. Theodore Dreiser, "I Find the Real American Tragedy," *Mystery Magazine*, XI (February, 1935), 9, 10–11, 90.

2. From Dreiser's typed manuscript describing how he came to write *An American Tragedy*, Box 183, U. of P.

3. See *Dawn* (New York, 1931), p. 352.

4. Theodore Dreiser, *An American Tragedy* (New York, 1925), p. 187. All quotes are from the New American Library edition (1964), pages indicated in parentheses after the quote.

5. U. of P., Box 396.

6. The function of Rev. McMillan had been misread by several commentators. Van Wyck Brooks, e.g., maintains that "it was left for

the supposedly godless Dreiser to portray in his Duncan McMillan the Protestant minister as he ought to be." See "Theodore Dreiser," *University of Kansas City Review,* XVI (Spring, 1950), 197. Lionel Trilling, about to refer to Rev. McMillan, says "this is not the first occasion on which Dreiser has shown tenderness toward religion and a responsiveness to mysticism." See "Reality in America," *The Liberal Imagination* (New York, 1953), p. 29.

Chapter 11

1. Theodore Dreiser, "Ernita," *A Gallery of Women* (New York, 1929), reprinted as a Premier Book by Fawcett World Library in 1962, pp. 205–6.

2. See the San Francisco *Journal,* December 4, 1921.

3. "Dreiser on Hollywood," *New Masses,* IV (January, 1929), 17–18.

4. Theodore Dreiser, "This Florida Scene," *Vanity Fair,* May, June, July, 1926. This passage was from the June issue, p. 43.

5. Theodore Dreiser, "Paris—1926," *Vanity Fair,* XXVII (December, 1926), 136.

6. Theodore Dreiser, "American Restlessness," New York *American,* April 10, 1927, Section E, p. 3. This essay appeared in other Hearst papers.

7. Theodore Dreiser, *Dreiser Looks at Russia* (New York, 1928), pp. 75 and 79.

8. *Ibid.,* pp. 153–54.

9. *Ibid.,* p. 170 .

10. New York *Times,* March 16, 1930, p. 7, column 1.

11. San Francisco *Daily News,* May 30, 1930.

12. New York *Times,* November 7, 1932, p. 12.

13. Theodore Dreiser, *Tragic America* (New York, 1931), p. 410.

14. Bennett Stevens, "The Gnats and Dreiser," *New Masses,* IX (May, 1932), 24.

Chapter 12

1. Theodore Dreiser, "Challenge to the Creative Man," *Common Sense,* II (November, 1933), 6.

2. Theodore Dreiser, "America and Her Communists," *Time and Tide,* October 31, 1931, pp. 1247–48.

3. See Max Eastman, *Love and Revolution* (New York, 1964), p. 443.

4. "Letters from Writers," *International Literature,* no. 4, 1933 (Dreiser's letter was dated July 4, 1933), p. 123.

5. Theodore Dreiser, "America and Her Communists," pp. 1247–48.

6. "Letters from Writers," *International Literature,* no. 1, 1933 (Dreiser's letter was dated October 11, 1932), p. 126.

7. Theodore Dreiser, "The Epic Sinclair," *Esquire,* II (December, 1934), 32.

8. Theodore Dreiser, "Challenge to the Creative Man," *Common Sense,* II (November, 1933), 6–8.

9. Theodore Dreiser, "Flies and Locusts," a column Dreiser wrote for the New York *Daily Mirror* (August, 1933), while Walter Winchell was on two weeks' vacation.

10. Theodore Dreiser, "Why Capitalists Praise Democracy," *Common Sense,* III (July, 1934), 19–20.

11. Theodore Dreiser, "Individualism and the Jungle," *New Masses,* January 2, 1932, pp. 3–4.

12. Theodore Dreiser, "What Is Democracy?" *The Clipper,* I (December, 1940), 5.

13. Theodore Dreiser in *How*

The Great Corporations Rule The United States (Girard, Kansas, 1931), pp. 1–7.

14. New York *Times,* August 30, 1936, II, p. 2.

15. *Ibid.,* September 16, 1938, p. 10.

16. Theodore Dreiser, "America —And War," *Labor Defender,* VIII (August, 1932), 143, continued on 157.

17. Theodore Dreiser, "The Soviet-Finnish Treaty and World Peace," *Soviet Russia Today,* VIII (April, 1940), 8–9.

18. Theodore Dreiser, "Equity Between Nations," *Direction,* I (September–October, 1938), 5.

19. Theodore Dreiser, "The USSR Today," *Current History and Forum,* December 10, 1940, p. 30. This article was originally published in *Soviet Russia Today.*

20. Theodore Dreiser, *America Is Worth Saving* (New York, 1941), p. 18. All further references to this book are from this edition, page numbers indicated in parentheses after each quote.

21. *New Masses,* XX (July 2, 1941), 2.

22. Cf. letter to Dallas McKown, June 2, 1932. Scott Nearing had had the same kind of experience. See Joseph Freeman, *An American Testament* (New York, 1936), pp. 342–43.

Chapter 13

1. Theodore Dreiser, *Jennie Gerhardt* (New York, 1911), reprinted in Dell in 1963, p. 114.

2. U. of P., Box 395.

3. See Theodore Dreiser, "You, the Phantom," *Esquire,* II (November, 1934), 25–26.

4. Theodore Dreiser, "Man and Romance," *Reedy's Mirror.* This is one of the essays Dreiser clipped from the journal and saved among

his papers at U. of P. It was written in Aug. 1919, concurrent with *Hey Rub-A-Dub-Dub,* although there is no date on the tear sheets.

5. "You, the Phantom," p. 25.

6. Theodore Dreiser, "The Myth of Individuality," *American Mercury,* XXXI (March, 1934), 337–42.

7. Theodore Dreiser, "The Myth of Reality," a typed manuscript in "Notes on Life," U. of P., Box 399.

8. U. of P., Box 399.

9. *Ibid.,* Box 396.

10. Arthur Schopenhauer, *The World as Will and Idea,* II (London, 1883), 164.

11. U. of P., Box 401.

12. *Ibid.,* Box 400.

13. *Ibid.,* Box 402.

14. *Ibid.,* Box 403.

15. *Ibid.,* Box 396.

16. *Ibid.,* Box 395.

17. *Ibid.,* Box 395.

18. *Ibid.,* Box 395.

19. *Ibid.,* Box 404.

20. Cf. Lionel Trilling, "Reality in America," *The Liberal Imagination* (New York, 1953), pp. 15–32. Cf. also Robert Shafer, *"An American Tragedy:* A Humanistic Demurrer," *Humanism and America,* ed. Norman Foerster (New York, 1930).

21. Theodore Dreiser, Foreword to *A Bibliography of the Writing of Theodore Dreiser* by Edward D. McDonald (Philadelphia, 1928), p. 12.

Chapter 14

1. Letter to Dreiser, Box 365, U. of P. All further correspondence from Miss Tatum is from this source.

2. See Lionel Trilling, "Reality in America," *The Liberal Imagination* (New York, 1953), p. 26.

3. W. A. Swanberg, *Dreiser* (New York, 1965), p. 484.

4. *Ibid.,* p. 484.

5. Theodore Dreiser, *The Bulwark* (New York, 1946), pp. 137–38. All quotes are from the Popular Library edition (1960), pages indicated in parentheses after the quote.

Chapter 15

1. Theodore Dreiser, "The Great American Novel," *American Spectator,* I (December, 1932), 17.

2. William Dean Howells, *A Modern Instance* (Boston, 1881), p. 394.

3. William Dean Howells, *A Hazard of New Fortunes* (New York, 1952), p. 385. All further references are to this text, pages indicated in parentheses after the quote.

4. Granville Hicks, *The Great Tradition* (New York, 1935), p. 77.

5. Quoted in Hicks, p. 108.

6. Henry James, *The Princess Casamassima* (New York, 1908), I, p. 291.

7. Theodore Dreiser, "Mark Twain: Three Contacts," *Esquire,* IV (October, 1935), 162A.

8. Theodore Dreiser, "Mark the Double Twain," *The English Journal,* XXIV, no. 8 (October, 1935), 626.

9. See Philip S. Foner, *Mark Twain Social Critic* (New York, 1958), p. 177. Many of the above facts have been taken from this book. For a different portrait of Twain's political views, see Louis J. Budd, *Mark Twain: Social Philosopher* (Bloomington, 1962).

10. Mark Twain, *A Connecticut Yankee in King Arthur's Court* (New York, 1960), p. 304.

11. Edith Wharton, *The Custom of the Country* (New York, 1913), p. 94. All further references are to this text, pages indicated in parentheses after the quote.

12. Henry Blake Fuller, *The Cliff Dwellers* (New York, 1893), p. 324.

13. Henry Blake Fuller, *With the Procession* (New York, 1894), p. 293. All further references are to this text, pages indicated in parentheses after the quote.

14. *Letters of Theodore Dreiser,* ed. Robert H. Elias (Philadelphia, 1959), p. 612. See also Dreiser's "The Great American Novel," in which he discusses both Wharton and Fuller.

15. Theodore Dreiser, "The Saddest Story," *The New Republic,* III, no. 32 (June 12, 1915), 155–56.

16. Dreiser's correspondence with *The Atlantic Monthly,* U. of P.

A BIBLIOGRAPHICAL ESSAY

I. Dreiser's Books and Novels

Dreiser wrote eight novels, published between 1900 and 1947: *Sister Carrie* (1900), *Jennie Gerhardt* (1911), *The Financier* (1912), *The Titan* (1914), *The "Genius"* (1915), *An American Tragedy* (1925), *The Bulwark* (1946), and *The Stoic* (1947). He also published four volumes of short stories: *Free, and Other Stories* (1918), *Twelve Men* (1919), *Chains* (1927), and *A Gallery of Women* (1929). He also wrote two volumes of autobiography—*Dawn* (1931) and *A Book About My-self* (1922)—and three books of travel—*A Traveller at Forty* (1913), *A Hoosier Holiday* (1916), and *Dreiser Looks at Russia* (1928). Dreiser's interest in the city, in modern political developments, and in scientific theories are developed in the following four books: *The Color of a Great City* (1923), *Tragic America* (1931), *America Is Worth Saving* (1941), and *Hey Rub-A-Dub-Dub* (1920). Dreiser also wrote a book of poetry —*Moods, Cadenced and Declaimed* (1935)—and two books of plays— *Plays of the Natural and Supernatural* (1916) and *The Hand of the Pot-ter* (1918). There are two separate editions of Dreiser's letters: *Letters of Theodore Dreiser*, ed. Robert H. Elias, and *Letters to Louise*, ed. Louise Campbell (both published by the University of Pennsylvania Press in 1959).

II. Dreiser's Contributions to Books

Dreiser contributed as many as forty articles (or forewords or intro-ductions) to books. The most significant of these are his articles for Orison S. Marden's success books (discussed in the footnotes); his essays of literary criticism—such as, the introduction to Doubleday-Doran's Volume eight of the *Collected Editions of Frank Norris* (1928) and his introductions to the Limited Editions Club's Samuel Butler's *The Way of All Flesh* (1936) and Somerset Maugham's *Of Human Bondage* (1938); and his essays dealing with political or scientific matters—such as, those in Haldeman-Julius' *How the Great Corporations Rule the United States* (1931), the NCDPP's *Harlan Miners Speak* (1932), Walter Wilson's *Forced Labor in the United States* (1933), Anton Refregier's *Tom Mooney, Story in Pictures* (1933), *I Believe* (1939) edited by Clifton Fadiman, and *The Living Thoughts of Thoreau* (1939) edited by Dreiser with a 32-page introduction.

III. Dreiser's Contributions to Periodicals

Between 1896 and 1946, Dreiser wrote more than five hundred essays or stories for the leading magazines and periodicals. From 1896 to 1897, he contributed regularly to *Ev'ry Month* (discussed in footnotes). From 1898 to 1905, Dreiser wrote articles on such varied subjects as Nathaniel Hawthorne, Benjamin Eggleston, William Dean Howells, the harp, the making of small arms, the apple industry, carrier pigeons in war time, the Chicago River, the railroad and the people, and life in the tenements. These articles were published mainly in *Ainslee's, Cosmopolitan, Demorest's, Harper's Weekly* and *Harper's Monthly, Metropolitan, Munsey's, Pearson's, Reedy's Mirror, Success,* and *Truth.* From 1905 to 1909, Dreiser wrote primarily for *Smith's, Broadway,* and the *Delineator,* as well as the *Bohemian,* in which he had a financial interest. From 1910 to 1925, he devoted most of his time to his novels. The articles that he did write during these years, however, take on a philosophical and political cast, particularly those contributed to the New York *Call* and *Reedy's Mirror.* Dreiser at this time also wrote book reviews for the *New Republic,* travelogues for *Century,* and autobiography for the *Bookman.* Between 1926 and 1930, he wrote about Florida and Paris for *Vanity Fair.* From 1930 to his death at the end of 1945, Dreiser's essays (many of which are listed in the footnotes above) deal primarily with political and scientific matters.

IV. Dreiser's Journalism

From 1892 to 1894, Dreiser wrote for such newspapers as the St. Louis *Globe-Democrat,* the St. Louis *Republic,* the Toledo *Blade* (briefly) and the Pittsburg *Dispatch.* The best published list of Dreiser's early contributions to newspapers is in the notes of Robert H. Elias' *Theodore Dreiser: Apostle of Nature,* pp. 312–17. In 1928, Dreiser discussed his trip to Russia for the North American Newspaper Alliance (see the New York *World,* March 19–28, 1928). Also, Dreiser's 1938 trip to Spain was widely reported in the papers, as was his trip to the Harlan coal fields and his visit to Tom Mooney (see footnotes above).

V. Biographies of Dreiser

During Dreiser's life, Dorothy Dudley published *Forgotten Frontiers: Dreiser and the Land of the Free* (New York: Harrison Smith and Robert Haas, 1932). After his death, Dreiser's wife, Helen, published *My Life With Dreiser* (Cleveland: The World Publishing Company, 1951). Another personal recollection of Dreiser written by a woman who knew him is Marguerite Tjader's *Theodore Dreiser: A New Dimension* (Norwalk, Connecticut: Silvermine Publishers, 1965). The best "scholarly" biography is still Robert H. Elias' *Theodore Dreiser: Apostle of Nature* (New York: Alfred A. Knopf, 1949). The most extensive treatment of Dreiser's life, however, is the brilliantly detailed *Dreiser* by W. A. Swanberg (New York: Charles Scribner's Sons, 1965), a far from sympathetic book.

VI. Critical Books on Dreiser

The earliest full-length critical study of Dreiser is F. O. Matthiessen's *Theodore Dreiser* (New York: William Sloane, 1951), an excellent book, but one surely handicapped by the personal troubles Matthiessen was having while he was working on this manuscript. Other very fine studies of Dreiser include Charles Shapiro's *Theodore Dreiser: Our Bitter Patriot* (Carbondale, Illinois, Southern Illinois University Press, 1962); Philip L. Gerber's *Theodore Dreiser* (New York: Twayne, 1964); and John J. McAleer's *Theodore Dreiser: An Introduction and Interpretation* (New York; Holt, Rinehart and Winston, 1968).

VII. Critical Articles on Dreiser

Four very good general discussions of Dreiser are Eliseo Vivas' "Dreiser, An Inconsistent Mechanist," *Ethics*, XLVII (July, 1938), 498–508; Charles C. Walcutt's "The Three Stages of Theodore Dreiser's Naturalism," *PMLA*, LV (March, 1940), 266–89; Alexander Kern's "Dreiser's Difficult Beauty," *Western Review*, XVI (Winter, 1952), 129–36; and William L. Phillips' "The Imagery of Dreiser's Novels," *PMLA*, LXVIII (December, 1963), 572–85. Those interested in the response of contemporary novelists to Dreiser should see Saul Bellow's "Dreiser and the Triumph of Art," *Commentary* XXVI (May, 1951), 502–03 and Norman Mailer's "Modes and Mutations," *Commentary*, XLI (March, 1966), 37–40. For critical discussions of *Sister Carrie* see Claude Simpson's "*Sister Carrie* Reconsidered," *Southwest Review*, XLIV (Winter, 1959), 44–53; William A. Friedman's "A Look at Dreiser as Artist: The Motif of Circularity in *Sister Carrie*," *Modern Fiction Studies*, VIII (Winter, 1962), 384–92; and Ellen Moers' "The Finesse of Dreiser," *American Scholar*, XXXIII (Winter, 1963), 109–14. For a critical study of *Jennie Gerhardt* see Charles Shapiro's "Jennie Gerhardt: The American Family and the American Dream," *Twelve Original Essays on Great American Novels*, ed. Charles Shapiro (Detroit: Wayne State University Press, 1958), pp. 177–95. For a critical discussion of *An American Tragedy* see Richard Lehan's "*An American Tragedy*: A Critical Study," *College English*, XXV (December, 1963), 187–93; Irving Howe's "Dreiser and Tragedy," *New Republic*, CLI (July 25, 1964), 25–28; and Lauriat Lane's "The Double in *An American Tragedy*," *Modern Fiction Studies*, XII (Summer, 1966), 213–20. And for a critical study of *The Bulwark* see Sidney Richman's "Theodore Dreiser's *The Bulwark*: A Final Resolution," *American Literature*, XXXIV (May, 1962), 229–45. The only collection of critical essays on Dreiser is the useful *The Stature of Theodore Dreiser*, ed. Alfred Kazin and Charles Shapiro (Bloomington: Indiana University Press, 1955).

VIII. Biographies and Checklists

Most of Dreiser's own writing and the criticism and reviews of it up to 1928 are listed in Edward D. McDonald's *A Bibliography of the Writing of Theodore Dreiser* (Philadelphia: The Centaur Book Shop,

1928). This can be supplemented with Vrest Orton's *Dreiserana: A Book About His Books* (New York: The Chocurua Bibliographies, 1929). For works of or about Dreiser published after 1929, the reader can find help in R. N. Miller's *A Preliminary Checklist of Books and Articles on Theodore Dreiser* (Kalamazoo, Michigan: Western Michigan College Library, 1947); Kazin and Shapiro's *The Stature of Theodore Dreiser; The American Novel Through Henry James*, ed. C. Hugh Holman (New York: Appleton-Century-Crofts, 1966), and Hugh C. Atkinson's *Theodore Dreiser: Checklist* (Columbus, Ohio: Charles E. Merrill, 1969).

INDEX